Neural Networks

New Technologies for Social Research

New technologies are transforming how social scientists in a wide range of fields do research. The series, New Technologies for Social Research, aims to provide detailed, accessible and up-to-date treatments of such technologies, and to assess in a critical way their methodological implications.

Series Editors:
Nigel G. Fielding, *University of Surrey*
Raymond M. Lee, *Royal Holloway University of London*

Recent volumes include:

Computer Analysis and Qualitative Research
Nigel G. Fielding and Raymond M. Lee

Computer Modeling of Social Precesses
edited by Wim B.G. Liebrand, Andrzej Nowak and Rainer Hegselmann

Neural Networks
An Introductory Guide for Social Scientists

G. David Garson

SAGE Publications
London • Thousand Oaks • New Delhi

© G. David Garson 1998

First published 1998

 SAGE Publications Ltd
6 Bonhill Street
London EC2A 4PU

SAGE Publications Inc.
2455 Teller Road
Thousand Oaks, California 91320

SAGE Publications India Pvt Ltd
32, M-Block Market
Greater Kailash – I
New Delhi 110 048

British Library Cataloguing in Publication data

A catalogue record for this book is available
from the British Library

ISBN 0 7619 5730 8
ISBN 0 7619 5731 6 (pbk)

Library of Congress catalog card number 98–61097

Typeset by Mayhew Typesetting, Rhayader, Powys
Printed in Great Britain by Biddles Ltd, Guildford, Surrey

Contents

1
Introduction to Neural Network Analysis

Social scientists find neural networks attractive because of their relevance to commonly encountered types of problems. Neural networks
can be used for classification problems which involve mapping a large
number of inputs onto a small number of output classes. In a similar
vein, neural networks handle completion problems (identifying correct
categories into which to map incomplete or corrupted inputs). As such
neural networks are an alternative to factor analysis and discriminant
function analysis. Neural networks also excel at prediction problems,
particularly when there are a large number of inputs which are related
in nonlinear ways which cannot be easily expressed in structural equations. In prediction, neural networks are an alternative to the multivariate general linear hypothesis (MGLH) models, structural equation
models and expert systems. Finally, neural networks solve constraint
satisfaction problems involved in complex activities such as scheduling,
routing and resource allocation to meet complex demand constraints
and are thus an alternative to linear programming and dynamic systems
analysis. In general, neural models may outperform traditional statistical
procedures where problems lack discernible structure, data are incomplete, and many competing inputs and constraints related in complex,
nonlinear ways prevent formulation of structural equations, provided
the researcher can accept the approximate solutions generated by neural
models.

Neural network analysis can be traced back to the work of Warren
McCulloch, a neurobiologist trained as a psychiatrist and neuroanat-
omist, and Walter Pitts, a statistician and mathematics prodigy who,
using an analog to the brain's neuron, argued that modelling brain
functionality could be represented mathematically. Working at the
University of Chicago in the late 1930s and early 1940s, McCulloch and
Pitts demonstrated that calculations could be performed by a network of
artificial binary-valued neurons (McCulloch and Pitts, 1943; Pitts and
McCulloch, 1947). Their threshold logic units contained the essential
elements of what were later called perceptrons.

1   Computations are carried out in discrete time intervals.
2   If a neuron receives an inhibitory signal from any input unit, it does not fire.
3   Computations follow a linear threshold law: the unit fires when at least a threshold number of input neurons send excitatory signals, and no inhibitory signals are received.
4   Unlike later more advanced models, in a McCulloch–Pitts network there is no learning from experience, though the model does respond to difference between the present input pattern and the prior one.

McCulloch–Pitts models, though simple, prefigured later models in a number of respects, including having input, hidden and output layers as do most contemporary neural networks.

The essence of the McCulloch–Pitts analogy to biological neurons is the concept that a processing entity, designated an 'artificial neuron', can be programmed to fire (release a signal) when its inputs reach a threshold level. The dendrites linking neurons in a biological system can be imitated through programmed connections. Connections between inputs and neurons can be assigned weights to simulate the biological phenomenon of synapses varying in strength, with some allowing a large signal to pass through and some allowing only a weak signal. Moreover, the connections can be programmed to be positive or negative, imitating the biological phenomenon of some synapses being excitatory, adding to the signal received from the dendrite, while other synapses are inhibitory, reducing the received signal.

After the war, in 1949, Donald O. Hebb wrote *Organization of Behavior*, presenting a biological model seeking to explain plausibly how learning can take place in a network of perceptrons. In his book Hebb presented what has become known as Hebb's rule, a predecessor of the backpropagation rule. This rule set forth the concept that short-term neural memory could be imitated by arranging that when a pair of neurons is simultaneously excited, the connection between them should be augmented to represent learning. This was the first formal presentation of the concept of synaptic modification, contrasting with the McCulloch and Pitts model, which used fixed weights. Hebb also believed that imitation of long-term neural memory would require structural modifications of the artificial neural network, not just adjustment of connection weights. That is, just as the physical contact areas of the knobs of a frequently used synapse in neurobiology were thought to become enlarged to make the connection more efficient, so in an artificial network Hebb posited that stable long-term memory would require some structural change in connection equations which would reinforce the connection.[1] Although Hebb's concept was too simple for practical use, it was the basis on which all future neural network algorithms were built. At the time Hebb's work was primarily of interest to psychologists and had little impact on the nascent field of computer engineering.

Neural networks were brought to national attention in 1956 when Marvin Minsky, John McCarthy, Nathaniel Rochester and Claude Shannon organized the first international conference on artificial intelligence – the Dartmouth Summer Research Project on Artificial Intelligence, sponsored by the Rockefeller Foundation. The mandate of the conference was 'to proceed on the basis of the conjecture that every aspect of learning or any other feature of intelligence can in principle be so precisely described that a machine can be made to simulate it'. Rochester, an employee of IBM Research, presented at the conference the first neural network, although at that time it was not understood how to interpret its numerical output. Rochester's simulation, however, did show that Hebbian learning required inhibitory as well as excitatory feedback in order to work properly. Rochester's model was the first computer simulation of a neural system (Rochester et al., 1956). The year 1956 also saw (1) related work by Uttley (1956), who showed that classification of binary patterns could be accomplished by a neural network whose synaptic connections were modified in response to presentation of patterns; (2) the first publication of the work on associative memory by Taylor (1956); and (3) von Neumann's (1956) solution to the problem of network reliability through redundancy.

A year later Frank Rosenblatt (1957; 1959; 1961) of Cornell University published his first work on perceptrons, naming them such. This represented the first major neural computing research project, which centred on optical pattern recognition using an array of 400 photocells. In this project Rosenblatt developed neural learning algorithms in various ways, including the idea of using randomly selected neurons in the learning process. He constructed an artificial neural system with three types of processing entities. Sensory neurons accepted input signals. Response neurons propagated output signals. Associative neurons processed signals internally. Rosenblatt was able to show that his neural model could learn to classify simple shape patterns and that it functioned robustly even in the face of data noise or when some components were disabled, because information was distributed throughout the network.

The excitement and significance of Rosenblatt's work was the demonstration that a neural computer system could learn to classify inputs through induction from example rather than through the usual top-down programmed algorithmic instructions as used, for example, in statistical packages. However, Rosenblatt's perceptron models could not generalize their classifications to new patterns in the absence of complete data, and for complex patterns required excessive numbers of neurons.

Contemporaneously with Rosenblatt, Samuel (1959) developed a checkers-playing program which attracted widespread attention.

Samuel's intelligent checkers program learned as it proceeded with play. While it was a precursor of a wide variety of forms of symbolic processing programs, Samuel's program played a role in neural networks' historical development in so far as it was based on the common underlying principle of adjusting weights in recognition of patterns presented to the program, which compared new input vectors of board positions with previously stored patterns.

Real-world applications were pioneered by Bernard Widrow at Stanford University, based in part on ideas of McCulloch and Pitts in the 1940s. His 'Adaline' (adaptive linear neuron) system was a one-layer neural network utilizing a more sophisticated learning algorithm than Rosenblatt's perceptrons. Widrow's later two-layer version was called 'Madaline' (multiple Adaline; see Widrow, 1962). Widrow and Hoff (1960) developed the least mean square (LMS) mathematics of the linear perceptron, as neural networks were initially labelled, in particular the Widrow–Hoff learning rule, better known today as the delta rule, which in generalized form became the learning rule underlying backpropagation, the most widely used neural architecture (Werbos, 1994). Widrow published his work on adaptive linear neurons in 1962 and in the same year developed the first application of neural networks to a major real-world problem, meteorological forecasts. Widrow and his associates also applied neural analysis to character recognition, speech recognition and other problems.

Other less known researchers also sought to apply Hebbian learning to McCulloch–Pitts perceptrons in this period, including Selfridge (1959) in the UK. Minsky and Papert, discussed below, based their abstract computational geometry in part on Selfridge's work.

The perceptron model lacked adequate complexity, having only an input and an output layer. Minsky[2] and Papert (1969), of MIT's Research Laboratory of Electronics, published their book, *Perceptrons*, critiquing such models as capable of solving only linearly separable problems.[3] Minsky and Papert proved a theorem showing that as the input layer (which they called the 'retina') became large enough to present geometrically important classes, the number of nodes in the perceptron had to become arbitrarily large. That is, the perceptron architecture treated by Rosenblatt and others was shown to be inherently incapable of separating classes which were related in defined but nonlinear manners.

The powerful critique of perceptron applications by Minsky and Papert led to a period of sharply diminished research in the 1970s. However, in the 1988 republication of their book, Minsky and Papert noted that it was not so much their study of the limitations of the perceptron which led to the subsequent decline of neural network research as it was the concentration of neural network researchers on refining perceptron training and building better machines rather than on the fundamental theory of neural networking.

Early neural systems, such as that developed in 1957 by Frank Rosenblatt (1961), had only two layers, input and output, connected by a linear step function. These two-layer neural networks were called perceptron systems. These simple systems were proved to be incapable of handling exclusive-OR (XOR) discrimination problems, as highlighted by Minsky and Papert (1969). (The XOR problem in relation to perceptrons is discussed more fully in Chapter 3 on the backpropagation architecture.) This critique dampened neural net research for most of the ensuing decade as computer scientists and others misinterpreted the scope and significance of Minsky and Papert. The Minsky–Papert research was indeed a severe criticism of perceptrons for their inability to handle a fundamental class of logical problems. Overlooked by many at the time was the fact that this criticism was confined to two-layer neural systems using linear activation (transfer) functions.

Neural network scholars eventually responded to the Minsky–Papert critique by constructing more complex models involving one or more middle or 'hidden' layers, providing the capacity for handling more complex knowledge representation problems. Unlike early perceptron models, the newer models also relied on a nonlinear activation (transfer) function.[4] Neural networking was popularized in this period by the work at Brown University by James Anderson, creator of the 'brain-in-a-box', and by the founding of Nestor, Inc., by Brown University professors Leon Cooper and Charles Elbaum in 1975.

Stephen Grossberg (1969a; 1969b; 1970; 1971; 1972; 1976a; 1976b; 1982) also played a prominent role in continuing neural net research in this era, including a focus on self-organizing networks, adaptive resonance and the Cohen–Grossberg theorem which demonstrates that external inputs to certain types of networks will converge toward equilibrium. His adaptive resonance theory (ART) models trained without supervision on a single pass of the data, much in contrast to the supervised, iterative approach of multi-layer perceptrons. Adaptive resonance referred to the amplification of neural activity through excitatory connections when the input pattern is matched by learned output. Grossberg (1980) and Anderson et al. (1977) also contributed to the application of neural networks to problems arising in the field of psychology.

Other researchers continuing neural network research in the 1970s and early 1980s, when it was out of favour in many quarters, were von der Malsburg (1973) with his pioneering work on self-organizing maps, Amari (1972; 1974) with his work on random selection of neurons, and Fukushima (1975) with work on machine vision.

Notable leaders of the neural network revival in the 1980s included Teuvo Kohonen et al. (1988) and Teuvo Kohonen (1989) with work on competitive learning, based on earlier work by David Willshaw and von der Malsburg. Kohonen's work at Helsinki Technical University gave further impetus to alternative neural models based on self-organization of topographic mappings of attribute space and, more broadly, to the family of unsupervised neural network models alternative to supervised models of the multi-layer perceptron family.

A background factor in the revival of neural computing in the 1980s had to do with the development of the field of artificial intelligence (AI). Mainstream AI used complex top-down if–then algorithms webbed together to form expert systems capable of imitating human decision-making. The algorithmic approach to AI made rapid progress initially, but by the 1980s it had become apparent that initial hopes were unlikely to become realized. In spite of impressive successes in certain well delimited areas (for example, winning chess games, diagnosing symptoms of illness), in less well defined problems, such as computer vision, algorithmic AI failed to generate the progress that had been anticipated. The time was right for new directions. And in fact AI received a new lease of life in the 1990s as researchers found ways to combine expert systems with neural networks.

Widespread academic interest in neural computing revived after John Hopfield (1982) presented his work on crossbar associative networks to the National Academy of Sciences – the first neural network paper published by the Academy since Minsky and Papert's critique over a decade earlier. Hopfield's work demonstrated the utility of neural networks when nonlinearities are added to neural models through feedback. Hopfield also set forth the mathematics of what are now known as Hopfield networks, including the description of network states in terms of a global energy function whose minima defined local or general optimal solutions (see Careur and Kelley, 1989: 243–4). Other concepts developed by Hopfield included content-addressable memory and error resistance. Overall, Hopfield did much to repopularize neural network research through his numerous talks as well as original research. In particular, his demonstration of the link between recurrent networks and Ising models used in statistical physics helped encourage an influx of physicists into the field of neural networks, transforming it.

The development of Boltzmann machines by Hinton et al. (1984) constituted another milestone. Boltzmann models allowed neural network researchers to generate working neural networks from a set of training examples for the first time. Gallant's (1986) work on optimal linear discriminants solved another limitation of perceptrons noted by Minsky and Papert, the difficulty in handling nonseparable sets of training patterns. Other prominent researchers in the 1980s included Kunihiko Fukushima (1988), and James A. Anderson with his work on the linear association, a parallel distributed model based on Hebbian learning (Anderson and Rosenfeld, 1988). A variety of reviews in this period further popularized the subject (see Dayhoff, 1989; Wasserman, 1989; Wasserman and Oetzel, 1989; Russell, 1991).

Boltzmann machines were characterized by slow learning times. The problem facing neural researchers after the Minsky–Papert critique went beyond creating multi-layer models with nonlinear activation functions. The additional problem was to develop a training algorithm appropriate for these more complex neural nets. Werbos (1974), in his Harvard doctoral dissertation, had developed the mathematics of a faster algorithm, the progenitor of backpropagation, but did not apply it to generating weights in hidden middle layers of a network.

Werbos's work remained hidden from the field at large for over a decade and came to prominence only after backpropagation had been described by Rumelhart et al. (1986a; 1986b), who are credited with working out the mathematics of actually estimating such complex networks, including the algorithms underlying backpropagation. Rumelhart and his colleagues at the Carnegie–Mellon Parallel Distributed Processes (PDP) Group created the backpropagation training model – still the most common neural model in general usage – which was originated in work beginning in 1981 and summarized by Rumelhart and McClelland (1986), who showed how objections raised by Minsky and Papert could be overcome by use of hidden layers and nonlinear activation functions. Backpropagation models were also developed independently in this period by Parker[5] (1982; 1985) and LeCun (1985; 1986).

Radial basis function (RBF) networks were described in 1988 by Broomhead and Low (1988), delineating a system of layered feedforward networks. RBF models set the stage for a wave of studies seeking to show their links to the field of numerical analysis and the study of adaptive linear filters.

By 1989, the neural network modelling movement was fully revived from the setback suffered in the 1970s. In a milestone work, Hornik et al. (1989) demonstrated that neural network models are universal approximators of input–output connections for both linear and non-linear relationships. Kuan and White (1994) later demonstrated that linear regression, binary logit and binary probit models are special cases of neural network models. Moreover, the appearance of how-to articles (Bailey and Thompson, 1990) and a variety of microcomputer-based neural network development tools made this form of analysis widely available (Neuralware, Inc., 1990) in this period. An article by Geoffrey E. Hinton (1992), considered by many to be the best popular introduction to neural network analysis, was published by the *Scientific American*, further popularizing the new field.

Part of the revival of neural network research has been the development of models bridging related fields. Feldman and Ballard (1982) popularized 'connectionism' (also known as subsymbolic processes) as a way of integrating artificial intelligence with neural network models, modifying traditional symbolic AI to focus on learning processes. Hybrid systems were promoted by Kandel and Langholz (1992). Within a decade of the advent of connectionism, texts such as those by Gallant (1993) and Fu (1994) presented neural networking in a manner thoroughly integrating neural networks with knowledge-based approaches like expert systems. Hybrid systems take advantage of rule-based domain knowledge where it is effective in prediction and classification, but also use neural network architectures to handle noise and uncertainty in the input data in a manner better than knowledge-based systems alone can process.

Some of the excitement of the neural network movement is found in the account of David Jenkins:

> I cut my teeth on William Allman's *The Apprentices of Wonder* and then Ed Rosenfeld and Jim Anderson's *Neurocomputing* – two wonderful books. They swept me away from my mundane database work with the idea that neural networks represent a new way of thinking: a wildly polygamous conjunction of computer science, biology, linguistics, engineering, psychology, and statistics that had the thrill of 1960s rock and the roar of a thousand central processors hooked up in parallel. (1991: 50)

In this monograph we explore what the 'rock and roar' is all about.

The Case for Neural Network Analysis

Neural networking involves algorithms under which information is accumulated in programmed objects or nodes which are capable of 'learning' through many iterations using simulated or real data. This form of artificial intelligence can handle problems for which relationships are less known compared with relatively highly structured expert systems or equation-based approaches. Neural net models can fit linear, polynomial and interactive terms without requiring the researcher to model them. Neural net models are also well adapted to handle analyses of topics in social science where input information is incomplete and output results are approximations.

In comparison with procedures such as log-linear analysis neural models enable reconstruction of social processes within a global frame which simultaneously considers all available relevant variables. Scott Toborg and Kai Hwang (1989: 611–12) have outlined seven points on which neural models differ from conventional statistical computing:

1   *Massive parallelism,* which means complex neural models may utilize hundreds of thousands of neurons
2   *High interconnectivity,* which means that neural models involve tracking the connecting paths, which are often a large multiple of the number of neurons

3 *Simple processing,* which means that each neuron engages in relatively simple calculations, summing inputs, then applying a threshold function to determine if the neuron will fire (have output)

4 *Distributed representation,* which means that connection weights are modified based on error or new information, which in turn means that data leading to predictions are not a stored 'answer' at a memory location but are based on data throughout the network

5 *Fault tolerance,* which is a corollary of distributed representation, and means that neural network systems continue to function even when particular neurons 'die' (cease having output)

6 *Collective computation,* which means that problems are solved not by sequential instructions but rather through the joint activities of all the neurons in the system

7 *Self-organization,* which means that neural network systems are capable of changing structure to reflect new input patterns.

Where neural nets are appropriate they may be superior to conventional statistical techniques for pattern matching. Neural network models are universal, nonparametric and robust (Bengio, 1996: 92). They work even with noisy, overlapping, highly nonlinear and noncontinuous data because processing is spread over a large number of processing entities, making neural networks relatively fault-tolerant (see Moore, 1988). There is no constraint on the number of input variables, which may include nominal-level data.

In neural models, outputs are not greatly influenced in most cases by any single input value but rather depend on patterns of inputs, with the result that neural networks are tolerant toward coding errors, missing data and noise. The built-in redundancy of neural models provides the ability to withstand component failures without crashing the system. The social scientist should consider neural models wherever a precise computational answer is not feasible. This occurs in pattern recognition problems, classification problems and when working with 'fuzzy variables'.

As shown by Hornik et al. (1989), neural network models are universal approximators of input–output connections for both linear and nonlinear relationships. The nonparametric nature of neural models makes them particularly suited for social science data, where the assumptions of normality and linearity cannot be assured. On neural models as efforts to create consistent nonparametric estimators, see Geman et al. (1992). Where traditional statistical and even expert systems models require well defined or at least partially defined domains to be effective, neural models can handle highly unstructured data. There is evidence that neural models are robust in the statistical sense (Lippman, 1987) and are not easily confounded by varying underlying data distributions.[6] There is also evidence that neural models are robust when faced with a small number of data points (Church and Curram, 1996; Chiang et al., 1996; see contrary findings of Pugh, 1991).

Not all studies comparing neural networks with traditional statistical techniques find neural nets to be superior. Griffin (1995), for instance, found that for Navy flight training data, neural models yielded better prediction of flight performance but not significantly so. There are other studies coming to much the same conclusion.

- Pugh (1991) found that while neural networks were comparable with regression analysis in general, they did worse in predicting medical diagnoses for small data sets, where they tended to overfit the data and not generalize as well.
- Dwyer (1992) compared backpropagation networks with logistic regression and nonparametric discriminant analysis in prediction of backpropagation. She found backpropagation outperformed discriminant analysis but was only on a par with logistic regression.
- Heckert (1994) compared neural models with discriminant function analysis (DA) of police personnel records and found neural models did not outperform discriminant analysis, and fared worse than discriminant analysis when data had missing cases.
- A review of the literature on use of neural models in forecasting by Hill et al. (1994) found evidence that neural models performed on a level comparable with conventional statistical time series techniques.
- Nour (1994) compared a modified version of a Kohonen self-organizing neural network with regression and discriminant analysis, finding the three approaches were comparable in power.
- David Scarborough (1995), using employee selection data for sales personnel, compared neural models with ordinary least squares (OLS) regression and with a nonlinear model, finding that while neural network analysis outperformed both alternatives, the margin of superior performance was significant only in comparison with OLS.
- Church and Curram (1996) compared neural network models with econometric forecasts of the rate of growth of consumers' expenditures in the late 1980s. They found that neural models described rates as well as but no better than traditional econometrics.
- Hana (1996), in a study related to nicotine in flue-cured tobacco, found quadratic discriminant analysis outperformed backpropagation in two of three test models.

Church and Curram reflect a growing consensus in the research methodology community when they emphasize that whatever methodological procedure is used, the critical factor is judicious selection of the menu of independent variables.

In light of findings such as these, Sohl and Venkatachalam (1995) have argued that no one model provides the most accurate forecasts for all situations. Instead, they urged use of neural models as meta-research tools, as a way of assisting the researcher in the selection of appropriate time series characteristics on the input side and appropriate time series forecasting methods on the output side. Likewise Reynolds (1993) demonstrated that neural network analysis could be effective in selection of ARIMA (auto-regressive integrated moving average) time series forecasting models for business and industrial applications. And a number of authors have demonstrated that integrating statistical techniques like discriminant function analysis with neural models can lead to results superior to using neural network analysis alone (Cortez et al., 1995; Srivastava, 1996).

With due appreciation for studies showing neural models are not panaceas, are not always superior to traditional statistical techniques, and do not substitute for wise variable selection and accurate measurement of data, it can be argued persuasively that neural network models are often superior to alternatives in terms of predictive power. Although neural models are a type of multivariate approach which is still less well known than multiple regression and other now-traditional members of the multivariate general linear hypothesis (MGLH) family of procedures, several studies have demonstrated them to be the methodology of choice, performing more powerfully in common settings than MGLH models and other traditional and modern techniques.

- Lapedes and Farber (1987) compared a backpropagation neural network model with conventional linear and polynomial time series methods and found that for chaotic series, backpropagation outperformed traditional methods by orders of magnitude.
- Shea and Lin (1989) reported on the Thermal Neutron Analysis (TNA) project developed by Science Applications International Corporation (SAIC). SAIC had been contracted by the Federal Aviation Administration (FAA) to develop software for analysis of neutron radiation directed at travellers' luggage at airport security checkpoints. Initially it used a linear discriminant function technique, but this proved too inefficient and slow. SAIC then turned to a neural-network-based methodology which proved successful.
- Porter Sherman of the University of Bridgeport, CT, found that in recognizing liver disease the neural network he developed produced results with 86–90 per cent accuracy, compared with SAS statistical results of 77–84 per cent accuracy (Xenakis, 1990: 42).
- Schrodt (1990) compared neural network analysis with discriminant analysis and expert systems approaches and found neural networks to outperform the other two in split-sample tests of predicting international conflict outcomes for the Butterworth data set (ICPSR #7586).

- Fowler (1991) compared a neural network model with discriminant analysis to predict dental college students' academic outcomes from preadmission data, finding the neural model to exceed prediction rates using discriminant analysis.
- Garson (1991a) compared a neural network model with an expert system model (based on the ID3 algorithm) as well as with MGLH models and found that, for a controlled data set, neural network analysis consistently outperformed the alternatives.
- Hutton (1992) found that neural network classifiers often outperform classical techniques.
- Gordon (1992) compared discriminant function analysis with neural network backpropagation and found that as decision thresholds for classification were made more stringent, neural models retained accuracy of prediction better than discriminant models, suggesting their being a methodology of choice for prediction of low base rate human behaviours.
- Collins and Clark (1993) compared multiple regression models of white collar crime with models based on neural network analysis and found cross-validation correlations and correct classification were significantly greater for neural models.
- Peterson et al. (1993) reviewed the literature and concluded that methodology comparisons are in favour of neural models.
- Guan (1993) compared neural networks with discriminant analysis in predicting bankruptcies, finding neural networks to be superior.
- Xiong (1993) compared backpropagation neural networks with Box–Jenkins time series forecasting and found the former outperformed the latter by a significant margin.
- The US National Institute of Standards and Technology (NIST) undertook two studies comparing traditional and neural network classification techniques. One study focused on classification of FBI fingerprints, while the other focused on classification of handwritten digits in a US postal context. The NIST studies compared a variety of classification techniques, including Euclidean minimum distance (EMD), quadratic minimum distance (QMD), normal parametric classifier (NRML), single nearest neighbour (1-NN), k nearest neighbour (k-NN), weighted several nearest neighbour (WSNN), multilayer perceptron (MLP), radial basis functions (RBF1, RBF2) and the probabilistic neural network (PNN). In both cases the NIST found probabilistic neural network models to be the superior classification technique (NIST, 1993; 1994).
- Anderer et al. (1994) compared backpropagation with z statistics and discriminant function analysis for purposes of discriminating between demented and normal patients in a pharmacological study. The authors found backpropagation to outperform the two alternatives investigated.

- Everson et al. (1994) compared backpropagation with multiple linear regression and with discriminant function analysis in a study of classification of educational performance. Results showed neural computing methods may lead to higher rates of classification accuracy, particularly when underlying models are nonlinear.
- Kilmer (1994), in a metamodel of computer simulations, found neural network analysis to outperform regression analysis.
- Meley (1995) compared backpropagation neural models with linear multiple regression, using nonlinear simulated data, and found backpropagation produced consistently superior predictions.
- Wheeler (1994) compared neural network analysis with discriminant function analysis for purposes of predicting graduate student success in passing bar examinations. She found neural models yielded significantly better predictions for this purpose. However, in related comparisons (for example, predicting minority student success rates), no significant difference was found.
- Ye (1994) compared neural analysis with traditional linear methods for predicting foreign exchange rates, finding that the outperformance of the neural network model over other traditional linear models may come from the successful detection of the nonlinearities existing between the spot exchange rate and its lagged values.
- Forsstrom and Dalton (1995) surveyed work on positron emission tomography (PET scan) and found neural networks have outperformed trainees and discriminant function analysis, and have even performed significantly better than human experts.
- Greene (1995) found in a psychometric study that (1) neural network methodology is a viable alternative to traditional psychometric procedures in the demonstration of the discriminant validity of a multidimensional psychological test in the affective domain of self-concept; and (2) neural network methodology can be expected to provide promising results in the identification of items that are most discriminating or least discriminating in relatively homogeneous scales in psychological measurement.
- Longo (1995) compared neural and discriminant function models for selecting winning stocks, concluding that neural networks used for forecasting were shown to be highly effective, while the models based on discriminant analysis were ineffective.
- Paik and Marzban (1995) analysed television nonviewership with a neural model and with discriminant function analysis, finding the neural model to be superior in performance.
- Hiemstra (1996) compared the most common form of neural network model with linear regression for purposes of stock market prediction. After establishing that strong nonlinear effects were absent from the data, Hiemstra was able to show that the neural model outperformed linear regression by a wide margin.

- Bejou et al. (1996) used neural network analysis in predicting relationship quality, finding it superior to multiple regression.
- Chiang et al. (1996) compared neural networks with regression models for purposes of predicting end-of-year net asset value of stocks. They found neural models to outperform significantly regression models.
- Dybowski et al. (1996) compared neural network analysis with logistic regression in prediction of mortality of critically ill patients based on medical case history information, finding that neural networks performed better in terms of prediction.
- Greene (1992) and Greene and Michael (1996) compared neural network models with traditional multivariate and psychometric statistical procedures and found that neural model estimates were consistently equivalent to or better than traditional procedures in analysing the same databases. A predictive improvement of 15–20 per cent was found on the average.
- Kohzadi et al. (1996) compared neural net models with ARIMA models for forecasting commodity prices, finding the former to be significantly better.
- Luciano (1996) studied clinical depression, comparing a neural model with multiple linear and quadratic regression, finding the neural model to outperform the alternatives studied.
- Marzban and Stumpf (1996) compared neural network analysis with a rule-based expert system, the National Severe Storms Laboratory's mesocyclone detection algorithm for predicting tornados, finding the neural model outperformed the expert system, as well as discriminant analysis and logistic regression.
- Meraviglia (1996) compared neural network analysis with path analysis of social mobility patterns, finding it to be higher in explicative power.
- Pattie and Haas (1996) compared neural net models with multiple regression for purposes of forecasting wilderness recreation use, finding the former to be significantly more accurate by a factor of two.
- Quinn (1996) studied IRS cases, comparing a neural model with ordinary least squares regression, discriminant analysis and logistic regression (logit), finding the neural model to outperform the alternatives.
- Xia (1996) studied insurance insolvency and found a backpropagation model to outperform discriminant analysis, logistic analysis and some other rating methods in its prediction accuracy.

Neural networks present the social scientist with a tool which has been shown to be powerful across a broad range of problems, frequently to outperform many standard procedures, and to be appropriate even for fuzzy data environments common in the social sciences. Indicative is William Hedgepeth's (1995) study of 400 years of data on military combat, finding that traditional statistical methods may equal or even surpass neural models when data are clean, filtered and perfect, but that neural models outperform their statistical counterparts when data are noisy and imperfect. In addition, of course, neural models outperform multiple regression and other linear techniques when there is underlying nonlinearity in the data, and, in fact, neural modelling is a test for neglected nonlinearities (Lee et al., 1993). Moreover, unlike regression, neural models do not assume an absence of interaction among the input variables, can handle interaction effects as well as nonlinearities, and are not restricted to analysis of a single output at a time.

Haykin (1994: 4–5) summarizes by outlining eight useful properties of neural networks:

1   *Nonlinearity* includes the ability to handle data sets whose underlying nonlinearities cannot be described in advance.
2   *Input–output mapping* is accomplished without assumption of any particular probabilistic distribution model for the inputs or outputs, putting network analysis in the same class as nonparametric statistical inference.
3   *Adaptivity* allows neural networks to operate effectively in nonstationary environments, easily capable of being retrained to deal with environmental changes.
4   *Evidential response* allows neural networks not only to make classifications but also to provide confidence information about these classifications, information which can be used to reject future ambiguous patterns.
5   *Contextual information*, including interaction effects, is handled automatically by neural networks as every neuron in the network is affected globally by all other feature detectors.
6   *Fault tolerance* means neural networks degrade gracefully because information is distributed throughout the network, and operating problems like outliers have less effect on outputs than in statistical models.
7   *VLSI implementability* means neural network analysis is well suited for very large scale implementation (VLSI), allowing real-time analysis of complex information.
8   *Uniformity of analysis and design* means there are common building blocks which enable integrated modular designs.

To these eight, Haykin adds a ninth: *neurobiological analogy* provides proof, in the form of the human brain, that fault-tolerant parallel processing is possible, fast and powerful, even though present neural models are capable of capturing only a tiny fraction of that power.

Obstacles to the Spread of Neural Network Analysis in the Social Sciences

Given the strong case for neural network analysis in application to problems where prediction is critical, it is hardly surprising that it has become the methodology of choice in fields such as financial analysis of stock portfolios. While one might think that neural models might quickly displace traditional approaches throughout the literature of social science, this has not happened. The student of neural models quickly encounters several reasons why this is so. One, of course, is the relative novelty of this approach. Rumelhart and McClelland edited their influential collection, *Parallel Distributed Processing: Explorations in the Microstructures of Cognition,* only in 1986, and neural network software became generally available to social scientists only in the early 1990s. Beyond novelty, there are four other obstacles to the spread of neural network analysis in social science.

First, neural models lend themselves to prediction but not to causal analysis. It can be difficult to understand how neural nets arrive at their results. Systems designed thus far do not include the capacity of alternative techniques like expert systems to provide an audit trail fully explaining how the system arrived at its conclusions. Moreover, neural nets are not designed to take advantage of existing expertise as are expert systems. The 'hidden layers' do more than conjure up a 'black box' imagery: the algorithms of neural analysis result in neural weights to which it is difficult to assign a causal interpretation. In a later section of this monograph, this problem is faced head-on. While there are approaches to causal analysis using neural models, it is still fair to state that the social scientist's core concern with explication, not simple prediction, has been the primary reason why neural models have not spread more than they have. In this vein Andrew Hunter (1997) observes of neural networks:

> It is accepted that it may never be possible to completely understand how such a machine actually operates. Provided networks can be built which can learn to perform the necessary functions, we need not actually understand how exactly they perform them. From a viewpoint of a classically-trained scientist, building things without understanding them is almost tantamount to heresy.

Second, neural models are many and complex. The backpropagation model is the most common, but neural network analysis is not 'a' technique. There are many, many neural models. One could devote a lifetime to experimenting with the alternatives, optimizing them, and exploring the effects of different parameters. Ultimately, neural modelling is an art form and the social scientist who embraces it is an artist whose work is never finished, or at least, is an artisan who is never sure the analysis he or she presents to the public might not be suboptimal. The social scientist titillated by the appeals of neural models is often soon repelled by their complexity.

Third, at a practical level, neural models have been slow to become incorporated in *SAS*, *SPSS* and other much-loved standard statistical packages which, for many social scientists, define the very bounds of research methodology. Fortunately, however, this is now changing and as a result one may expect a substantial upsurge in interest in neural models. See, for example, the work of Sarle (1994b) using *SAS* to implement neural network analysis. *SPSS* has now acquired a neural network module, called *Neural Connection* described later in this monograph, and *SAS* is likewise implementing neural network programming.

Fourth, of lesser but still nontrivial importance, another obstacle to the spread of neural modelling in social science is confusion arising from the fact that as the methods arose in fields alien to social science, a very different jargon of the trade is encountered by social scientists who begin to read neural network literature.

1   Cases or observations are called patterns.
2   Variables are called features.
3   Independents are inputs.
4   Dependents are targets or outputs.
5   Residuals are errors.
6   Estimation is training, learning or self-organization.
7   Validation is generalization.

And the reader must make the connection between regression and discriminant analysis on the one hand and supervised learning on the other; between principal component analysis and unsupervised learning; and between cluster analysis and competitive learning. These and other terminological problems can make neural network analysis a difficult read for the novice social scientist.

Uses of Neural Network Analysis

Neural network analysis is useful throughout the social sciences for several purposes, the primary of which is prediction, including time series forecasting, whether of the performance of a stock index or the occurrence of international events. As such it is an alternative to multiple regression, logistic regression and members of the multivariate general linear hypothesis family of statistical procedures. Second, neural network analysis is useful for a broad range of classification problems as, for example, an alternative to discriminant analysis. Related to this, neural network analysis can be used to address segmentation tasks which involve identifying clusters of data attributes as an alternative to factor analysis, cluster analysis and related statistical techniques.

Uses of Neural Network Analysis: Economics and Business

Neural networks are increasingly common in a broad variety of other business-related domains from financial analysis to market research to economic modelling, widely publicized in business journals (Cringely, 1994) as well as information technology periodicals (Widrow et al., 1994) and economics generally.[7] Among the many applications are these:

- accounting control assessment (O'Callaghan, 1994)
- banking applications (O'Heney, 1990)
- bankruptcy prediction (Odom and Sharda, 1990; Dwyer, 1992; Guan, 1993; Luther, 1993; Nour, 1994; El-Temtamy, 1995; Boritz and Kennedy, 1996)
- bond rating (Dutta and Shekhar, 1988; Nour, 1994)
- commodity price forecasting (Kohzadi, 1994; Kohzadi et al., 1996; Ntungo, 1996)
- decision science (West, 1996)
- document retrieval (Kim, 1994)
- econometric modelling (Wang, 1996; Verkooijen, 1996b)
- employee classification (Quinn, 1996)
- employee selection (Scarborough, 1995)
- exchange rate prediction (Ye, 1994; De Matos, 1994; Seiler, 1994; Verkooijen, 1996a; Rivera-Piza, 1996)
- financial management (Lin and Lin, 1993; Chang-tseh, 1993)
- finance and investment (Trippi and Turban, 1993)
- forecasting economic time series (White, 1994)
- forecasting insurance fraud (Xia, 1996)
- forecasting US Treasury bonds (Cheng, 1996)
- institutional simulation (Luna, 1996)
- interest rate option forecasting (White, 1996)
- market research conjoint analysis (Powell, 1995)
- market research as an alternative to the Brunswik lens model (Ali, 1995)
- merger prediction (Theng, 1996)
- modelling consumer choice (Blankenship, 1994)
- modelling production functions (Brummett, 1994)
- money demand functions (Soto, 1996)
- mortgage underwriting (Collins and Scofield, 1988)

- mutual fund net asset value forecasting (Chiang et al., 1996)
- production process control (Hamburg, 1996)
- public offering optimal pricing (Jain and Nag, 1995)
- relationship quality in relationship marketing (Bejou et al., 1996)
- risk assessment (Davis, 1993; Hegazy, 1994)
- sales forecasting (Breedt, 1994)
- stock market index forecasting (Chua, 1992; Corcella, 1994; Van Eyden, 1994; Zhuo, 1995; D'Souza, 1995; Tak, 1995; Haefke and Helmenstein, 1996a; 1996b; Qi, 1996; Westheider, 1997; Gottschling, 1997)
- stock selection (Longo, 1995; Srivastava, 1996)
- valuation of mortgage-backed securities (Chan, 1996).

Ward Systems Group, publishers of *NeuroShell*, cites among examples of its users those who employ the software for stock buy/sell decisions, predicting the risk of bankruptcy, predicting sales revenue, predicting service calls and customer transactions, optimizing manufacturing processes, selecting target markets, forecasting reservations, scheduling staff members, predicting fish catch and selecting audit targets. Wherever prediction is central to economic analysis, neural network models are apt to be found.

Financial analysis is one of the few social science domains in which neural network analysis has become the preferred mode of multivariate investigation – for the obvious reason that the profit motive as mediated through stock selection places a premium on predictive power, which is where neural models excel. Hiemstra (1996), for instance, has applied a neural network model to the prediction of quarterly stock market excess returns and has shown it to be superior to previously used regression techniques. By predicting the sign of the excess return prediction, Hiemstra utilized an asset allocation policy to switch among stocks and long bonds, improving investment performance by a wide margin over regression-based results.

Risk assessment and risk management is another prediction-oriented area in which neural models are commonly applied. Jagielska and Janusz Jaworski (1996), for instance, used two neural network systems, one to emulate the decisions of a legacy risk assessment system and the other to predict performance of credit card accounts based on historical data. The authors found that neural network modelling can identify problem credit card applicants at a very early stage in the credit account life cycle. Neural models have also been used to study auditors' selective attention and to measure auditors' knowledge structures in control risk assessments (Davis, 1993).

A third arena of economics and business in which neural networks are coming into use is as tools for general managerial decision-making. Huston (1993), for instance, has used neural models to implement concurrent verbal protocol analysis, with a view to selection of best problem-solving tools to apply to particular business problems. More generally, Usher and Zakay (1993) have developed a neural network model for multi-attribute decision processes.

A fourth area is managerial applications. For instance, the Airline Marketing Tactician (AMT) is a computer system combining neural network backpropagation with expert systems to monitor and recommend departure booking levels, controlling airline seat allocation. Another example from a different sector is the set of neural network models developed by Robert Hecht-Nielsen, founder of the HNC Company. These include the Credit Scoring System to screen mortgage applications.

Uses of Neural Network Analysis: Sociology

Neural network models have been used in social work to screen decisions regarding child abuse, and in criminology to select criminal investigation targets. Other neural model research in sociology has included:

- predicting violent criminal behaviour based on demographic variables, criminal history, psychometric scales, and family and work variables (Gordon, 1992)
- prediction of child sexual abuse (Kelly et al., 1992)
- predicting white collar crime (Collins and Clark, 1993)
- modelling human decision-making and learning in relation to sociological theories of religion (Bainbridge, 1995)
- investigation of prisoner dilemma scenarios in game theory (Macy, 1996)
- study of use of Forest Service and Park Service recreation lands (Pattie and Haas, 1996)
- study of feelings of hopelessness among high school adolescents, based on such standard instruments as the Millon Adolescent Personality Inventory and the Parental Bonding Questionnaire (Kashani et al., 1996)
- explication of patterns of social mobility and inequality (Meraviglia, 1996)
- human services applications (Steyaert, 1994).

Uses of Neural Network Analysis: Political Science

Greene R & D International, Inc., of San José, California, has used neural models to analyse voting behaviour. Neural models have also been used to select optimal legal strategies. Other neural research in political science has included:

- event analysis in international relations (Schrodt, 1990; 1991)
- analysis of municipal jurisprudence (Bochereau et al., 1991)
- prediction of the likelihood of passing bar examinations (Wheeler, 1994)
- prediction of administrative success of candidates for local school principals (Stone, 1993)
- identifying legal precedents for cases of interest (Hobson and Slee, 1994; Rose, 1994)
- modelling data on the history of military combat (Hedgepeth, 1995)
- predicting the outcome of cases at law (Hunter, 1997).

Uses of Neural Network Analysis: Psychology

Neural network models have been used for psychiatric diagnosis, for predicting psychiatric treatment outcomes, and in teaching cognitive psychology. Colin Martindale, for instance, integrated neural network modelling with cognitive psychology in *Cognitive Psychology: A Neural-Network Approach* (1991). Among the other uses of neural network analysis are:

- artificial vision techniques for recovering the general structure and three-dimensional shape characteristics of objects depicted in line drawings (Tambouratzis, 1991)
- chromatic perception (Pessoa, 1996)
- cognition: the context effect for letter recognition (Murre, 1992)
- combat psychology (Hedgepeth, 1995)
- comparison of natural and artificial neural networks better to understand both (Happel and Murre, 1994)
- construct validation (Greene, 1995)
- depth perception (Gotts and Bremner, 1995)
- designing neurodynamic architectures (Happel and Murre, 1994)
- development of artificial intelligence capabilities, such as autonomous navigation of a vehicle through obstacles (Ziegler, 1991)
- development of external memory strategies in problem-solving (Anumolu, 1993)
- enhancing expert systems used in defence sector decision-making (Trafton, 1995)
- human information acquisition (Shaw et al., 1995)
- identification of structure in personality data (Laudeman, 1994)
- language acquisition under the competitive model (Blackwell, 1995)

- methods of improving neuropsychological assessments implemented through standard word association instruments (Bobis, 1991)
- modelling memory and amnesia (Lynn, 1994)
- modelling reciprocal determinism (Meley, 1995)
- modelling of unipolar depression (Luciano, 1996)
- modelling the Wisconsin Card Sorting Test, a widely used neuropsychological instrument (Parks et al., 1992)
- models of development (Elman, 1996)
- models which simulate Gestalt rules for visual grouping of stimuli, such as proximity, good continuation, and symmetry (Lehar, 1994)
- models of recognition and cued recall (Chapell and Humphreys, 1994)
- models of spatial colour and brightness information processing (Arrington, 1993)
- models of speech motor skill acquisition and speech production (Guenther, 1995)
- models of textural segmentation in the study of figure–ground discrimination processes (Mesrobian, 1992)
- models designed to improve adaptive intelligent application environments for better human–computer interfaces (Chiu, 1993)
- natural language processing, inferring rules about language (Rumelhart and McClelland, 1986)
- network models of rule learning and encoding (Levine, 1995)
- neuromorphic modelling of biological nervous systems (Russell, 1996)
- Pavlovian environments (Burgos, 1996)
- perception of musical sequences (Page, 1994)
- predicting employee misconduct (Heckert, 1994)
- prosodic variation in human speech (Fleming, 1997)
- reinforcement in learning theory (Styer, 1995)
- role of the frontal lobes in sequence classification (Bapi, 1994)
- simulation of hallucinated 'voices' and associated speech perception impairments in schizophrenic patients (Hoffman et al., 1995)
- simulation of spatial learning (Brown, 1995)
- simulation of stroke-induced dyslexia (Wallich, 1991)
- spoken word recognition (Taschman, 1993)
- symbol manipulation (van der Velde, 1995)
- temporal processing in speech perception and motor control (Boardman, 1995)
- test validation and instrumentation (Greene and Michael, 1996)
- text-to-phoneme conversion (Bullinaria, 1995)
- visual figure–ground separation and auditory pitch perception (Wyse, 1994)
- visual perception (Mcloughlin, 1995).

2

The Terminology of Neural Network Analysis

This chapter lays the groundwork for the rest of the monograph by providing a terminological tour of neural networks. Synonyms for neural networks include neurocomputers, artificial neural systems (ANS), and natural or artificial intelligence. In fact, synonyms abound in such other terms as parallel distributed processing systems, connectionist systems, computational neuroscience, dynamical computation systems, adaptive systems, neural circuits and collective decision circuits.

Neural network approaches are inspired by biology, with components loosely analogous to the axons, dendrites, and synapses of a living thing. As Figure 2.1 illustrates, in biological neural networks dendrites collect signals which they feed to the neuron, which processes it by sending a spike of electrical current along an axon, discharging it at a synapse connecting it to other neurons, which in turn are excited or inhibited as a result. In an artificial neural network, input signals are sent to a neural processing entity, also called a neuron, which after processing sends an output signal on to later neurons in the network. While artificial neural networks process events several orders of magnitude faster than the best current computers, the human brain has some 10 billion neurons and perhaps 60 trillion synapses (Shepherd and Koch, 1990), giving it a complexity and what Faggin (1991, cited in Haykin, 1994: 1) terms an energetic efficiency about 10 orders of magnitude greater than current artificial neural networks.

The biological analogy centres on the fact that neural networks do not operate on programmed instruction sets as do statistical packages. Rather they pass data through multiple processing entities which learn and adapt according to patterns of inputs presented to them. Data are not stored in these entities, nor is an 'answer' stored at a particular address in the computer's memory. Rather as inputs are presented, processing functions assume a pattern throughout the system reflecting the nature of the inputs.

The three basic components of a neural net are the neuron itself, which is the processing element, the interconnection topology and the

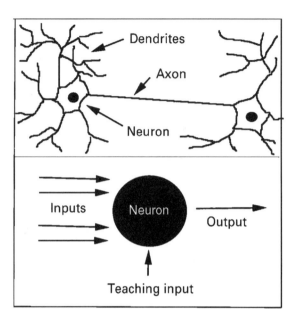

Figure 2.1   Biological and neural networks

learning scheme. The processing element accepts inputs and cumulates them in relation to positive or negative weights assigned to each class of input. Through associative recall, neural nets match incoming inputs with past patterns. Input sets need not be complete for some of the processing units to send output onto the network. Incomplete input, therefore, may still lead to appropriate output. Interconnections vary by extent of feedback loops and parallel processors. The number of inter-connections in a neural net is analogous to amount of memory in conventional computing, and the interconnections/second is analogous to instructions/second processor speed. The architecture which specifies the interconnection structure is called the network paradigm.

Neural Networks

A neural network is a parallel distributed processing system composed of processing entities called neurons, the connection strengths between which are weights which are adjusted to store experiential knowledge and make it available for later use in prediction and classification.[8] Neural network models are called *neural* because their initial formulation was inspired by analogies to the neural architecture of the human brain as applied to problems of cognition and learning. Although no

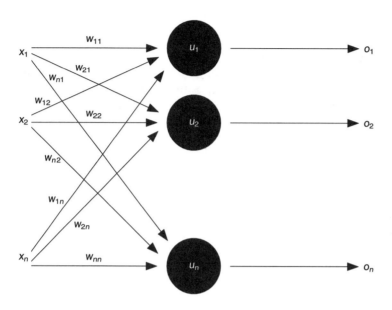

Figure 2.2 A one-layer neural model

longer confined to problems associated with biology and cognition, the language of neural network analysis still retains its roots in terms such as 'genetic algorithms', 'neurons', 'perceptrons', and the like. In fact, neural network models are sometimes called 'multi-layer perceptrons'. Neural network models involve *networks* because their structure links nodes in an input layer to nodes in a hidden middle layer to nodes in an output layer – a structure which is diagrammed as a network of nodes and connecting arrows.[9] Neural network models are *models* because neural network analysis is not reducible to a simple formula or even single procedure. Rather they are true models: rigorously defined sets of relationships assumed to exist between the input and output layers that join a set of variables of interest. 'Models' is plural because there are a large number of variations in how those relationships may be assumed to come about, and consequently there are many parameters which the researcher may set to modify the dynamics underlying a model portrayed in a neural network diagram. Figure 2.2 illustrates the elements of a one-layer neural network with 1 to n inputs (x) to as many neurons (u), with corresponding outputs (o).

Neural net software is based on multiple *neurons*, also called *processing entities* (PEs) or *nodes* or *cells*, which pass data to one another, adjusting values according to the logic assigned to each. These emulate on a much smaller scale the massive parallelism of the human brain, which uses 10 billion neurons and 10 trillion interconnections. Each neuron can accept up to $n - 1$ *inputs* in a system with n neurons, and the path from each is assigned a *weight* value. Weights determine the relative strength of the connection from an input neuron to the neuron under consideration. Weights are initialized to random values at the outset of the neural network training process, but become meaningful as learning progresses. Weights are positive if the connection is *excitatory* and negative if the connection is *inhibitory*. The rectangular array of weights is called a *connection matrix*, for which synonyms are weight matrix, decision matrix and connectivity matrix.

Weights are ordinarily *variable weights* which are adjusted during the neural network training process as part of learning. However, there are other types of weights which can be determined by the researcher. *Fixed weights* are constants for the duration of training. *Modified weights* are weights which, while fixed, are modified according to the *modifier factor* in the learning and recall schedule. This allows for weights which do not learn, but which shift in fixed value over the course of training. *Set weights* are similar to modified weights but are multiplied by an *input clamp*, which is simply another coefficient in the learning and recall schedule. (Input 'clamp' derives its name from being used to clamp initial inputs into a layer; the term originated with brain-state-in-a-box neural models but is now used to refer to any model in which given neurons are clamped to assure they retain current activation levels and are not adjusted through feedback.) *Pruning* is an option which sets a criterion for eliminating weights below a given threshold value.

Weighted inputs must be aggregated by the neuron through a *summation function*, sometimes also called a combination function, linear combiner or adder, which computes the *net input*. That is, for target neuron j, the basic summation is simply the sum of the path weights from all its input neurons i times the outputs of these i neurons:

$$\text{net input}_j = \sum_{i=1}^{n} w_{ji} o_i$$

While this summation function is often a simple sum, such as that above, it may reflect some other function such as maximum, minimum, majority, product, normalization or other. Summation is usually applied to all weights, but in some models it is only applied to set weights. After summation, random *noise* may be added to the sum, as determined by the learning and recall schedule's *temperature* coefficients. *Uniform noise* is the adding of linearly distributed random numbers, while *Gaussian noise* is adding random numbers distributed along the bell-shaped normal curve.

The summed weights are forwarded to the next layer of neurons by an *activation function*, also called a transfer function or squashing function, which converts the summed weighted inputs into an *activation value*, also called the transfer weight. 'Squashing' refers to the activation function squashing or limiting the permitted range of the output signal. The activation function usually introduces nonlinearity into the neural network model, allowing it to transcend the limitations of early perceptron models, which lacked a hidden layer.

If the activation value is above some *threshold value*, the neuron will *fire*, which means it will general an output – often the binary value 1. Depending on the transfer function a *gain factor*, specified by the learning and recall schedule, may be used as a multiplier of the summed weights. The transfer function may be sigmoidal (S-shaped, the most common), step threshold, linear threshold, Gaussian, logistic or many other forms (see White, 1989). After the transfer function is applied the transfer weight may be *scaled*, which involves multiplying by a *scale factor* and adding an *offset* value. In addition, the transfer weight may be *limited* to truncate it to fixed bounds.

The *output function* then takes the transfer weight and sends it along according to some rule. The rule may be direct output of the transfer weight, output of only the highest weight in a layer, output of only the highest two weights in a layer, or other rules of *competition*. Some algorithms introduce a *firing rate*. A firing rate of 0.5, for instance, would cause the neuron to fire at random only half the number of times it would otherwise be expected to fire.

Data

Neural networks operate on an input–output model. *Inputs* are the presumed predictor variables, while *outputs* are the neural model's estimates of the dependent variable or variables. Inputs may be numeric, text or pictorial (in full-featured neural software). The inputs can cause a neuron to assume one of a small number of possible states. An activation function, also called a *transfer function*, based on net inputs and the current state determines one output, which is sent to other neurons in the network. The *parent node* is the initiator and the *child node* is the recipient of a connection. If a parent node is not also a child, then it is a *root node*. The input–output process leads to similar processes in other neurons, which in turn send outputs onto the network. In the spreading activation design, the activation function is applied simultaneously to all neurons in the net. Either way, stability is eventually reached.

Data Sets

The *training data set* is the set of data used by the neural modelling software to compute model weights. It includes data on both the predictor variables and the dependent variable or variables. The training data set may be as simple as a list of input–output pairs. The *test data set* is the set of data to which the final neural model, and its associated weights, is applied for purposes of generalization. In more complex designs, the researcher may also randomly sample the test data set to create one or more *cross-validation data sets* which are also used in computation of model weights before generalization to the test data set. Cross-validation sets are used, for example, in an iterative process by which error in generalizing to the cross-validation set is fed back to adjust neural weights in the next iteration of the model under construction. Some neural packages, such as *NeuroShell 2*, refer to the use of cross-validation data sets as *calibration*.

It should be noted there is some confusion in the literature on nomenclature regarding test data sets. Because test data sets are used for validation in the final stage of development of a neural model, test data sets are also sometimes called validation data sets. However, other authors shorten the naming of the cross-validation data set used to estimate generalization during the training process and they call this the validation set. Likewise, the term 'test set' is sometimes applied to the cross-validation data set because it is used to test generalization during training, and sometimes to the final validation set used after training. In this volume we shall refer to the data used during training for purposes of estimating generalization as the 'cross-validation data set' and call the final post-training data set the 'validation data set' or 'test data set'.

Finally, some authors reserve the term 'cross-validation data set' to refer to the sets of training patterns derived by repeated retrainings, each with a different set sampled. When a researcher sets the validation set aside and trains only once, then it is called the 'split-sample validation set'. In this volume, however, 'cross-validation' will be used as a general term for *n* training iterations of a sampled cross-validation set, comprehending split-sample validation, which is the instance where *n* is 1.

An *epoch* is the number of training data sets presented to the model between updates of neural weights.

Models

The basic neural network model is one in which an input layer of nodes generates signals to a hidden middle layer of nodes which compute weights sent to a final output layer of nodes which aggregate the hidden layer weights to generate final output layer weights used to compute the desired predictions. A *node* may be thought of as an 'artificial neuron' or processing entity which performs a computational function.

A *layer* is one of three sets of nodes: input, middle (also called hidden), and output. It is not the case that the more layers, the more effective the model. While some neural network software packages allow dozens of layers, most applications work well with only three to five layers. Note there is some confusion in the terminology associated with counting layers. In this volume we would speak of a neural network with a set of input neurons, a set of hidden neurons, and a set of output neurons as a 'three-layer network'. However, some do not count the input layer and thus would refer to it as 'two-layer'. Others would refer to it as a 'two-layer' network for an entirely different reason: they count layers of connection weights, not layers of neurons, and for this example there are only two layers of weights: from input to hidden, and from hidden to output.

A *neighbourhood set* is a set of adjacent neurons in a given layer. In certain models, such as Kohonen self-organizing models, learning is linked to the neighbourhood set to which a neuron belongs. A *slab* is a set of neurons in a given layer which share distinguishing functions and/or connections, with a view to each slab serving to detect a unique input feature of interest.

Connections between neurons can be of several types. *Forward* connections go from a neuron in one layer to a neuron in a subsequent layer and are of two types: (1) *inhibitory connections* which tend to prevent the firing of a neuron, and (2) *excitatory connections* which cause the neuron to fire. *Jump connections* are a special type of forward connection, directly connecting a neuron in the input layer with a neuron in the output layer, skipping over the middle layer.

Feedback connections should not be confused with *backpropagation*. Whereas feedback connections feed data outputs back to earlier layers, backpropagation feeds information on error back to earlier layers so as to cause earlier layer neurons to adjust the functions on which they operate. Since backpropagation feeds effects forward from input to hidden to output layer, it is called a feedforward model. The term 'backpropagation' comes from the fact that in this model the error between output layer predictions and training set actual values is propagated backwards through the connections to update the weights used by earlier layers.

It is also possible to have *lateral connections* within the same layer, also known as *intralayer connections*, in contrast to *interlayer connections* between neurons in different layers. Some researchers use the term *supralayer connection* to refer to the situation where the interlayer connection is not between adjacent layers. Connections are said to be *symmetrical* if for every connection from neuron i to neuron j there is also a connection from j to i. The weights associated with a pair of symmetrical connections are equal. *Asymmetrical connections* are, obviously, those which are not symmetrical.

Lateral connections connect a neuron to other neurons in its layer, usually inhibiting the others from firing: hence this is also called *lateral inhibition.* This inhibiting of other neurons to reduce the number of active neurons in a layer is a type of *competition.* In models with competition, usually only one neuron in a layer is enabled to fire in a given iteration. A variant model allows multiple neurons to fire under competition, but constrains the sum of outputs to 1.

Feedback connections go from a forward layer neuron back to a neuron in an earlier layer. Network models which use feedback connections are called *feedback models* (e.g. Hopfield networks, recurrent neural models) and exhibit more complex behaviour than do *feedforward networks* (e.g. backpropagation networks) in which data flow only in a forward direction. In feedback networks the output of a given node is dependent on the previous state of the network; they are less affected by new data inputs; and they may not converge to the same point as a feedforward network. Feedback networks are also less likely to reach a point of stabilization but under certain circumstances may oscillate endlessly unless stopped. When feedback and input patterns reinforce each other, *adaptive resonance* is said to occur. The complexity introduced by feedback connections can lead to model instability. Feedforward models, such as the standard backpropagation network, are much more commonly used.

An issue with regard to connections is how to handle timing. If a neuron receives signals at different times, the neural modeller must decide if an early signal which is below the firing threshold is to be discarded or retained for accumulation with later signals, whose summation may exceed the threshold. In practice, most neural models handle the timing problem by updating signals in distinct waves such that signal propagation, summation and activation are all calculated simultaneously across the entire network.

Raw error is the difference between actual and desired output. However, raw error may be subjected to an *error function* which adjusts it to become what is called the *current error.* The backpropagated error is the current error, sometimes scaled by the derivative of the transfer function, which itself may be adjusted by an *offset* parameter. The backpropagated value is multiplied by each connection weight and added to the neuron's error field. *Learning rules* are then applied which adjust the neuron weight according to the error field and one or more learning coefficients.

Self-connections are also a possible model element, albeit used infrequently, in which a processing entity's output is also one of its inputs.

Fan-out connections are the set connecting an individual neuron to the neurons in a layer, such as connections of a single input layer neuron to neurons in the hidden layer. *Fan-in connections* are the set of connections from the neurons in a layer to a particular neuron, such as the connections of neurons in the input layer to a single neuron in the hidden layer.

The simplest neural network functions occur in the *input layer*, which simply generates the training data set. The computational function of nodes in the *middle, hidden layer* is to sum the weighted incoming signals from the input layer and then generate a corresponding signal to the output layer. The hidden layer picks up interdependencies in the model. Summation functions produce an *activation value*. This value is usually 0 or 1, which is a type of *bounded, discrete activation value*, characteristic of *discrete state neurons*. However, in some models the activation value can assume an unlimited range and is an *unbounded, continuous activation value*, characteristic of *continuous state neurons*.

The number of layers and the number of nodes per layer are referred to as the network's *framework*, and the framework along with the inter-connection scheme linking the layers and their nodes is called the network's *topology*.

When the *activation level* of a neuron is reached, a signal is generated and sent. The *activation function*, also called *transfer function* or *learning rule*, determines how and when the summed weighted input values merit the sending of an output signal or *firing*. Firing occurs when the activation level is above the *threshold level* set by the learning rule. A signal may be added, called *input bias*, to raise or lower the threshold level of a neuron. The transfer function also may include a *momentum* term, which reduces change by carrying forward previous weights of the neuron in question.

Firing activates the transfer function which determines actual output to the next layer. The activation level may vary over time, influenced by feedback from other nodes, and the activation rule itself may vary from model to model. Activation functions are reinforced by similar patterns of input, but they tend to decay over time when not reinforced. *Saturation* occurs when further reinforcement above a certain level has no further effect on the output value. In addition to depending on inputs, feedback and the previous output value of the neuron in the last iteration, the activation function may also incorporate the effects of random noise (sometimes called a stochastic factor or, in some packages, the jog weights tool) used to help networks get out of local minima and proceed toward optimal learning.

Neural networks vary in the way layers allow neurons to fire. Under *competition* only a single neuron, or perhaps just a few, are allowed to fire, depending on some criterion. A common criterion is declaring the neuron with the highest activity to be the *winning neuron*. In contrast, under *normalization* all neurons in a layer may be allowed to fire, but the vector of values associated with all the neurons in the layer is adjusted so that they add to a constant.

Self-organization is the automatic adjustment of weights in a neural model in response to inputs and is associated with unsupervised network models such as Kohonen nets. Self-organization is a way of handling complex and noisy data for which a mathematical description is otherwise not possible. *Synchronous* networks release all output values of a given layer or slab simultaneously, whereas *asynchronous* networks allow each neuron to fire independently of all other neurons.

The computational function of nodes in the *output layer* is to aggregate the signals of the hidden layer and generate neural weights used for prediction. *Recall* is the network's processing of the input vector into an output vector, including comparison of actual with desired output responses to create an error signal for backpropagation in the next time iteration. *Learning* is the network's adjustment of neural weights in each iteration of the model. To put it another way, recall and learning are two phases of neural processing: recall is the phase of passing signals from the input layer to the output layer, and learning is the adjustment of neural weights, usually in response to the error term associated with the recall phase. The *learning and recall schedule* is a lookup table of coefficients used in each phase.

Training tolerance is a parameter the researcher can set in most neural software. It simply specifies the degree of difference between actual and estimated output values in the training data set which will be allowed to be considered small enough to be equivalent to no difference, that is, to a correct answer.

The term 'model' operates at two levels in neural network analysis. On the one hand it may refer to selecting backpropagation versus some other system of neural network calculations. This is sometimes called the selection of *architecture*. 'Model' also refers to the set of weights associated with a particular iteration of a particular architecture. In this latter sense, a backpropagation system applied to a given data set might generate many models, among which the researcher would seek out the optimal one. The *backpropagation* model is the most common architecture.

Modular neural models are a more complex architecture in which multiple modules process inputs simultaneously, and there are both intramodular and intermodular connections. In CALM models (discussed in Chapter 4), for instance, intramodular connections operate on predefined weights and are mostly inhibitory, whereas intermodular connection weights vary and such connections are excitatory, changing the learning rate. The complexity of modular neural models is thought to better model the processes of the cerebral cortex (Eccles, 1984; Murre, 1992), whereas few if any neuroscientists would assert that three-layer backpropagation networks of classic neural network modelling are likenesses of human neural processes.

Partitioned typologies, such as the form supported by SPSS's *Neural Connection* package, are a class of modular neural model in which three parallel models are developed. Each has a separate set of inputs (e.g. demographic, socioeconomic and cultural) with the same target output.

Inputs may be assigned to sets on the basis of theory or on the basis of correlative techniques ranging from inspection of scatterplots to factor analysis. Outputs from the separate partition models are merged to derive a final prediction of the value of the dependent.

Whereas statistical procedures such as multiple regression are programmed, neural models are trained through presentation of examples. *Training* is the process of refining the weights in a neural model through a process in which training data are fed into the model, analysed and reprocessed through a number of iterations. Training may be supervised, unsupervised or by reinforcement.

In *supervised learning*, the correct output answer for each input pattern is supplied to the model. That is, the desired target response for the vector of training cases is also presented to the network, allowing network weights to be adjusted not only in response to the training vector but also on the basis of an error signal defined by the target vector. The most common neural models, such as backpropagation, use supervised learning because central to their algorithms is the concept of error, defined as the difference between model predictions and supplied correct answers. Supervised learning is of four types, or some combination or variation:

1   *Hebbian learning* is the oldest form, named after its creator, neuropsychologist Donald O. Hebb. Hebbian learning reinforces a neuron's weight if its input is high and subsequent (defined by some time-dependent mechanism) desired output is high, so connections are strengthened every time they are activated. Thus Hebb wrote:

> When an axon of cell A is near enough to excite a cell B and repeatedly or persistently takes part in firing it, some growth process or metabolic changes take place in one or both cells such that A's efficiency as one of the cells firing B is increased. (1949: 62)

2   Subsequent neural researchers (Stent, 1973) have added to the original Hebb rule a corresponding second one, which holds that a neuron's weight should be reduced whenever its input is high and the desired output is low, or vice versa. *Anti-Hebbian learning* networks are models which reverse the associations, such that positive correlations lead to weakening of weights, and vice versa. *Associative learning* is the term more often used now, avoiding specific reference to Hebb's algorithms, for learning which increases connection strengths according to correlated activity of the connecting neurons.

3   *Error-correction learning*, also called *delta rule learning*, reinforces a neuron's weight in proportion to an error signal expressed as some

function of the difference between the target and actual outputs, such as mean square error (the mean square value of the sum of squared errors). This function is commonly called the *cost function*. The cost function is usually minimized by *gradient descent* procedures (Widrow and Stearns, 1985; Haykin, 1991).

4   *Competitive learning*, growing out of the early work of von der Malsburg (1973) and Grossberg (1972; 1976a; 1976b), reinforces the neuron which gives the strongest response to a given input. That is, unlike Hebbian and delta rule learning, only one neuron is selected to activate; simultaneous activation does not occur. The losing output neurons remain unchanged and no learning occurs. For the winning neuron j, its connection weights are changed according to the learning rate, r:

$$\Delta w_{ji} = r(x_i - w_{ji})$$

Supervised network architectures include backpropagation, generalized regression neural networks (GRNN), probabilistic neural networks (PNN) and group method of data handling (GMDH) models.

Unsupervised learning is a process which is automatic, with classification depending on induction from examples in the training data set without reference to expected correct classifications. That is, networks trained by unsupervised learning cluster input examples according to similarity. As such they are algorithms for information compression. Under unsupervised learning, neural nets learn a compressed representation of the input data. The researcher specifies the number of clusters and the algorithm attempts to identify that number of clusters by assessing their proximity in n-dimensional space. Such models are also called *self-organizing* networks. There is some evidence that hybrid supervised/unsupervised neural models may support better generalization (Taschman, 1993). Kohonen networks are an example of implementation of unsupervised learning.

Reinforcement learning is a middle type in which, while correct outputs are not provided, a reward signal is given for desired classifications. That is, the network is not given a target vector with desired outputs for each pattern but is told how well it is performing. An example is the pole balancing problem described by Barto et al. (1983). In this example the network receives data on pole position and angle at each step, and it computes the pressure to apply to the base of the pole at each step. Data about whether the pole falls down, however, are presented after a series of steps. In reinforcement learning the algorithm does not have 'correct' responses available simultaneously with the training set itself, but it does receive global reinforcement signals indicating if its output is the desired one for a given input. The linear reward–penalty algorithm is an example of reinforcement learning (Narendra and Thathachar, 1974).

Reinforcement learning may be subdivided into two types: nonassociative and associative. Nonassociative reinforcement learning is limited to problems where the network seeks a single optimal output regardless of input stimuli (Holland, 1975; 1992; Narendra and Thathachar, 1989). Associative reinforcement learning deals with problems where the network seeks an optimal output which differs according to different constellations of inputs, thus involving mapping of outputs to input stimuli (Barto and Anandan, 1985; Watkins, 1989; Werbos, 1989; 1992; Barto et al., 1990; Sutton et al., 1991). Reinforcement strategies tend to be inefficient for large data sets, with danger of settling on suboptimal local minima.

Convergence is the speed with which a model arrives at a stable set of weights such that further iterations do not improve performance. However, speed of convergence is not equivalent to model effectiveness. In fact, a model which converges fast may train too tightly on the training data set and lack what usually is really wanted, which is good generalization. The *learning rate* is a parameter set by the researcher in most neural packages, with the default usually being 1, or at least in the range 0.1 to 1, which determines the magnitude of the adjustments made in weights in response to error. The *learning schedule* in some implementations reflects a more complex, superior approach in which the learning rate changes as the network is trained. Some packages allow the learning schedule to be edited during training. *Stochastic approximation* is a method of convergence under which the learning rate is slowly reduced.[10]

Dynamic stability is the capacity of a model to return to convergence after being presented with extreme input values. *Normalization* is a process which keeps output values within a prescribed range.

Fault tolerance is the capacity of the model to converge, perhaps with reduced accuracy, when one or more neurons is disabled.

Generalization is the extent to which the neural network model is effective in predicting data in the test data set and other future unseen data sets, not just data in the training data set. *Overfitting* occurs when the model is allowed to draw too many characteristics specific to the training data set. As the model is trained, often the underlying structure of the data is reflected in the neural network model at an early iteration. Later iterations may focus on refinements which, in essence, seek to fit the model to data noise. If enough hidden nodes are used, a neural network model can be made to fit a training data set as close as one wants. However, overfitting will occur. Some neural network software packages utilize algorithms which seek to save the model at the iteration before which overfitting starts to occur (Hutton, 1992).[11]

Pretrained networks are simply neural models, perhaps supplied with a neural network software package, which have been developed by someone other than the end-user researcher. That is, someone has already selected and applied a neural model to a set of data similar to that of the end-user research (e.g. to stock market data), and in the process has identified the purportedly best predictive indicators and has trained the network to find the purportedly optimal neural weights. Pretrained networks are thus a form of 'canned' research which either (1) reduces the time and trouble of the end-user researcher, or (2) entices the end-user researcher to fail to do the tedious spadework of identifying for himself or herself the best neural model, the best indicators and the best weights.

The basic terminology of neural networks may be summarized and reflected through a synopsis of the generic algorithm for neural learning. A network composed of neurons (nodes) grouped in layers is constructed and connections between neurons are identified. Connection weights are initialized, usually to small random values. For $i = 1$ to n training patterns, the ith pattern is presented to the input layer. The weighted input is fed to the hidden layer. The activation levels of hidden layer nodes are calculated. When activation exceeds the threshold value, the neuron fires using a sigmoidal or other activation (transfer) function. Patterns are fed through the network, looping until a minimum error stopping criterion is met or the network fails to stabilize. If training does not fail, the trained network is used to classify, predict or otherwise make inferences regarding data sets other than the training data set.

3

The Backpropagation Model

The backpropagation model, a feedforward multi-layer perceptron architecture using mean square error and gradient descent, provides both the single most common form of neural model and also a vehicle for a more detailed look at the architecture of neural models in general. Consequently, this chapter, in addition to presenting the standard backpropagation model, also discusses common variations including many more often associated with other models.

Learning Rules

The *Hebbian learning rule* was a predecessor of backpropagation. It is used mainly in teaching about neural networks. Under the Hebb rule, the change in weight w for output layer neuron i with respect to input layer neuron j is the learning rate r times the activation for neuron i times c, the correct (desired) output of neuron i:

$$\Delta w_{ij} = r a_{ij} c_i$$

This delta weight is added to the existing w_{ij} weight. Thus if the activation is 1 and the desired output is 1, then the learning rate is added to the existing weight. A threshold function may be applied to a_{ij} and to c_i to force them to 0 and 1 values. In the simplest forms of Hebbian learning, there is no learning rate factor present (that is, the learning rate is 1). When both neurons i and j are activated, the weight of the connection between them is increased under the Hebb rule. The Hebb rule always works when input vectors are mathematically orthogonal (i.e. the patterns are linearly independent) and the number of patterns to be learned is under 20 per cent of the number of neurons (see McClelland et al., 1986). When input data patterns are not orthogonal, the Hebb rule works poorly owing to interference. Hebbian learning does not take inhibitory connections into account.

The *Hebb/anti-Hebb rule* is implemented through a formula which augments the weight when the input is 1 and the desired output is 1, but decrements the weight if the input is 0.

$$\Delta w_{ij} = r(2a_{ij} - 1)c_i$$

The *Hopfield rule* is another variation on the Hebb rule:

$$\Delta w_{ij} = r(2a_{ij} - 1)(2c_i - 1)$$

This formula has the effect that if the input is 1 and the desired output is 1, then the weight is increased by the learning rate r. If the input is 0 and the desired output is 0, then the weight is also increased by the learning rate r. If neither is true, then the weight is decremented by the learning rate. Because of the nature of this rule, Hopfield networks can have trouble distinguishing between a pattern and its complement.

The *bipolar Hopfield rule*, also called the brain-state-in-a-box (BSB) rule, is still another variant on Hebbian learning. In the following formula, m_{ij} is a momentum term set equal to the previous weight change for w_{ij}:

$$\Delta w_{ij} = r_1 a_{ij} c_i + r_2 m_{ij}$$

Under BSB learning, if the input is 1 and the desired output is 1, then the weight is incremented by a first learning rate r_1. The same occurs if input and desired output are both −1. If both are 0, the weights are unchanged. If the input and desired output differ, the weight is decremented.

The *BSB/Widrow–Hoff rule* is another variant on the brain-state-in-a-box rule:

$$\Delta w_{ij} = r_1 u_{ij}(c_i - u_i) + r_2 m_{ij}$$

In this formula, a_i is the activation output of neuron i. The BSB/Widrow–Hoff rule makes weight changes depend upon output error $(c_i - a_i)$, since r_2 is normally set to 0, disabling the momentum term.

The *Adaline rule* was also invented by Bernard Widrow:

$$\Delta w_{ij} = (r/n)a_{ij}(c_i - \sum w_{ij}a_{ij})$$

The learning rate is usually set to 1 but the Adaline rule discounts the learning rate r by the number of inputs n for the current neuron. Weight changes depend upon a different definition of output error – namely the difference between the desired output c_i and the weighted summation for the ith neuron. Adaline networks may fail to converge if there are $n + 1$ or more training patterns, where n equals the number of weights, unless the learning rate is set to a value smaller than 1 (e.g. to 0.1).

The *competitive learning rule* may be mentioned here by way of comparison, though it is used in architectures other than backpropagation. Under competitive learning, the change in weight w for neuron j with respect to neuron i is equal to the learning rate r times the activation level of neuron j times an error factor equal to the difference between the activation level of the input neuron i and the weight of neuron j for the path from neuron i:

$$\Delta w_{ij} = ra_j(a_i - w_{ij})$$

The competitive learning rule is applied in a winner-take-all strategy such that only the neuron closest to the input pattern is fired. The competitive learning rule comes in different flavours (for more detail, see McClelland et al., 1986; Wasserman, 1989; Freeman and Skapura, 1991).

The *delta rule*, also known as the least mean square (LMS) rule, originated with Widrow and Hoff (1960) in connection with their Madaline neural network, which had linear outputs like perceptrons but which were not constrained to threshold values of 0 and 1. The delta rule as applied in backpropagation makes the change in weight w for input neuron j with respect to output neuron i depend on the learning rate r times the state of activation (input value) of input neuron i times an error term. The error term is the difference between the desired and actual outputs of the output neuron j. In addition, a second learning rate (which may differ, be the same, or be set to 0) times a momentum term may be factored in.

$$\Delta w_{ij} = r_1 a_i e_j + r_2 m_{ij}$$

The *delta weight* is the change in weight between the current iteration and the one prior. The delta rule is an efficient method of finding the best weights for two-layer models with linear activation functions using the delta weights to generate a momentum term. Compared with use of the Hebb rule, the delta rule allows networks to learn more associations. Whenever inputs are linearly independent, the delta rule can learn them (see McClelland et al., 1986).

The *cum delta rule* accumulates the delta weights across iterations and uses the sum to generate an adjustment to the weights. Some neural packages allow the researcher to zero the delta weights at any iteration desired. The cum delta rule is significantly less sensitive to the order of presentation of training patterns than the delta rule.

A brief illustration of how the delta rule works illuminates the basics of neural network processing in general. First consider a simple two-layer perceptron with two input neurons and one output neuron. Let the inputs represent presidential votes of husband–wife pairs, where

Democrat = 1 and Republican = 0. Let the desired output equal 1 if both husband and wife vote Democrat. Let the weights from each input to the output be initialized to 0.8. In such a very simple network, only an input pattern in which both husband and wife voted Democrat will be at or above the threshold value of 1.0. That is, the input of 1 times the weight of 0.8 plus a similar product for the other input equals 1.6. Any other input pair will result in an output value below the desired threshold, failing to cause the output neuron to fire (that is, failing to generate an output of 1).

The simple network just described can handle the AND condition of a paired pattern of husband–wife votes. Suppose, however, that the desired output of 1 is to indicate an OR condition – either husband or wife voting Democrat, or both. The delta rule can be used to retrain the AND network above to new weights which will conform to the desired input–output relationship. Using the delta rule formula above, let the learning rate r be a customary value such as 0.35. Let the network be trained for the following four patterns, representing all possible husband–wife voting patterns:

Husband	Wife	Desired output (OR)
1	1	1
1	0	1
0	1	1
0	0	0

Applying the delta rule to each of the four patterns in the training set will retrain the AND network to recognize the OR condition:

1   The first training pattern (1, 1) will not affect the weights in the network. This is because the error term will be 0 since the network correctly predicts the AND condition reflected in this pattern. When the error term is 0, the delta weight adjustment will be 0 and nothing will be added to the existing weights.

2   The (1, 0) pattern of the husband input neuron to output neuron path gives a delta weight equal to the learning rate of 0.35 times the input value of 1 times the error term of 1, which equals 0.35. The (1, 0) pattern for the wife input neuron to output neuron path gives a delta weight of 0.35 times 0 times 1, or 0. The error term is 1 in both cases because the existing AND network we are starting with generates an activation level of 0.8 for this pattern, below the threshold level of 1.0, so the output neuron does not fire, which is an output of 0. The desired output for the OR condition of (1, 0) is 1 and the actual output is 0, the difference of 1 being the error term. Applying the delta rule for this pattern will not affect the path from the wife input neuron to the output neuron since the delta weight is

0, added to the existing weight of 0.8, which leaves the weight as 0.8. For the husband input neuron to output neuron path, however, the delta weight of 0.35 is added to the existing weight of 0.8, adjusting it to 1.15. Thus after the presentation of the (1, 0) training pattern, the model weights have become 0.8 for the wife neuron path and 1.15 for the husband neuron path.

3   The (0, 1) pattern is then presented to the adjusted network. The computations are similar, resulting in a delta weight for the husband input neuron to output neuron path of 0 and a delta weight of 0.35 for the wife input neuron path – the opposite of the (1, 0) pattern, as one would expect. Adding these delta weights to the now adjusted path weights gives 0 + 1.15 for the husband input neuron path and 0.8 + 0.35 = 1.15 for the wife input neuron path. That is, after presentation of the (0, 1) pattern, both weights in the network have become 1.15.

4   The presentation of the (0, 0) case results in delta weights of 0 and no further changes in the network weights.

The new network has weights of 1.15 for each of the paths after training. For these weights, if both husband and wife vote Democrat, an activation of 2.30 will occur, above the threshold of 1.0, so the output neuron will fire, giving an output of 1. For either of the OR conditions of only the husband or only the wife voting Democrat, the activation will be 1.15, the output neuron will fire, and the output will be the desired OR value of 1. If neither vote Democrat, the activation will be 0, the output neuron will not fire, and the output will be 0, as desired. That is, application of the delta rule has retrained the network to new weights which recognize both AND and OR training patterns.

The two-layer network just described cannot be trained to recognize exclusive-OR (XOR) patterns however.[12] This is where the desired output is 1 *only* when either the husband votes Democrat and the wife does not, or vice versa, but not when both vote Democrat. XOR conditions require training for a model involving hidden layers. A generalized delta rule is needed. Parker (1985) and LeCun (1985) advanced learning systems adapted for intermediate connections. However, the principal advance may be attributed to Rumelhart et al. (1986a: Chapter 8), who used backpropagation to generalize the delta rule to a model with hidden layers.

The *backpropagation rule*, also called the error propagation learning rule, least mean square (LMS) algorithm, or generalized delta rule, is today the most common form of learning in neural networks, by a wide margin.[13] A form of feedforward, nonlinear, supervised network, the backpropagation model is the standard against which the performance of other models is often assessed. Sometimes this model is abbreviated 'BPN', for *back*propagation *n*etwork. Backpropagation is usually the default for neural network software. When neural network analysis is presented and the model is not specified, the author is almost always utilizing a backpropagation model in which there are one or more hidden layers and all neurons in a given layer are connected to the neurons in the next layer. Backpropagation modifies input weights on the basis of error signals arising from the output layer. Also, when a neuron fires it may fire any output value on a continuum from 0 to 1, not just fire a 1 or not fire for a 0 output.

Backpropagation Process

The general backpropagation process is relatively simple in concept, as illustrated in Figure 3.1. Weighted inputs are summed, processed by an activation function, and output to the next layer of neurons. That is, the backpropagation model assumes a layer of input nodes, a middle layer of hidden nodes and a layer of output nodes.

One of the input nodes is bias (sometimes this is diagrammed as a side factor rather than one of the input nodes). For any hidden layer or output layer neuron, the n inputs it receives define an n-dimensional input space. In essence, the neuron will draw a hyperplane through that space such that a given set of signals can be classed as 'on' (1) or 'off' (0). If a bias input is not present, the hyperplane must be drawn through the origin of the input space. Often this is not the optimal way to draw the hyperplane. For sigmoid activation functions, a fixed nonzero bias will avoid this problem (Hornik, 1993). The outline of a simple three-layer (input, hidden, output) network is shown in Figure 3.2.

Initial network weights and biases are set to small random values. Users provide a training set of examples of input and output. On this basis neural net algorithms attempt to model the process by which the former (input) is mapped onto the latter (output) (Kemske, 1989). With regard to the training set, note that if retraining is necessary both existing patterns and new patterns must be fed into the network, which otherwise will forget already-learned patterns.

Initialization

The neurons (nodes) in the backpropagation model are initialized to small random values. The more inputs to a neuron, the smaller the weights should be initialized. A rule of thumb is to initialize the weights to lie within the range $-2/n$ to $+2/n$ for a neuron with n inputs (Gallant, 1993: 220). After this, the input nodes distribute the input vector of values from the training data set.

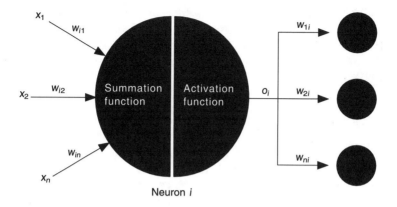

Figure 3.1   The artificial neuron

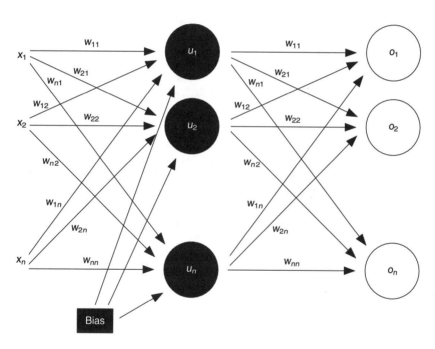

Figure 3.2   A three-layer network

The hidden nodes accept the vector of weighted input node values, sum them and apply an activation rule, also called a transfer function or squashing function. The activation rule may be sigmoid (increasing continuously from 0 to 1 as input levels increase, according to a sigma or S-shaped curve; this is the most common type), threshold (output shifts from 0 to 1 when an input threshold level is reached), linear threshold (output shifts from 0 when an input threshold level is reached, and increases linearly to 1 at some constant rate), Gaussian (adds noise, hoping to increase generalization) or logistic in nature, to name some of the possibilities. There are many possible rules (Hertz et al., 1991).

Weighted Summation Function

In the basic backpropagation model, within a hidden node each input value is multiplied by a weight. In formulaic terms, the net input I to hidden layer neuron j is the sum of paired products of the output signals o from the input neurons times the respective weights w which apply to them, for all inputs i from 1 to n:

$$I_j = \sum_{i=1}^{n} o_i w_{ji}$$

A bias term b_j acting as an additional input, such as the constant +1, is often added to the formula, so that it becomes:

$$I_j = b_j + \sum_{i=1}^{n} o_i w_{ji}$$

The output of the neural network will be some activation function $f(I_j)$ of this net input. Activation functions are discussed in the next section.

Computation of net input is the core of neural network analysis because it determines why selected neurons become associated with given input patterns. Note that the neuron whose weight vector is closest to the input vector will have the highest net input. This is because, in the formula above, the largest sum occurs when low values of w_{ji} are matched with low values of a_j and high values are matched with high values. Thus the input level I_j is determined by the correlation of the input and weight vectors.

While simple weighted summation is the usual weighted summation function, there are other possible rules:

Majority weighted summation   This is similar to simple summation, but what is added is not the weight times output signal products but only the sign (sgn) of these products. That is, majority weighted summation is equal to the net count of activation signal × weight pairs, counting those greater than zero as +1 and those less than zero as −1:

$$I_j = \sum_{i}^{n} \text{sgn}\,(o_i w_{ji})$$

CumSum weighted summation   The input I_j in iteration t is added to the previous sum in iteration $t - 1$:

$$I_{j_t} = I_{j_t} + I_{j_{t-1}}$$

Maximum weighted summation   The input I_j is set equal to the maximum of the product of the output signal times the weight among the j inputs:

$$I_j = \max_j(o_i w_{ji})$$

Minimum weighted summation   The input I_j is set equal to the minimum of the product of the output signal times the weight among the j inputs:

$$I_j = \min_j(o_i w_{ji})$$

In computing the weighted summations, in some implementations a threshold value for the node may be subtracted from the $(o_i w_{ji})$ term. In such cases one can make the threshold value adjustable by adding a bias neuron to the input layer, such that its output is always 1 and the weight for its connection to hidden layer neurons is the negative of the threshold value. There are several other possible summation functions, not characteristic of backpropagation models, including cascade, city block, DNNA, LVQ, product (shunt), SOM and SPR (spatio-temporal pattern recognition) summation functions.

Normalizing and Noise Functions

After summation and before the transfer function is applied, inputs may be normalized and noise added.

Normalization in this context refers not to the normalization of raw input values but rather to normalizing summation functions. This comes in several flavours but is not usually part of backpropagation modelling and therefore is not discussed here.

Noise may be added and often is in backpropagation modelling. When a noise function is attached to a layer, a random value (positive or negative) may be added to the weighted sum. The purpose is to help jog neural weights over local minima toward learning, leading to desired output values. Noise may follow uniform (linear) or Gaussian (normal) distributions and is set to an amount which is a function of *temperature coefficients* in the learning and recall schedule.

Activation (Transfer) Function

The output signal o_j of neuron j in the next time period $t+1$ is a function of the current weighted sum of inputs I_j.

$$o_j = f(I_j)$$

The simplest form of transfer function would, of course, be the linear one in which $o_j = I_j$. However, for reasons discussed earlier, linear transfer functions are inadequate to allow neural systems to work for certain common classes of problems. In practice, the *sigmoid transfer function* is the most common in backpropagation, used to calculate the activation level a_j, which is compared with a threshold value to determine if the neuron will fire (generate an output of 1 in many system designs):

$$a_j = 1/(1 + e^{-I_{ji} \times \text{gain}})$$

In this equation the gain is a coefficient taken from the learning and recall schedule of coefficients, modifiable by the researcher in most software packages. In basic implementation, the gain term is omitted. This sigmoid function maps input into output in a range between 0 and 1, distributed as an S-shaped curve.

The derivative of the sigmoid function at x is

$$f'(x) = \frac{d}{dx}(1 + e^{-x})^{-1}$$

$$f'(x) = -(1 + e^{-x})^{-2} e^{-x}(-1)$$

Since the expression $(1/(1 + e^{-x}))$ is equivalent to the activation a_j, the derivative of the sigmoid function at x is identical with

$$f'(x) = \frac{1}{1 + e^{-x}} \left(1 - \frac{1}{1 + e^{-x}} \right)$$

$$f'(I_j) = a_j(1 - a_j)$$

For derivation of the backpropagation algorithm, see Gallant (1993: 217–19).

Backpropagation's algorithm can be summarized in four steps:

1 Backpropagation starts by randomly assigning small weights to a_j.
2 Taking a training pattern, one computes neuron activations in a forward pass to compute the weighted sums I_j and the activation levels a_j for each neuron.
3 One then computes error gradients in a backward pass. This gradient is used to update the weights, with the new weight for neuron i with respect to neuron j equalling the former weight for neuron i with

respect to j, plus the learning rate r times the activation level a_j from neuron j times the error term e_i for neuron i.

(a) If neuron i is an output neuron, the error term is computed by taking the correct output minus the current activation level, and multiplying this difference by the derivative of the sigmoid function, $f'(I_j)$.

(b) If neuron i is a hidden layer neuron, then the error term is computed as the sum of weights for neuron i with respect to each of k inputs times the corresponding error terms for these paths, and that summation times the derivative of the sigmoid function.

4   One proceeds through the training patterns in this manner until the updates are smaller than some cutoff criterion.

At the end of the process we judge that the gradient descent has resulted in weights which represent an estimate of the minimum squared error. The sigmoid function and alternative transfer functions are discussed in the section 'Learning from Error' in this chapter, and further in Chapter 5 'Methodological Considerations'.

Stornetta and Huberman (1987) have noted that restricting the sigmoid transfer function to the range −0.5 to +0.5, instead of 0 to 1, can halve training time simply because there is no need to modify weights from neurons whose activation levels are zero. This restriction is accomplished by subtracting 0.5 from the result of the function above. For similar reasons, the hyperbolic tangent (tanh) transfer function is also faster than the sigmoid.

After the activation (transfer) function is applied, the output value may be scaled and/or limited. Linear scaling is, of course, simply multiplying a_j by a scale factor and optionally adding a positive or negative offset value. The scale factor and offset value are stored in a lookup table, the learning and recall schedule. After scaling, a_j may be truncated to lie within a specified upper and lower limit. Nonlinear scaling functions, such as logistic or tanh functions, may be applied as an alternative to linear scaling to achieve the same scaled range (0 to 1 in the case of logistic, −1 to +1 in the case of tanh). Nonlinear scaling by logistic or tanh functions has the effect of stronger scaling at the high and low ends of the data range, 'squeezing' the data, and for this reason is used to diminish the effect of outliers in the data set without arbitrary truncation or removal.

If competition is applied, only the one or two neurons with the highest output a_j will learn, and all other neurons will be set to their current weights (not be allowed to learn). That is, a_j is set to zero for these neurons, or to the offset value if one is present in the learning and recall schedule. Ordinarily, backpropagation models do not employ competition.

Learning from Error

After competition, if any, the current error is computed as a basis for adjusting weights in the hidden layer neurons. Error is the difference between the current output and desired output. Optionally, an error function may be applied to raw error prior to computing the weight change factor, though standard procedure is no transformation. Possible error transformation functions include quadratic (squaring the error but retaining the sign), cubic (cubing the error), tolerant (a tolerance coefficient in the learning and recall schedule is used as a cutoff to stop learning when error reaches the coefficient), and user-loadable error functions of a custom nature.

The general idea of backpropagating the error is to leave weights the same when correct output is achieved by the model, but to diminish weights for appropriate nodes as error of overestimation increases and to increase weights when error of underestimation increases. The purpose of backpropagation is to minimize the overall error of the neural model (i.e. to minimize global error). Neuron weights have to be changed according to a learning coefficient based on the magnitude and direction of the negative gradient of the error surface, which is a plot of the cost function (the measure of the error signal, commonly mean square error) versus the neural weights. The principle of gradient descent involves using a derivative of the ratio of error to weights as a criterion for reducing output error in the next pass of the training data. In equation terms:

$$\Delta w_{ji} = r e_j a_i$$

The change in weight is equal to the learning rate r, derived from the learning and recall schedule, times the local error gradient of neuron j times the activation level signal a from neuron i.

The local error of an output neuron j on the output layer, with respect to hidden layer neuron i, equals the activation level of neuron j times one minus that level, times the difference between desired target output t and actual activation level:

$$e_j = a_j(1 - a_j)(t_j - a_j)$$

The local error of the corresponding hidden layer neuron j at unit k, to which a connection from neuron j points, equals the activation level of neuron j times one minus that level, times the sum of weighted local errors at all neurons k to which connections from neuron j emanate:

$$e_j = a_j(1 - a_j)\left(\sum_k e_k w_{kj}\right)$$

The comparison of the local errors of the output and hidden neurons forms an error gradient.

Example: XOR Problem

This background puts us in a position to understand by example how backpropagation learning handles the XOR problem which perceptrons cannot. The example which follows is adapted from an implementation by Fu (1994: 84–5). Recall the example of husband–wife paired voting data, but adapted for the case where the desired output is 1 only when either husband or wife vote Democrat (1) but *not* both:

Husband	Wife	Desired output (XOR)
1	1	0
1	0	1
0	1	1
0	0	0

Since the desired output is a single value, there will be a single output layer neuron (neuron 1). Let there also be a bias neuron (neuron 2) with an output of 1. Since the training pattern comes in pairs, there will be two input layer neurons, which we will label neurons 3 and 4. Let there be one hidden layer neuron (neuron b).

Let there be skip connections from the input to the output layers as well as connections from the input to the hidden layer, and from the hidden layer to the output layer, so one has a fully connected network. Then let the network weights be initialized to small random values as follows:

$$w_{13} = 0.02$$
$$w_{14} = 0.03$$
$$w_{12} = -0.02$$
$$w_{23} = 0.01$$
$$w_{24} = 0.02$$
$$w_{1b} = -0.01$$
$$w_{2b} = -0.01$$

Let there be no gain factor, for simplicity.

The activation levels are calculated as follows for the first pattern [1, 1]:

$$a_4 = 1$$
$$a_3 = 1$$

$$a_2 = 1/(1 + e^{-(1 \times 0.01 + 1 \times 0.02 - 1 \times 0.01)}) = 0.505$$
$$a_1 = 1/(1 + e^{-(0.505 \times -0.02 + 1 \times 0.02 + 1 \times 0.03 - 1 \times 0.01)}) = 0.508$$

Given a learning rate of $r = 0.3$, the error gradient terms are computed:

$$e_1 = 0.508(1 - 0.508) \, (0 - 0.508) = -0.127$$
$$e_1 = 0.505(1 - 0.505) \, (-0.127 - 0.02) = 0.0006$$

The corresponding weight changes will then be:

$$\Delta w_{13} = 0.3 \times -0.127 \times 1 = -0.308$$
$$\Delta w_{23} = 0.3 \times 0.0006 \times 1 = 0.0002$$

Other weight changes are computed in a like manner. Weight changes are added to existing weights before further training. The threshold is adjusted also, set equal to the negative of the bias unit weight. There are a very large number of iterations of this process. Eventually the weights stabilize, similar to those below:

$$w_{13} = 4.98$$
$$w_{14} = 4.98$$
$$w_{12} = -11.30$$
$$w_{23} = 5.62$$
$$w_{24} = 5.62$$
$$w_{1b} = -2.16$$
$$w_{2b} = -8.83$$

These weights will solve the XOR data problem with a high accuracy. For an additional example, see Gallant (1993: 214–17).

Thus, after the error term is computed, it is backpropagated from the output layer to the hidden layer(s). The purpose is to adjust the connection weights so that in the next pass through the data, predictions will, hopefully, be even closer to the desired results. While the back-propagated error term is normally signalled directly, the backpropagation value might be scaled by the derivative of the transfer function, or might even be the desired output. Under backpropagation, the error value may be modified by an input clamp or modifier factor taken from the learning and recall schedule lookup tables.

Learning Algorithms

Note that the learning process just described is based on algorithms which discover local minima by a simple gradient descent process. It should be noted that gradient descent algorithms involve lengthy computation time. Moreover, as model complexity increases through linear expansion of the number of neurons, training time increases nonlinearly. This is because the number of weights in a network is approximately the square of the number of neurons in the largest layer, and the number of dimensions of the gradient surface is a function of the number of weights in the network.

The most common learning algorithm is based on 'steepest descent', which simply means that weights are changed in the direction of the steepest gradient on the error surface. (Recall the error surface is a plot of the cost function – the measure of the error signal, commonly mean square error – versus the neural weights.) Solution is easy when the network is composed only of neurons with linear activation functions since then the error surface will be a quadratic function of the network's weights, forming a bowl-shaped plot with a single minimum. However, in the usual case where the network has nonlinear processing units, the error surface will be a more complex plot with not only a global minimum but also multiple local minima. Gradient descent can get stuck in a local minimum and never reach the global solution. To avoid this, a momentum term may be factored in to push the network beyond local minima in search of the global solution.

Alternatively, *conjugate gradient* learning alters weights according to an average of the steepest descent gradient and the previous direction of change (momentum) for that neuron. The conjugate gradient algorithm slows convergence but in some cases assists the model in avoiding purely local minima (Shanno, 1990; Johannson et al., 1992). Conjugate gradient learning is most appropriate when there is a large number of weights in the model and the error surface is such that long valleys lead to the global minimum. However, it appears that when the error surface is more complex, or flat (as often happens when there are multiple hidden layers), conjugate gradient learning is often unable to find the true global minimum (see benchmark tests by Schiffman et al., 1993).

In most implementations of backpropagation, the gradient descent process is accomplished using a batch update (also called a deterministic update) of all weights after the gradient has been computed over all test patterns.[14] However, better results may be obtained if the backpropagation algorithm instead uses a stochastic update (also called an online update) in which weights are adjusted after each input pattern is fed into the network. The stochastic process results in a noisy estimate of parameters, and the noise may help the network avoid becoming stuck in suboptimal generalization and may improve learning speed. By updating after each pattern, stochastic updating performs a more exhaustive local search along descent paths than is the case with batch updating.

In particular, stochastic updating seems to improve model performance when the training set is large, when the learning rate is slowly decreased as training proceeds, and when training is halted before the network proceeds to overtrain by learning the noise in the particular training set it is fed.[15] Social scientists should note, however, that stochastic updating diminishes precision, making the method more appropriate for pattern recognition problems (where precision is less critical) than for prediction problems for continuous outputs.

Regardless of learning algorithm, there is no assurance of a global solution and, in fact, the researcher should assume that the first solution found is *not* optimal. Although noise functions and other tinkering with the basic backpropagation model may help the algorithm hop over local minima in search of better global solutions, standard research procedures call for multiple reruns of the model from different starting points (that is, from different orderings of the training data and/or different initial random seed values). The process is repeated by feeding in new input data until a local minimum is achieved. At the end of each iteration, data from the cross-validation (not test) data set are fed into the system to calculate validation error, and weights at that iteration are retained in memory. The best set of weights are those that minimize validation error.

Fast backpropagation is a variant proposed by Tariq Samad (1988). It modifies the equation for computing local error by adding error from the previous layer:

$$\Delta w_{ij} = L[e_j(a_i + e_i)]$$

Samad found this variation could improve time to reach convergence dramatically. Yet other fast backpropagation models add a multiple of the prior layer local error e_i. Some experimental work suggests adding $1.5e_i$ works well in many situations.

The problem with the straight application of the backpropagation algorithm as presented thus far is that the learning coefficient is adjusted based on assumptions that error is locally linear. What one would prefer is an algorithm which kept the learning rate low where the error surface might have high curvature, and high where it may be linear. A constant high learning rate can miss nonlinear error, and a constant low learning rate can involve very slow learning. A method of seeking to vary the learning rate appropriately is to add a *momentum term* (Rumelhart et al., 1986a):

$$\Delta w_{ij(t)} = re_ja_i + M\Delta w_{ij(t-1)}$$

Not only is the change in a neuron's weight in time t set equal to the learning rate r times local error multiplied by the input activation signal, but also a momentum coefficient M times the change in the neuron's weight compared with the previous time period is added. M is often set at a figure such as 0.9.

The momentum term must be in the range 0 to 1, otherwise the change in neural weights will grow toward infinity. A momentum term close to 0 will have little consequence. A more customary setting toward 1, such as 0.9, will work well for most situations. However, if the problem is characterized by a steep error gradient, then momentum may carry the network past the desired point of minimum error. The higher the momentum coefficient, the more prior weight change is carried forward with the consequence that short-term fluctuations tend to cancel each other out, but genuine trends do not. That is, without a momentum term, the backpropagation algorithm will zig-zag in pursuit of simple gradient descent on the error surface,[16] whereas with momentum added, the process is stabilized in the direction of average gradient descent. One can then set a low learning rate, sensitive to nonlinearities, yet obtain faster learning than would otherwise occur at such a learning rate setting. In particular, with noisy data, a rule of thumb is to set a low learning rate (e.g. 0.05) and a high momentum term (e.g. 0.5).

I_k is set as the input vector propagates forward through the network, as are the output signals s_k. After the forward wave reaches the output layer, the scaled local error is computed as above and then can be backpropagated by computing the change in weights as above. The delta weights are, of course, added to their respective previous weights.

In summary, in a backpropagation model the output nodes accept the vector of adjusted values from the middle layer and convert them into neural weights used for prediction. In some models there are 'skip layer' connections directly from the input nodes to the output nodes. This may be done, for instance, to incorporate linear regression as an explicit component of the neural model (cf. Verkooijen, 1996a: 55). Weights are computed through an iterative process in which, using a training set of data, estimators are channelled from input to hidden to output layers, then error terms are computed and backpropagated in the opposite direction for a new iteration. This cyclical process has been shown by White (1987) to be a form of stochastic approximation.

What does the output of a backpropagation model look like? To take a simple backpropagation example, shown in Figure 3.3, system learning results in input weights becoming modified on the basis of error signals arising from the output layer. This particular backpropagation network is constructed with three input nodes which correspond to the three causal variables in the model, LUCK, INCOME and ECONOMY. The output from a neural network software package is shown in Figure 3.4. The top of Figure 3.4 shows the input layer connections, which are the connection weights from each input node to each of the four nodes in the hidden layer. The bottom of Figure 3.4 shows the output layer connections, which are the connection weights from each of the four hidden nodes to the output node, which corresponds to the dependent variable, VOTE. The middle section of Figure 3.4 shows the hidden layer

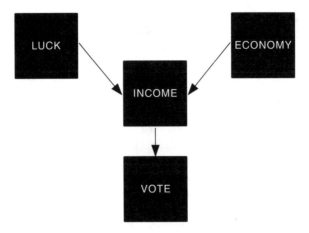

Figure 3.3   A simplified four-variable model

connections, which simply repeat the figures in the top and bottom portions of the figure. The reader will also notice that there are bias weights, which have to do with the error feedback process association with the backpropagation algorithm used by most neural networking packages. The result of application of the backpropagation algorithm is a set of predicted values of the dependent variable.

Backpropagation Model Variants

Today there are numerous variants of the backpropagation model.

Adaptive Backpropagation

The adaptive backpropagation model (Silva and Almeida, 1990) attempts to assign small learning rates where the error gradient is steep and large learning rates where it is gradual, doing this by assigning an individual learning rate to each weight, increasing it when the sign of the gradient remains the same and decreasing it when the sign of the gradient changes between iterations.

Super Self-Adapting Backpropagation (SuperSAB)

Super self-adapting backpropagation (Tollenaere, 1990) is a variant which combines the adaptive backpropagation technique with a momentum method. In this approach the learning rate is exponentially

```
Learning events completed: 160497
```

```
======================= Input layer connections =======================

 LUCK
 FROM :      4.82        15.1       -6.38       -24.9

 INCOME
 FROM :     -27.6       -4.21      -30.5       -11.2

 ECONOMY
 FROM :      13.7       -7.58      -12.0       -11.4

======================= Hidden layer connections =======================

 Hidden node # 1
 BIAS :     -3.29
 TO    :     4.82       -27.6        13.7
 FROM :     -1.32

 Hidden node # 2
 BIAS :    -13.7
 TO    :    15.1        -4.21       -7.58
 FROM :     -2.69

 Hidden node # 3
 BIAS :      3.75
 TO    :    -6.38       -30.5       -12.0
 FROM :     -2.56

 Hidden node # 4
 BIAS :      3.34
 TO    :   -24.9        -11.2       -11.4
 FROM :     -2.29

======================= Output layer connections =======================

 VOTE
 BIAS :      0.83
 TO    :    -1.32       -2.69       -2.56       -2.29
```

Figure 3.4   Neural coefficients associated with Figure 3.3

increased until the sign of the gradient changes, then momentum is used
to cancel the last weight adjustment and the learning rate is decreased
exponentially. SuperSAB has been found in some circumstances to
converge faster than standard backpropagation.

Ward Models

Coined by Ward Systems Group and its *NeuroShell 2* neural network
modelling software, discussed in Chapter 6, Ward models are a variant
of backpropagation which support multiple hidden layers, each capable

of different activation functions. That is, Ward models are backpropagation or jump connection models where there are two or more hidden layers. Since each hidden layer activates its nodes using a function (e.g. sigmoid function) different from the function used in the other hidden layer(s), a different vector of weights is sent to the output layer for each hidden layer, based on the same input data. Ward Systems' *NeuroShell 2* offers three variations: (a) two hidden layer slabs with different activation functions; (b) three hidden layer slabs with different activation functions; or (c) two hidden layer slabs with different activation functions plus a jump connection between the input and output layers. These complexities may or may not be better than experimenting with different activation functions within a backpropagation or jump connection model, but the software's authors suggest that such models can discover novel features in a single pattern passed through a network when other models cannot. They suggest, for instance, using a Gaussian activation function in one hidden layer slab to detect midrange outputs and using a Gaussian complement function in the other hidden layer slab to detect upper and lower extremes of the desired output values.

Jump Connection Models

The standard connection configuration in a backpropagation model is one in which each layer is connected directly to the preceding layer. However, other connection variants are sometimes used. In a model with jump connections each layer is connected to all preceding layers, not just the immediately preceding layer. There are direct connections from an earlier layer to a later layer, skipping one or more middle layers. Direct connections from the input to the output layer, for example, can be used to incorporate linear input–output relationships explicitly into a neural model.

Recurrent Models

Recurrent models have a duplicate slab of input neurons (or a window of N slabs representing states in N time periods). The duplicate slab holds values from the previous training pattern (case) and is connected to the hidden layer in the same way as the current input slab. There are three subvariations: (a) the duplicate slab contains weights from prior pattern input; (b) the duplicate slab contains weights from the prior pattern output layer; and (c) the duplicate slab contains weights from the hidden layer in the prior pattern (this is the *Jordan–Elman recurrent network*, and is usually the most powerful of the three subvariations: Jordan, 1986; Elman, 1988; 1990). Jordan–Elman nets are often used for time series data because they can learn recurring sequences of data. In essence, recurrent models remember previous input patterns, allowing them to respond differently to the same input pattern depending on whether or not that pattern has occurred previously. Recurrent models have been used extensively in signal processing, for example.

Recurrent models train on the current pattern augmented by prior patterns. This goes beyond incorporating a predetermined number of time-delayed inputs into the input layer.[17] Rather in recurrent models the algorithm itself uses neural weights and their changes to determine the extent to which past inputs should be considered in calculation of the weights of current inputs. The degree to which recurrent models emphasize historical patterns compared with current patterns is determined by two researcher-set parameters called *feedback links*. The proportion of current neuron values assigned to one feedback link will determine the emphasis on current values, while the proportion assigned to a second feedback link will determine the emphasis on historical values. The two proportions add to unity.

As with most neural architectures, recurrent models come in numerous flavours. BPS (backpropagation for sequences), for instance, is a model in which hidden layer neurons have self-loops. BPS models have been found to be effective for problems characterized by short-term dependencies, generalizing better than static neural models incorporating time-delay inputs. BPS is described in Gori et al. (1989), Bengio et al. (1990; 1996) and Bengio (1996: 70–5).

Recurrent networks make sense and can be more effective than standard backpropagation models when the training patterns are a time series. Using a recurrent model on data which are not a time series is equivalent to training a neural model on noise since prior patterns retained by the duplicate input slab will be random. If a recurrent model does not outperform a static model for input data composed of historical values, this is evidence that the data lack a temporal structure (that is, the data do not contain time dependencies).

Recurrent models are difficult to train owing to their tendency to converge on suboptimal weights which reflect short-term time dependencies rather than long-term data patterns (Bengio et al., 1994). Also, Ohlsson et al. (1994) have found that even for time series prediction, simple multi-layer perceptron models (like backpropagation) produce as good solutions as recurrent networks, within much shorter training times, provided the researcher uses appropriate time-lagged inputs.

Other Variants

There are innumerable other variations on backpropagation. Jacobs et al., (1991), for instance, have developed a modular approach to three-layer neural networks which differentiates intramodular and inter-modular backpropagation of error terms. In fact, it is relatively easy for researchers to program their own custom variations. Schrodt (1990) provides the code for such a model, written in Pascal, for instance. O'Brien (1990) provides code for a C++ version. Pseudocode for any language is given in Henseler (1995: 65).

4
Alternative Network Paradigms

In addition to backpropagation, there are a very large number of other algorithms used to regulate connectivity in neural networks (how the nodes are linked together) – far more than can be described here. At the present writing, the author is aware of 42 distinct classes of network topology, grouped by learning algorithm. Bailey and Thompson (1990) have presented a development methodology for selecting among 15 such algorithms, including backpropagation, counterpropagation, Boltzmann machines,[18] Cauchy machines, perceptron paradigms and others. Thus there is no one neural network methodology. Some of the most common alternatives used today are discussed below.

Generalized Regression Neural Network (GRNN) Models

Generalized regression neural network (GRNN) is a term coined by D.F. Specht (1991) for kernel regression (Nadaraya, 1964). GRNN architecture is often used when data are sparse and outputs are continuous. Not to be confused with traditional regression analysis, GRNN models fit multidimensional surfaces through the data. They may find better solutions than backpropagation for certain types of problems such as the approximation of continuous functions, but they can require very long training times for large training data sets (e.g. more than 2000–4000 cases). More important, they minimize error through a distance metric rather than gradient descent, a metric which involves comparing the training pattern with the set of all input variables, including any that are irrelevant to the output variable. As GRNN cannot ignore irrelevant variables, it is a poor methodological choice when there are many independents, some of which may well be irrelevant.

GRNN models have a three-layer architecture. The input layer has as many neurons as there are inputs in the problem at hand. The number of neurons in the hidden layer is arbitrary, but one rule of thumb is to have at least as many as there are patterns (cases) in the training data set. The output layer has as many neurons as there are outputs for the problem. Training cases are passed through the network only one time, unlike backpropagation.

For GRNN models, the researcher sets scaling as for backpropagation or PNN architectures. Rather than rely on a preset smoothing factor, in some software packages such as *NeuroShell 2* the program will calculate the best smoothing factor and retain it for use on the test set if the researcher so desires. It does this through a conventional goodness-of-fit procedure applied to the trained network. After training, the algorithm searches for the smoothing factor which gives the lowest mean square error (difference of actual and predicted values for the output variable, which is mapped to the 0 to 1 range) for all test set cases for all outputs. That is, each pattern error is squared. If there is more than one output, the mean of squares is calculated for the set of outputs for a given pattern. This is repeated for each pattern and the grand mean is calculated for all training patterns. This may be repeated for many generations until the best smoothing factor is approximated. Stopping may be manually determined by the researcher, or may follow some rule (e.g. stop if the minimum mean square error to date is not reduced by at least 1 per cent after 20 generations of the training set). In addition to an overall smoothing factor, some implementations also support individual smoothing factor adjustments to each input variable.

The algorithm used by GRNN focuses on calculation of a measure of how far a given training case is in n-dimensional space (for n inputs) from other training cases. Euclidean distance is normally used. That is, for two patterns represented in two input vectors $(x_{i1}, \ldots, x_{in})$ and $(x_{j1}, \ldots, x_{jn})$, the Euclidean distance is:

$$d_{ij} = \sqrt{\left[\sum_{n=1}^{N}(x_{in} - x_{jn})^2\right]}$$

As the two input vectors match, the Euclidean distance will compute to a smaller value. The 'city block' approach is an alternative based on the sum of absolute differences between the input case and the weight vector for the associated neuron. The GRNN algorithm will generate weights similar to those for prior patterns when the distance between the new input pattern and prior cases is small.

Probabilistic Neural Network (PNN) Models

Coined by D.F. Specht (1990), probabilistic neural network (PNN) models are a form of kernel discriminant analysis (Hand, 1982; McLachlan, 1992). PNN models are attractive where the researcher wishes the output to be an actual probability. This three-layer architecture is often used when data are sparse and outputs are categorical, such that each of multiple outputs is the probability that the input case falls in the associated value of the dependent variable. That is, in the output layer there is one neuron for each category of the dependent variable and the activation function is a probability density function estimate such that the highest value indicates the output layer neuron with the highest probability for the input pattern (case). This, of course, indicates the best classification for the pattern. If the best classification still displays a low probability density, this may indicate the classification involves extrapolation and is suspect. PNN models are often efficient in locating local pattern characteristics, whereas backpropagation, by way of comparison, is often more effective in finding global characteristics.

Because PNN models utilize a distance metric rather than gradient descent, they are more closely related to radial basis function models (see below) than to backpropagation. Unlike backpropagation, PNN cannot ignore irrelevant inputs and is a poor methodological choice when the researcher has many independent variables, some of which may be irrelevant to the output variable. This drawback to PNN arises from the fact that in classifying a new training case, it uses a probability density function which measures the distance of the case to all inputs, including irrelevant inputs.

Prior to training, the researcher sets the scaling function factor much as in backpropagation models.[19] The researcher also determines the smoothing factor to be applied. The smoothing factors apply Gaussian noise to each of the inputs in the input vector in order to improve generalization. In fact, it is possible to derive the optimal smoothing pattern by testing a broad range of smoothing factors against a cross-validation data set (*NeuroShell 2* does this under its Calibration feature when invoked under PNN architecture models). Alternatively, a genetic algorithm can be used to search out the optimal smoothing factor. The genetic adaptive PNN extension of the basic PNN algorithm is more suitable when outputs are continuous, but training takes much longer than under the normal iterative search for optimal smoothing patterns.[20]

The PNN algorithm compares each new case with all of the training patterns. The hidden layer is composed of at least as many neurons as there are training cases to be presented. These characteristics mean training is slow on large training sets (e.g. over 2000 cases). The algorithm compares each pair of cases using a measure of distance between them. Distance metrics include the Euclidean (discussed below in the section on Kohonen networks) or the 'city block' method (based on the sum of absolute differences between the input case and the weight vector for a given neuron). The Euclidean approach is generally superior in performance. PNN models can train in a single pass of the training set and can function with as few as two training patterns.

Radial Basis Function (RBF) Models

RBF models, originated by Powell (1985), are supervised networks which partition the training set into clusters for purposes of analysis. Clusters correspond to regions of decision space defined by features of the data and are determined by radial basis functions which delimit circles within the decision space. The network designer must set the number of and centroid locations of radial basis functions judiciously within the decision space so as to maximize the utilization of input information. When a training case is presented which falls in the space for a given node, the node responds more strongly than other nodes associated with other clusters (see Moody and Darken, 1989).

Unlike in backpropagation, in RBF models the weights from the input layer to the hidden layer are not changed during training. In the hidden layer, a k-means clustering algorithm is used to group inputs according to similarity (see Duda and Hart, 1973). MacQueen (1967) originated k-means clustering, which has several variations. Convergent k-means clustering is perhaps the most common, described by Anderberg (1973). Convergent k-means clustering can be accomplished by the following steps:

1   The researcher decides the value of k, which is the number of clusters into which data are to be placed. Neural network software which supports the RBF model normally assists the researcher in determining the optimal number of radial basis functions as, for example, by an experimental approach which starts at five centres and repeats the analysis in increments of five to a maximum of 50. Such software records the success of various model iterations in generalizing to test data and identifies the most successful model to the researcher.

2   From the training data set, k patterns are chosen at random, constituting one-pattern clusters. While this initial centroid location is normally accomplished simply by taking random cases from the training data set and using their values as the centres, this can be done repetitiously in an experimental mode to identify relatively successful locations. Alternatively, some researchers use a random case as the starting point but then in successive experiments test locations in the input space not covered in the first iteration.

3   Take the first of the remaining training patterns and assign it to the cluster with the nearest centroid (see step 4).

4   Compute the centroid of the cluster to which this case has been assigned. The centroid is simply the mean value for all patterns in the cluster. If there is more than one input per pattern, then the centroid vector is a vector in which each element is the average of values for that input for all the patterns in the cluster.

5   Repeat steps 3 and 4 until all patterns have been assigned.
6   Take each pattern again and compute its distance from each of the k centroids. If it is closer to a cluster other than the one to which it is assigned, reassign it and recompute the centroids of each cluster.
7   Repeat step 6 until a pass through the entire training set fails to produce any reassignments (that is, until convergence is reached).

The k-means clustering algorithm will minimize the sum of squared distances from each training set pattern to the corresponding cluster centroid. While the algorithm does force the researcher to predetermine the number of clusters k, computational speed is such that the researcher can experiment with different values of k to achieve desired results.

Unlike backpropagation, RBF models do not employ a bias term in the computation of net input, which is measured in terms of the Euclidean distance between the input and weight vectors. However, some variants employ a *width* term. Where bias is added to the summation function in backpropagation, the width term is divided into the Euclidean distance.

As in other neural models, RBF network design involves a choice of activation functions, though the Gaussian is identified with RBF because it was the function used when this type of design was first advanced. Contemporary neural software packages which support radial basis function networks now offer a range of activation function alternatives. Again, only an experimental approach can determine the optimal function, which is specific to the problem at hand.

In the output layer a least mean square (LMS) or other supervised algorithm may be used such that the change in weight in the output layer is a function of a learning rate times the activation level from the hidden layer times the local error, in turn defined in terms of the difference between the target (desired) output activation level and the actual level. The solution can be accomplished by linear techniques such as multiple regression, which is precisely the path taken by SPSS's *Neural Connection* module.

Constructive algorithms provide a more advanced architecture for RBF models. In constructive architecture, neurons and connections are added during the course of training. By automatically allocating resources in a radial basis function network, constructive algorithms can generate optimal weights but may not necessarily improve generalization (Platt, 1991; Fritzke, 1994).

Naturally, RBF models excel at modelling data which contain underlying local clustering of cases by input attributes. They are used in preference to backpropagation models when the problem is one of classification, particularly classification with many dimensions. RBF models train much faster than backpropagation models but are highly sensitive to the location of basis function centres within the decision space. Just as backpropagation networks can achieve an arbitrary level of precision if enough hidden layer neurons are available (and hence are subject to overtraining), so in RBF models an arbitrary level of precision can be achieved for any continuous transformation if enough generalized radial basis functions are available to the application (Poggio and Girosi, 1989; 1990).

Group Method of Data Handling (GMDH) or Polynomial Models

Originated by A.G. Ivakhnenko of the Institute of Cybernetics, Ukrainian Academy of Sciences, in Kiev, Ukraine, GMDH networks were refined by A.R. Barron and others. Also called polynomial neural networks, GMDH models identify the most important predictor variables and compute a nonlinear polynomial expression using them to predict the output variable (see Farlow, 1984). That is, GMDH weds nonlinear regression analysis with the logic of neural networks. Unlike other neural architectures, GMDH models result in a polynomial expression which can be expressed in a regression formula. Some packages, such as *NeuroShell 2*, display the polynomial regression equation at the end of the process.[21] GMDH models work best with engineering and other problems which can be described in polynomial equations.

The GMDH algorithm constructs each polynomial term in the regression formula one step at a time. The input layer is composed of the raw variable values. The first hidden layer is composed of the best nonlinear regression estimates of the input variables. The second hidden layer is composed of the best nonlinear regression estimates of the values of the first hidden layer. Successive hidden layers are created in the same manner until prediction drops below a researcher-set cutoff value. At each stage, nonsignificant input variables are dropped. The output layer represents a single dependent variable.

As GMDH constructs each layer, and therefore each polynomial term in the nonlinear regression, it selects only the best terms. At each layer, the algorithm selects a given number n of inputs (n is usually two or three, determined by the researcher; three is a common default) and constructs all possible polynomial terms (within nonlinearity restrictions discussed below). It then constructs all possible formulas using these terms and evaluates which perform the best. These are called 'candidates for survival' in GMDH parlance. For practical reasons, software usually allows the researcher to predetermine the allowable complexity of formulas for any candidate for survival (e.g. *NeuroShell 2* allows high–medium–low model complexity settings). The longest formulas often overfit the data and violate the modelling principle of parsimony.

The GMDH algorithm then takes the best n inputs and repeats the process, and so on, until all sets of n have been evaluated. At that point, all the candidates for survival are compared and a number (preset by the researcher) of the best are selected as 'survivors'. Neural software may allow the researcher to preset the maximum number of allowable survivors, in order to bring training time within reasonable limits.[22] The survivor terms which compose the first hidden layer, along with the terms in the input layer, are then used as inputs for constructing the next hidden layer in a like manner. As each successive hidden layer is constructed, the complexity of the model increases hyperbolically. The layering process continues until performance drops below a researcher-determined evaluation criterion. For practical reasons, similar to treatment of candidates for survival, software may also allow the researcher to determine the severity with which remaining terms are trimmed from the survivors. *NeuroShell 2*, for instance, allows off–fast–smart choices corresponding to no trimming (not recommended: lack of trimming is apt to result in an unparsimonious, overspecified model), optimizing for calculation speed, and optimizing for a combination of speed and performance.

For practical reasons it is necessary to restrict the GMDH engine's search for the best polynomial fits since the number of polynomial expressions that could be tested is infinite. For instance, *NeuroShell 2* software lets the researcher restrict model nonlinearity to 'off', 'low', 'medium', and 'high' values:

Off Only linear regressions are performed.
Low Covariant and trivariant terms are included in the regression formula but not powers.
Medium Covariant and trivariant terms, and powers, are included.
High Covariant and trivariant terms, and higher powers, are included.

Some software will allow interaction terms higher than trivariants, resulting in extraordinarily complex models. Naturally, the higher the nonlinearity open for exploration, the longer the GMDH model will require for training.

Since overfitting is not a problem for the GMDH algorithm, cross-validation is not necessary. Indeed, one advantage of GMDH is precisely that it allows the researcher to train on his or her entire data set – often an issue when the number of available patterns is limited. However, one method of setting the cutoff value is to have a cross-validation data set anyway and use the best fit of the polynomial regression based on the training set to the test set as the cutoff. This method is called the 'regularity' selection criterion. More commonly there is no cross-validation set and the criteria used vary.

Mean squared error (MSE)   This is not the preferred criterion because MSE will almost always decrease as a function of the number of terms in the polynomial expression. This creates a bias toward unnecessarily complex prediction equations which may not generalize well to real-world data.

Prediction squared error (PSE)   This is normalized MSE plus an over-fitting penalty term estimated as:

$$c\sigma_o^2 m/n$$

That is, the penalty term is a constant c, times the variance of the output variable o, times the number of model coefficients m, divided by the number of training patterns (cases) n. The default for the constant c is 1 but this may be varied by the researcher according to his or her estimate of overfitting (that is, larger than 1 for more observed overfitting; values are rarely set below 0.1 or above 4).

Minimal description length (MDL)   This is PSE with a larger penalty term, achieved simply by multiplying the PSE penalty term above by $\ln(n)$, the natural logarithm.

Generalized cross-validation (GCV)   This is normalized MSE divided by a variation on the penalty term:

$$(1 - cm/n)^2$$

where c, m and n are described above under PSE.

Final prediction error (FPE)   Here the normalized MSE is multiplied by $(n+m)/(n-m)$. This is appropriate when it can be determined that the model is correctly specified and errors are Gaussian, in which case FPE is the minimum variance unbiased estimator of MSE.

Fill complexity prediction squared error (FCPSE)   This is a proprietary variation of PSE used by *NeuroShell 2*. In essence, the PSE formula is used but instead of m, the number of model coefficients, another index term is computed which reflects both the number of coefficients and their level of complexity.[23]

GMDH models also do not require scaling the input data to the usual −1 to +1 range, though some researchers have observed that data normalization can increase model stability. GMDH likewise does not require the setting of learning rate, momentum or a smoothing factor.

Adaptive Time-Delay Neural Networks (ATNN)

ATNN is a neural network architecture with dynamic temporal capabilities. It is rooted in the analogy to time delays in signal processing in biological neural systems. Lin (1994) applied ATNN to identifying exo-atmospheric targets, finding ATNN achieved better generalization than related neural networks.

Adaptive Resonance Theory (ART) Map Networks

ART models are self-organizing unsupervised learning neural designs, described by Gail Carpenter and Stephen Grossberg (1987a; 1987b; 1988; 1990; 1992), Moore (1988); Carpenter et al. (1991a; 1991b); and Kasuba (1993). They incorporate environmental feedback and associative learning (reinforcing connection strengths when two connecting nodes are correlated in activity) to solve classification problems for both binary and analog input values. Lacking a hidden layer, their ability to generalize to new data sets is limited, but they are quite useful when the classification problem centres on a given data set already in hand and when the data set under investigation is relatively noise-free. ART models lack a mechanism such as cross-validation to avoid overfitting, which is why relatively noise-free data are required. Also, ART models are quite sensitive to the order of data presentation.

In associative networks, partial input can still generate closest-relative matches. As training proceeds, the system's internal category structure is expanded in response to an error function, as a form of self-organizing hypothesis testing process. ART models use both predefined and variable intramodular weights. Representations of inputs are compared with expected input patterns and the difference is used to modify connection weights in subsequent iterations.

In ART models, data are fed into a 'clamping layer' which is not really part of the basic ART model but serves as a buffer. Inputs are passed on to the input layer (also called the comparison layer), processed and passed to the knowledge base layer (also called the output or recognition layer). This main data pathway carries what is called the information component from the clamping layer. In addition, however, there is a separate 'gain control' neuron associated with the input layer. The gain control receives an 'arousal' component signal from the clamping layer, based on nonspecific input. The gain control also receives an inhibitory signal from the output layer. The output of the gain control neuron is fed to each neuron in the input layer.

Another aspect of ART models is the 'attentional subsystem' neuron, also called the reset or vigilance parameter, which receives a nonspecific arousal signal from the clamping layer and a nonspecific inhibitory signal from the input layer. It compares the size of these two signals and if that from the input layer is the smaller of the two, the attentional subsystem neuron sends an inhibitory signal to the winning node in the output layer. The output layer has a winner-take-all organization such that only one output layer neuron can be active at any time. Each output layer neuron receives a signal from the input layer, each contains a self-excitation loop, and each competitively sends an inhibitory signal to the other neurons in the output layer. The winning neuron is the one which receives the strongest signals from the input layer, and in this competitive lateral inhibition process is the one that sends excitatory feedback signals back to the input layer neurons, sends an inhibitory signal to the gain control neuron, and receives an inhibitory signal from the attentional subsystem. All output layer neurons contain feedback connections to each input layer neuron.

The two-layer structure of ART networks, in combination with gain control and the attentional subsystem, enable them to distinguish between inputs which are already learned and novel inputs. The exact matching process by which this is accomplished depends on the flavour of the ART model, which comes in ART1, ART2, ART3, ARTMAP, SMART and other variants.

In the standard ART1 implementation, each input layer node is receiving three signals: the input from the clamping layer, feedback from the output layer, and gain control. Patterns presented to the clamping layer are binary data (see description of ART2 below for discussion of the use of ART with continuous data). The 'two-thirds rule' then dictates that an input layer neuron will fire to the output layer if two of the three signals activate it. Gain control and output feedback activation will not occur simultaneously because the latter inhibits the former, meaning all three signals cannot activate an input layer neuron at the same time. When an input layer neuron is activated by both the input signal from the clamping layer and an output feedback signal, it combines them, then compares the merged weight with the input from the clamping layer.

If the difference exceeds a threshold value, the inhibitory signal from the input layer to the attentional subsystem neuron is lowered and the attentional subsystem neuron sends an inhibitory signal to the output layer (called a 'reset wave'), suppressing the winning output neuron and restoring the input layer pattern. The threshold value is determined by the 'vigilance' parameter, where a small vigilance factor sets a threshold which tolerates large mismatches and a large vigilance factor allows only small mismatches before the inhibitory signal is sent to the attentional subsystem. Note that large vigilance values, which set lower thresholds, will require and create a finer mapping of input patterns onto output neurons.

In formula terms, the comparison made by ART networks is a vigilance test:

$$(\sum_i w_{ij} a_i)/(\sum_i a_i) > v$$

In this test the ratio of the sum of weighted activation levels to the sum of activation levels for input neurons i, for a given output neuron j, is compared with a vigilance parameter v. Note that for binary values, since some of the a_i values will be 0, indicating the absence of an attribute, the numerator in this comparison reflects the number of attributes possessed by both the input and the output layers, while the denominator reflects the number of attributes in the input layer vector. That is, the ratio is a measure of the similarity of the input and output vectors. When the input vector from the current training pattern passes the vigilance test, the pattern is assigned to that neuron and the weights are fine-tuned and updated for that output neuron.

The reset wave sets the environment for a different output neuron to win in the next search cycle. Several search cycles may be needed before one is selected such that the difference between expected and input patterns lies below the threshold and adjusted values of the input layer neurons are accepted. This cycling is the 'resonance' process after which this approach is named, and once the difference drops below the threshold the input and output layer neurons are said to be in a state of 'resonance'. If no output layer neuron satisfies this condition, the training pattern is stored as a new pattern in the output layer, or if all output neurons are already storing patterns, it is skipped. Note that the higher the vigilance and the lower the threshold, the more likely skipping is to occur because it is more likely that previously learned patterns will have captured and are represented by all available output layer neurons.

Another aspect of ART1 models is a bias toward binary input patterns with many 1s rather than 0s. This is because the ART1 algorithm measures similarity by matches of 1s in the input and weight vectors, but does not count matches of 0s toward similarity. While this asymmetry may be acceptable for certain tasks such as recognizing black letters against a neutral background, it is unacceptable for a wide range of other tasks. ART1 may be made symmetrical by the simple expedient of duplicating the training set, with 0s and 1s reversed in the duplicate, which is added to the original training set prior to analysis. For further description of ART1 models, see Moore (1988).

There are several flavours of ART besides ART1. ART2 networks (Carpenter and Grossberg, 1987b) generalize ART1 models to the case of continuous (analog) input variables. ART2A networks (Carpenter et al., 1991b) are ART2 networks optimized for faster computation. The ART2 algorithm differs from ART1 in that data are normalized prior to presentation, and only values above a given threshold are accepted while those below are suppressed, eliminating weak signals. Also, the weight adjustments in ART2 utilize a fractional constant to determine the degree to which weights move toward the training example, as well as a measure of similarity.

ARTMAP (Carpenter et al., 1991a) models join two ART networks in a supervised associative network, creating an adaptive resonance design which can take advantage of problems where supervised learning is appropriate. That is, the ARTMAP algorithm temporarily increases the vigilance parameter to rule out incorrect patterns which would otherwise be matches in the absence of provided training data on desired outputs. Instead, such patterns are placed into a new category which is then, of course, the closest when the pattern is seen again on the next pass of the training data. ARTMAP is thus an alternative to backpropagation (the standard supervised model), particularly when the researcher wishes to guard against the bias of backpropagation networks toward input patterns later in the training sequence. By the same token, ARTMAP designs may amplify noise in the training data set.

Finally, SMART1 networks (simplified modified ART1) were developed by Tapang (1989). SMART1 models eliminate the gain control neuron and the two-thirds rule in an effort to improve learning speed without losing ART1 functionality. SMART and other ART variations are treated in Postma and Hudson (1995).

ART architecture is capable of distinguishing rare events even when similar to other events with different consequences. Reynolds (1994) found ART to outperform other neural models in terms of speed, accuracy and code compression on three estimation problems that Reynolds used for benchmark purposes. When the training patterns arise from a real-time data flow, ART models are particularly appropriate since they are capable of learning and categorizing new patterns in real time, not being based on a preset number of categories as are Kohonen networks or other strategies based on the k-means clustering algorithm.

ART models have the drawback that once all intermediate nodes are committed to representation of an input, new inputs are rejected. At the same time this is also their strength, in that catastrophic forgetting is less apt to occur than in backpropagation networks. Compared with Kohonen self-organizing maps, clustering by ART models is more sensitive to data noise and to the order of presentation of training patterns.

Bidirectional Associative Memory (BAM) Models

Bidirectional associative memory networks were created by Bart Kosko (1987a; 1987b; 1987c; 1991), influenced by but differentiated from Grossberg's ART networks. Kosko used BAM networks to decode picture images. BAM architecture utilizes an input buffer layer, two bidirectional associative memory layers and a final output layer. Every neuron in the first BAM layer is connected bidirectionally to every neuron in the second BAM layer, constituting a fully connected network. The two BAM layers may differ in their respective number of neurons. If there are m neurons in the first BAM layer and n in the second, then an m-by-n matrix can store the connecting weights.

The BAM layers use the bipolar Hopfield rule for learning, a form of Hebbian learning,

$$\Delta w_{ij} = r_1 a_{ij} c_i + r_2 m_{ij}$$

to determine how weights in the model change, as defined and discussed in Chapter 3 on backpropagation networks. This learning rule is associated with the inability to differentiate between a pattern and its complement.

Kohonen Self-Organizing Map Models

Kohonen (1989) architecture is a form of unsupervised neural model, which is to say, it is not necessary to specify outputs in the training data. Unsupervised models automatically search data sets for patterns, associating related data attributes into clusters, in this sense functioning similar to factor analysis. Kohonen models have analogies to the processing of light and sound information by the human brain and, in fact, Vrieze notes: 'A Kohonen network can be interpreted as a mechanism to simulate the learning process that enables certain areas of the brain to handle in an orderly manner the sensory perceptions' (1995: 83).

Kohonen models, also called topology-preserving maps, are used for four major purposes. First, they are used for purposes of categorization and classification of a data set, assigning examples to categories. For instance, Kohonen models have been used to categorize electric power system states for purposes of security state analysis (Niebur and Germond, 1992). Second, Kohonen models may be used to establish clusters of variables, perhaps as an alternative to statistical cluster analysis or factor analysis. Third, Kohonen models may be used to reduce a large input vector, mapping it to a smaller number of clusters in a data preprocessing step prior to feeding results to a subsequent neural model. Fourth, Kohonen networks may be used in literal mapping problems, such as shortest-route problems of the travelling salesman problem type (Angeniol and Le Texier, 1988; Vrieze, 1995: 95–7).

As a clustering technique, Kohonen maps require specifying the number of clusters in advance. While this constraint does not suit all research problems, it does mean that Kohonen maps are more tolerant of noisy data than are techniques (such as adaptive resonance theory neural models) which do not require specification of the number of clusters. Kohonen nets also may be sensitive to the order of patterns in the presentation of the input vector, particularly for small training sets. Order sensitivity is associated with the fact that the Kohonen algorithm uses single-pass learning, processing the training set only once. The corollary benefit is that as a single-pass network, Kohonen mapping has a fast training time. This in turn means that it is feasible for the researcher to experiment with different preset numbers of clusters in order to arrive at a number which yields desired results.

Statistically, Kohonen nets are estimators of the probability density function for the input vector. With the input and weight vectors normalized to a constant length, usually one, then the normalized weight vectors will be distributed such that the weight vectors will be closest in proportion to the density of the corresponding input patterns. This is true regardless of the underlying distribution of the input data. The self-organizing nature of Kohonen nets means that if the input distribution changes over time, the Kohonen maps will also change to reflect this.

The Kohonen net is a 'self-organizing feature map' which has only one layer of neurons. That is, it uses intralayer connections for training and learning. Each neuron is connected to all the inputs so every neuron receives the same input. There is no output layer because the single layer generates the outputs directly. That is, every neuron also receives as input the output of other neurons in the network, itself included.

When a neuron fires in a Kohonen network, positive feedback occurs for all neurons whose distance to the firing neuron is smaller than some value. This value determines the width of a given neuron's 'neighbourhood'. The extent of stimulation of adjacent neurons diminishes with distance from the firing neuron. After a given distance, an inhibition factor is applied to neurons further away, but inhibition diminishes toward zero with further distance. The distribution of stimulation with respect to a firing neuron in a Kohonen net thus takes on a 'Mexican hat' distribution, with a highly kurtotic distribution of positive stimulus on either side of the firing neuron (this is the region of the neuron's neighbourhood), giving way to moderate negative stimulus for middle-distant neurons (lateral inhibition), and a return to positive but very low stimulus for distant neurons on either tail of the distribution.

Similar neurons are grouped in neighbourhood sets to reflect the underlying structure of the input data. In Kohonen nets, learning has two phases. In the first phase neurons are moved to create a map of the data. In the second phase neurons converge asymptotically.

The Kohonen algorithm can be summarized in the following steps:

1   Neuron weights are initialized to random values.
2   The weight vector and the input vector should then be normalized to a constant length, usually one. Note that the input vector may

represent topological locations in n-dimensional space, using n inputs per training pattern.

3   The learning rate is set to a relatively high value, such as 0.1 or even 0.5.

4   The value of the parameter setting neighbourhood size is also set to a large number, such as 90 per cent of the number of input layer neurons.

5   The number of training epochs is also preset (*NeuroShell 2* suggests 50 for small problems, and as many as 10,000 for large problems).

6   Data points are input to the net, selected at random.

7   Determine which neuron is least distant from the presented pattern. This is the neuron whose weight vector is closest to the input vector from the current pattern, measured in Euclidean distance. The Euclidean distance d of neuron j is determined by summing the squared distances from the input values x and the corresponding neural weights w:

$$d_j = \sqrt{\left[\sum_{i=1}^{n}(x_{ji} - w_{ji})^2\right]}$$

An alternative to Euclidean distance is the normalized distance metric, which is sometimes (but still rarely) used when all the input variables have been normalized. If they have not, Euclidean distance must be used.

Another way of thinking about this is to observe that the minimum distance corresponds to the maximum dot product of the normalized weight vector times the input (activation) vector. The lower the Euclidean distance, the higher the dot product, also called the inner product. In a process of lateral competition, the winning neuron is the one with the largest resulting activation, representing the neuron which is least distant from the presented point. This neuron alone (hence 'winner-take-all' competition) is fired.

8   Weights of neurons in the neighbourhood of the firing neuron are adjusted in value to become closer to the value of that point. That is, the input vector is mapped onto the single neural layer, a mapping which improves with repeated application of this procedure. It may be noted that while the winner-take-all method, also called the accretive mode, is most common, the interpolative mode is an alternative. In this alternative a set of neurons having the highest activation is chosen and the signal fired to neighbourhood neurons is an interpolation of the selected set. In the accretive mode, the existing weights of the winning neuron j and neurons in its predefined neighbourhood are adjusted as a function of the learning rate:

$$\Delta w_{ji} = L(x_i - w_{ji})$$

That is, the new weights will equal the old weights plus the learning rate times the difference between the input vector minus the weight vector. Neurons not in the neighbourhood under consideration are not changed in weight.

Kohonen models are very sensitive to the learning rate. The learning rate is decreased over time and the neighbourhood shrinks, according to parameters set in the learning and recall schedule (though, of course, it is possible to specify that neighbourhood size remain constant). The neighbourhood starts out widely defined but decreases spatially as learning iterations proceed, eventually reaching zero (that is, only the winning neuron is adjusted in the last stages of Kohonen models). As this happens, the Kohonen network becomes more sharply defined in differentiating new input examples. When the neighbourhood drops to one, the convergence phase begins.

In an alternative known as frequency-sensitive competitive learning, the chance of a given neuron winning is penalized by a factor related to the frequency with which it has previously been the winning neuron.

As an optimization strategy in Kohonen networks, additional neurons may be added during the training process. *Neural Connection*, for instance, allows the researcher to check a 'double network size' para-meter in the Kohonen dialog box, causing the program to add a new neuron between every existing node. It is also possible to specify the learning rate (Kohonen models are very sensitive to this parameter); to specify the error response function (whether the winning neuron is the one with minimum distance to the input, or the one whose product with the input is maximum); and the type of normalization (zero mean and unit variance for minimum distance functions; or spherical normal-ization for dot product functions).

Kohonen models are explained in detail in Wasserman (1989). For those wishing to program their own variations on Kohonen models, pseudocode is given in Vrieze (1995: 99–100).

Counterpropagation

Counterpropagation networks were developed by Hecht-Nielsen (1987) at the Hecht-Nielsen Neuro-Computer Corporation. These networks incorporate a Kohonen layer of predetermined size for purposes of competitive learning and clustering of normalized input data. Without normalization, the Kohonen layer may not function properly. The train-ing set must also represent a uniform distribution of class categories to be predicted, and there must be enough neurons in the Kohonen layer to form boundaries separating the classes. If there are too few Kohonen layer neurons, class categories will be too coarse. That is, because the Kohonen layer trains without supervision, a Kohonen neuron may train to become responsive to more than one class category, resulting in ambiguous outputs to the next layer, discussed below. Activation and weight changes in the Kohonen layer are computed as described in the preceding section on Kohonen networks.

Counterpropagation models feed the winning output from the Kohonen layer to a Grossberg outstar layer, which functions to decode the information into meaningful output categories. Activation in the Grossberg layer is simply the sum of weights times the activation signals from the Kohonen layer, and weight changes are a learning rate times the activation signal from the Kohonen layer times an error factor, which is the difference between the desired output of output neuron j and w_{ji}, the corresponding weight for an input from Kohonen layer neuron i to neuron j.

What is described above is the uniflow version of counterpropagation. The original formulation by Hecht-Nielsen called for a bidirectional flow. In this model inputs were also applied to the output layer and mapped back to the input side. The bidirectional flow of information in opposite directions gave rise to the name counterpropagation (see Stork, 1988).

Dwyer (1992) compared backpropagation with counterpropagation neural models in prediction of bankruptcies. She found counterpropagation clearly inferior in prediction. While agreeing that in general counterpropagation is less effective than backpropagation, Fu (1994: 210) notes that counterpropagation converges more rapidly. This strength, plus the fact that its Kohonen layer learns without supervision, has meant that counterpropagation has found valuable uses in image and data compression applications.

Learning Vector Quantization (LVQ) Network Models

Also originated by Tuevo Kohonen et al. (1988), learning vector quantization models are supervised networks which use competitive learning. As supervised networks, of course, the training data must contain the desired outputs (correct class labels) corresponding to each input pattern. LVQ models utilize one neuron in the input layer for each input variable and one neuron in the output layer for each value of the dependent variable. The middle layer is a Kohonen layer, different from backpropagation hidden layers in that every middle layer node is connected to every input neuron and to every output neuron.

LVQ models are initialized such that each output neuron is associated with one of the possible class labels in the problem at hand. There are also equal numbers of Kohonen layer neurons for each class label. LVQ models begin by computing the difference between the training vector of input value activations and the weight vector associated with each input neuron (for $j = 1$ to n) with respect to Kohonen layer neuron i:

$$d = \left[\sum_{j=1}^{n} (w_{ij} - a_j)^2 \right]^{1/2}$$

Using this distance measure, the best Kohonen layer neuron is identified. If the class label of the winning neuron corresponds to the correct class label of the training pattern, its weight is augmented by a learning rate factor times the difference between the normalized input and the weight. If not, it is penalized by a possibly different learning rate factor equal to the learning rate times the difference between the normalized input and the weight.

In their simple, unmodified form, LVQ models are not efficient. It is ordinarily found that some neurons dominate while others remain inactive throughout the training process. To some extent, this is a function of initialization. Neurons initialized close to the input vector are drawn even closer. Other neurons, initialized far from the input vector, never become winners in the Kohonen competitive learning process and never move. To avoid this, several variants have been suggested.

Extended LVQ

A simple extension can be used which classifies input vectors not on the basis of the winning neuron but on the basis of all the neurons. This is accomplished by computing a Bayesian likelihood function for each class.

LVQ without Repulsion

Another simple variant on the LVQ model is to disable repulsion. That is, no penalty is assigned to nonwinning neurons. This can be useful in promoting their movement across input regions to other regions where perhaps they will become winning neurons for particular input features. This modification is most apt to be used early in the LVQ training process, then repulsion is restored.

Boundary Refinement LVQ (Also Called LVQ2)

In simple LVQ models it is sometimes found that the winning neuron corresponds to the wrong value of the dependent variable, while the second-best neuron corresponds to the correct value. A boundary adjustment can be made which moves the boundary between the two neurons. Specifically, the weight of the winning neuron is moved away by subtracting the learning coefficient times the difference between the normalized input and the weight. For the correct but second-best neuron, the weight is moved closer by adding the same term. These boundary adjustments are made only if the input is near the average of the weights of the winning and second-best neurons, with 'near' defined as an input activation a satisfying the following:

$$-\frac{(w_1 + w_2)}{2} + t(a - w_1) \le a \le +\frac{(w_1 + w_2)}{2} + t(a - w_2)$$

Conscience Mechanism LVQ (Also Called LVQ1)

DeSieno (1988) proposed an LVQ variant in which winning neurons are penalized in ratio to the neuron's win frequency as a percentage of average neuron win frequencies. Specifically, a bias factor associated with this ratio is added to d, the distance between the training vector and the weight vector for that neuron. The bias term is a learning temperature coefficient (set by the researcher in the learning and recall schedule) times the Euclidean distance for the neuron calculated to be most distant from the input vector times $(1 - Np)$, where N is the number of neurons in the Kohonen layer and p is the estimate of the win frequency. The win frequency is initialized to $1/N$, and then is reset by multiplying it by $(1 - t)$, where t is the learning temperature, if the Kohonen layer neuron is not the in-class winner: or by multiplying it by $(1 - t)$ and then adding t if the neuron is the in-class winner. Learning temperature is a constant set between 1 and 0.

In conscience mechanism LVQ, the winning Kohonen layer neuron without the conscience bias is the 'global' (unbiased) winner, while the winning neuron after bias is added is the 'in-class' winner. If the in-class winner is also the global winner, the weight is adjusted by a learning coefficient times the difference between the normalized input and the weight. If the in-class winner is not also the global winner, the weight is adjusted by a possibly different and perhaps slightly lower coefficient times the same difference.

DeSieno's method is sometimes called the 'conscience mechanism', anthropomorphizing to the notion of 'feeling guilty about winning'. The conscience mechanism operates to distribute neural activity throughout LVQ networks. The researcher must be careful in setting the conscience bias. With too large a conscience bias, competitive learning will depend only on the win frequency, while too small a conscience bias will have no effect. Normally the researcher starts with a moderate conscience bias and decreases it as training progresses.

Categorizing and Learning Module (CALM) Networks

Murre (1992) has presented a neural network module for unsupervised categorization, called CALM (categorizing and learning module). It employs a network of modules where intramodular connections are primarily inhibitory but intermodular connections are excitatory. This model purports to imitate the architecture of the cerebral neocortex in this manner, though most commentators would argue that even CALM models are far from representing the complexity of the human brain. In comparison with traditional, simpler neural models, the modular approach taken by CALM better supports scaling. CALM employs pre-defined internal connections and weights, varying only the intermodular excitatory weights.

The algorithm used by CALM operates to increase the likelihood that the node which most represents an input will also win the competition for representation on subsequent presentations of the same input pattern. That is, the amount of competition for representation, not the difference between presentation and expected input patterns, is used to modify connection weights. CALM models tie the learning rate to competition of inputs, are able to discriminate nonorthogonal patterns, and do not reject new inputs even when all intermediate nodes are committed.

Hybrid Models

Though beyond the scope of this work, it should be noted that there are any number of variations in which one or another neural network architecture is used as a preprocessor for a nonneural procedure. For instance, Bengio (1996: 80–144) has developed extensively the methodology for combining recurrent neural networks as preprocessors for hidden Markov models (HMMs). A hidden Markov model is a parametric stochastic model for analysing time series and data sequences. Bengio's experiments suggest that a recurrent-neural-network/HMM hybrid system outperforms recurrent networks alone, overcoming some of their tendency to converge on short-term sequential patterns.

As mentioned in the historical introduction to this monograph, in the last 15 years considerable work has been done under the banner of connectionism (Feldman and Ballard, 1982) to integrate artificial intelligence (AI) techniques like expert systems with neural network models. These hybrids wed knowledge-based AI learning processes with neural network modelling (see Kandel and Langholz, 1992). Texts such as those by Gallant (1993) and Fu (1994) now integrate neural network models discussed in this monograph with knowledge-based approaches to take advantage of rule-based domain knowledge. Fu's text comes with a PC-based diskette containing an object-oriented neural network software package which allows building a knowledge-based neural network as well as backpropagation networks.

5
Methodological Considerations

This chapter covers a broad range of methodological topics, including treatments of data elimination, data transformation, scaling, validation sets, training parameters, learning rules, vector algorithms, weight decay and other parameters the user may control in neural modelling.

Applicability

The researcher should, of course, fit the methodology to the problem. It has been observed that neural models may be particularly appropriate when the researcher is dealing with fuzzy, noisy, overlapping, highly nonlinear and noncontinuous data. White (1981; 1989) has also shown that backpropagation networks are an alternative to nonlinear least squares when the number of cases in the training set is large. However, the broad applicability of neural models does not mean neural networks are always the optimal methodology for all situations. Neural networking has its limitations (Feldman et al., 1988).

Neural networks are applicable to three broad classes of problems, to which we may add a fourth:

Mapping: classification and completion Classification problems involve mapping a diversity of input onto a finite number of outputs, so as to simpify data for ease of analysis and treatment. Completion problems involve the related task of identifying the proper category into which to map incomplete or corrupted patterns. In this capacity neural networks are an alternative to factor analysis and discriminant function analysis.[24]

Prediction Prediction problems involve making estimates, often of a continuous variable. In this capacity neural networks are an alternative to regression and other multivariate general linear hypothesis (MGLH) statistical procedures. Feedforward networks like backpropagation are a type of general linear model when they lack a hidden layer. Since in practice such networks are implemented with hidden layers, they are nonlinear alternatives to linear regression.

Control   Control problems are those which require artificial intelligence to make decisions based on complex and often fuzzy data, such as involved in controlling a robot arm in manufacture or automated driving of an unmanned vehicle while avoiding obstacles. In this capacity neural networks are an alternative to expert systems procedures, both inductive algorithms like ID3 and systems engineered.

Constraint satisfaction   Constraint satisfaction problems are those that arise in such arenas as scheduling of complex activities, routing of complex transportation tasks, and assigning appropriate resources to meet complex demand patterns. In this capacity neural networks are an alternative to linear programming and dynamic systems statistical procedures.

Statistical procedures are more appropriate, however, when the problem has calculable parameters such that answers may be computed. That is, neural network models may not be the best research choice when problems are clearly defined and deterministic, and therefore are amenable to application of precise logic and statistical algorithms.

Neural models may outperform traditional statistical procedures where problems are unstructured, involve incomplete information, are ambiguous, and involve large sets of competing inputs and constraints, provided the researcher can accept approximate solutions (Iyengar and Kashyap, 1991: 1). In a review of statistical applications of neural networks, Chatterjee and Laudato similarly conclude: 'Neural networks are most useful when a massive quantity of very high dimensional data need to be modeled without any proper model specification available *a priori*' (1995: 12).

In addition, fundamental social science logic applies to neural modelling as well. For instance, input variables which are invariant for the range of the dependent variable should be dropped from neural models for the same reason they are dropped in other procedures – because they lack explanatory power. Second, the researcher should give consideration to throwing out outliers or setting them to some limit since extreme cases can distort the computation of neural weights used in prediction, as they distort coefficients in other statistical methods. Third, nominal values need to be converted to dummy variables, as in MGLH procedures such as multiple regression, though, unlike MGLH, all values may be retained as dummies since the problem of over-determination does not occur in neural models. Fourth, if the data used for training come from a different universe from those used for generalization and testing, generalization may well be poor. For example, if the training data come from one year and the generalization data come from a couple of years later, intervening events may have changed the dynamics among the variables under study, requiring a different predictive model than one developed two years previously.

Model Complexity

One of the choices the researcher must make in constructing a neural network model is the determination of the level of model complexity. Since inputs are related to outputs through the hidden layer nodes, it might be supposed that the more hidden nodes, the better the output specification. Nothing could be further from the truth. Increasing the number of hidden nodes will often lead to performance deterioration both in terms of generalization and in terms of training time. In general, for a given number of patterns in the training data set, as one increases the complexity of the model, training error will decline asymptotically toward zero. Test set error, which is the basis for measures of generalization, however, will likewise start to drop nonlinearly toward zero but will bottom out at a plateau at a point well before training error is minimized, and will then often increase. The objective of the researcher is to identify the point at which model complexity, reflected in the number of neurons, particularly hidden layer neurons, reaches the bottom plateau for the test set.

Input Layer

It is customary for the number of nodes in the input layer to equal the number of independent variables in the study. However, this forces the researcher to treat ordinal data as interval. To avoid this, and to handle nominal data, one may instead create as many input nodes as there are values for each independent variable – a much larger number. Schrodt (1990) experimented with differences in convergence and generalization using the latter binary method as compared with the more usual interval method. Schrodt found that while the binary approach did improve estimation for the training data set, it failed to improve generalization to the validation data set while at the same time, of course, enormously slowing the training process.

Hidden Layer(s)

Having no hidden layer may be appropriate for problems which have a linear solution, or for where a linear approximation is the best that can be undertaken given insufficient training patterns or too much noise in the input data. In fact, when the data may be properly classified by a simple hyperplane or hypersphere, a statistical model rather than a neural model will probably be more efficient. The more complicated the decision surface, the more a neural model will be helpful and, if it is complicated enough, two hidden layers may be more efficient than one. As a rule of thumb, classification problems have simpler decision surfaces than function fitting problems, so one hidden layer will normally suffice for classification problems. For more complicated function fitting problems, two hidden layers may be more efficient, but the model will be more difficult to train as a result.

It is rare to find that more than three layers – one input, one hidden, one output – improve model effectiveness. More than five is almost unheard of. The reason for this is that as the number of layers increases, the meaningfulness of backpropagated error terms decreases. Moreover, training time can increase by an order of magnitude for each additional hidden layer. There are three primary reasons, however, to consider having two hidden layers (or more) rather than the customary one:

1   The researcher knows that higher-order relations are present in the data structure. In such cases having two or more hidden layers sometimes improves generalization. That is, when the target function is one which has several hills and valleys, a separate hill or valley in the target may be fitted by each neuron in the second hidden layer. Correspondingly, a network with two hidden layers can achieve accurate results with fewer neural weights than can a model with only one hidden layer. See Chester (1990). Situations in which two hidden layers may be more efficient are discussed by Hartman and Keeler (1991), Lonnblad et al. (1992) and Ohlsson et al. (1994).
2   The researcher desires to have an additional layer which receives jump (skip) connections, so as to reflect the direct effect of a linear regression model on the output layer, though such connections can be developed for a three-layer model as well.
3   When a step or threshold activation function is used, full generality requires two hidden layers (see Sontag, 1992; Bishop, 1995: 121–6).

As with most neural modelling decisions, trial and error may be necessary to determine the optimal number of layers in the application. The optimum will be specific to each problem and there is, as yet, no general theory for determining the optimal number of hidden neurons.

Having too few hidden layer nodes may cause the network not to train well, perhaps stabilizing at the 40–75 per cent correct level rather than the expected 85–95 per cent level, because the model lacks sufficient complexity to reflect input–output patterns in the training set. On the other hand, if there are too many hidden layer nodes, the model will tend to overtrain and generalization will suffer as the model simply memorizes the input–output data in the training set. In fact, it can be shown that neural networks can achieve arbitrary levels of precision on continuous data problems when there are sufficient hidden neurons (Cybenko, 1989; Funahashi, 1989; Hornik et al., 1989; Stinchombe and White, 1989). While as a rule of thumb it is better to err on the side of a larger number of hidden layer neurons, there is no substitute for trial-

and-error experimentation with the optimal number. When cross-validation is used, this reduces the need for as large a number of hidden layer neurons.

There is no a priori method for determining the optimum number of hidden nodes in a neural model. Various authors have suggested different rules of thumb for making this determination. Some advance the rule that one should take the number of input nodes and the number of output nodes, average them, and use this average as the initial number of hidden nodes (Stanley, 1988: 172; Ripley, 1993). In general the more complex the relationships linking inputs to outputs, the more hidden layer neurons will be required. Also, when early stopping is used, more hidden layer neurons are an aid to avoiding bad local minima. There is no point, however, in increasing the number of hidden layer neurons beyond the number of training cases and a guideline when using weight decay is to limit the number of hidden layer neurons to no more than half the number of training examples.

The number of hidden layer neurons is also affected by the size of the training data set. Thus the default number of hidden layer neurons in *NeuroShell 2* software is the average mentioned above (the average of the number of input plus output layer neurons) plus the square root of the number of training set cases. Klimasauskas (1992) advances the rule of thumb that there should be at least five training examples for each neural network weight. Another rule of thumb is that the maximum number of hidden layer neurons should be

$$h = n/[(r(i + o))]$$

where h is the maximum number of hidden neurons, n is the number of cases in the training data set, i and o are the number of neurons in the input and output layers respectively, and r is a rate constant set by the noise level of the data. Typically, r is in the range from 5 to 10, but might be as high as 100 for very noisy data and as low as 2 for very clean data.

Parsimony is a good rule of thumb when it comes to determining model complexity. Though experimentation is necessary – and it *is* necessary, because the optimal number of nodes is specific to the problem at hand, – the typical result is a finding that simple models are as or more efficient than complex ones. For instance, Hiemstra (1996: 68) found that for a financial portfolio analysis a model with only two hidden nodes showed superior out-of-sample performance. After similar experimentation, Jagielska and Jaworski (1996) also found two nodes optimal in a risk assessment neural model, as did Verkooijen (1996a) in an application on exchange rates.

The experimental model of n-fold cross-validation (discussed later in this chapter in the section on cross-validation) is used when there are not enough available patterns for independent experimentation. In this method subsets of the training data are sequentially held back for use in cross-validation and the mean error is taken as an estimate of error of generalization. The researcher can undertake n-fold cross-validation for different numbers of hidden layer neurons, then use the number for the network with the lowest estimated error as the final network model.

Parsimony is achieved by pursuing one of two opposite strategies, *growing* or *pruning*. Both involve sequentially testing models of different sizes until one finds the level of complexity at which cross-validation set error is minimized. In the growing strategy, one starts with the smallest conceivable model (usually this equates to the model with the fewest conceivable hidden layer nodes), then adds nodes in various trials of the model. Alternatively, the researcher may add entire hidden layers instead of merely new hidden nodes within a single hidden layer. Direct weight pruning, by contrast, starts with a framework with a large number of hidden layer neurons.

The pruning method is more common. One starts with a number of hidden neurons larger than that expected in the final model. One then uses the smallest weight by magnitude to select neurons to be pruned sequentially. When no further pruning is possible without impacting generalization, the isolated nodes of the network are deleted to simplify the trained network. Both growing and pruning are trial-and-error methods which cannot provide the researcher with a preset optimal number of hidden layer nodes.

Pruning as described above is simple but not necessarily optimal. While eliminating neurons corresponding to the smallest weights is a simple criterion, a better criterion – one which allows for the real possibility that the network will be sensitive to small weights – is to use a measure of weight saliency instead of weight size as the criterion for neuron elimination. LeCun et al. (1990) have developed an *optimal brain damage* (OBD) criterion which defines sensitivity in terms of the sensitivity of the network to small changes in weights. Mozer and Smolensky (1989) have defined a straightforward but time-consuming alternative method called *skeletonization* in which relevance is a function of the difference between the error function with and without the neuron in question being in the network.

It is sometimes effective to create multiple parallel slabs within a hidden layer such that each slab uses different types and numbers of nodes. Impetus for this architecture derives in part from neurobiological findings that distinct sets of neurons within the brain are associated with feature detection.

Strong assertions are sometimes made (cf. Murre, 1992) that modular networks are superior to single-module networks. Modular networks separate a problem into smaller subtasks, using different neural models for each subtask. Training is easier and more efficient in such smaller models. Much of the case for modular networks rests on abstract arguments that the complexity of modular networks better emulates processes of the human cerebral cortex. At an empirical level, however, there is little evidence that modular models are consistently more effective at classification than are simpler models, though they may be for particular problems. Unfortunately, the selection of the architecture which excels at generalization for a given set of problems is one which must be determined by experimentation.

Output Layer

When there are the same number of output neurons as input neurons, the model is said to be *auto-associative*, and performs a type of mapping or encoding of inputs into outputs. When there are fewer outputs than inputs, the neural model performs a type of compression of inputs into outputs. For these reasons neural models are sometimes used for such applications as image compression. Of more general significance for social science is the fact that such models (fewer output neurons than input neurons) are ones which perform a type of principal components extraction. When extraction of principal components from noisy data is a research objective, neural networks may prove useful.

The Training Data Set

As with any form of data analysis, the meaningfulness of neural net output is tied directly to the extent to which the actual causal variables for the dependent variable of interest are included among the inputs. When a high proportion of the inputs are unrelated to the desired outputs, the network may become inefficient and generalize poorly as it devotes itself to representing irrelevant partitions of the input space. Nonetheless, as a rule of thumb, a larger number of inputs is better than a smaller number, assuming there is some intelligent effort to filter out irrelevant variables. Neural nets will learn to ignore superfluous input variables, but they will never generalize well if crucial inputs are omitted from analysis. Moreover, if inputs interact, as when ratios are known to be important correlates of the dependent variable, entering inputs as precalculated ratios rather than as separate component inputs will generally yield better neural net performance.

Number of Training Patterns

The availability of cases for the training data set is a constraint on the number of input variables. In general, for a given level of model complexity (number of neurons), increasing the number of patterns in the training set will increase training error but decrease generalization error for the test set. In other terms, if 'variance' is the number of possible polynomial expressions which the model's complexity makes possible and 'bias' is the minimum error possible for the given training set given the variance, then increasing the number of patterns reduces bias but increases variance. This is the bias/variance tradeoff discussed by Geman et al. (1992).

It is common to supply hundreds of cases for the training set, even thousands, and correspondingly supplying fewer than 50 – to take an arbitrary number – may result in very poor results. A liberal rule of thumb is that the number of training patterns should be at least 10 times the number of inputs. A conservative rule of thumb is that the number of training patterns should be at least 10 times the number of input and middle layer neurons in the network. Some conservative researchers even make the rule that there should be 30 times as many input patterns as network weights to avoid overfitting. Note that underfitting, which increases bias in the outputs (i.e. difference between the estimator and the correct output), will result if these rules of thumb are met by the artifice of arbitrarily reducing the number of network weights. There is no easy substitute for having an adequate number of training patterns.

Selection of Training Patterns

While neural models will learn to ignore superfluous input variables, performance may improve if variables known to be unimportant are removed from the training data set. Input variables used in the training data set ideally are continuous interval variables such that higher numbers represent more of the variable in question. Because neural models handle noisy and fuzzy data relatively robustly, rank data are frequently used as inputs even though arithmetic calculations are performed on rank values. As with regression models, however, use of multivalued nominal data can be accomplished only indirectly. For instance, when measuring religious denomination of respondents, each denomination can be treated as a 0–1 off–on dichotomous variable. Since overdetermination is not a problem, there is no need to drop a value from a nominal variable as is the case with dummy variables in multiple regression, for instance. Alternatively, one may create separate neural models for each value of the nominal variable.

Selecting the training data set cases requires some care (Crooks, 1992). Researchers are apt to assume that a randomly selected set of training cases will be the best, just as random sampling is best for survey research. However, the ideal set of training cases is not random but rather is a set in which each example can be used by the model to reinforce a different input–output relationship principle. As Stanley wrote: 'Nothing beats a hand-crafted set of particular examples, each of which is designed to make some conceptual point to the network' (1988: 168). A randomly selected set of training cases, in contrast, may well overemphasize certain underlying relationships and neglect others. It is usually better to utilize expert opinion to select a wide variety of patterns, including patterns with noise.

As discussed earlier, neural models are generally robust even for noisy data. Datasets with as much as 30 per cent missing data often may still yield satisfactory results. Nonetheless, researchers normally adopt one of the common social science methods for compensating for missing cases. For instance, mean or median values may be substituted, or one may randomly assign a substitute value in proportion to the distribution of the missing variable's values for the nonmissing cases. The learning process used in neural modelling is biased toward commonly encountered (modal) values, making the technique possibly less useful for prediction of unusual cases (Schrodt, 1990: 21) unless care is taken in the data preparation phase to train the network on a training set in which target cases are as well represented as nontarget cases. A rule of thumb is to equalize the number of cases in the training data set for each value of the dependent variable. On the input side, the training, cross-validation and test data sets should all reflect the full variance of all inputs.

In order to achieve this proportionality, sometimes researchers recycle training cases with less common values on the dependent variable so that the network is exposed to equal numbers of cases for each value. This is a form of overtraining. Schrodt's (1990) experimental work on such overtraining shows that it does increase accuracy of prediction for the training data set, but it often leads to lower generalization (worse performance) for the test or validation data set.

Order of Training Patterns

Order matters in training data sets. Supplying the training data in a different order sometimes results in different performance. In particular, if data cases are grouped in some manner rather than randomly interspersed, the network will start learning by the first group, then 'forget' this in favour of learning by a second group, and so on, with the consequence that by the end of the training data set, the network is biased toward the last grouping. This is the stability/plasticity dilemma – designing a system which is stable in its retention of patterns already learned but plastic enough to integrate new knowledge.

Also, randomization compensates for time dependencies in the data – that is, for patterns associated with the time sequence in which people were interviewed or the data collected. Bengio (1996: 31) and others recommend 'shuffling' the training patterns. That is, neural analysis is repeated multiple times (e.g. five times) using differently ordered data and/or different random initialization values as starting points, then the results are averaged.

Coding of Input Data

Coding output variables for neural networks should take advantage of the fact that, in comparison to regression, neural models are not restricted to a single output. For instance, if one is predicting presidential voting, one might set up a code of 1= Republican, 0 = undecided and −1 = Democrat. However such a coding would not provide a value for the case where a prediction could not be made; rather the network would probably generate a value approaching zero for such a case, confusing the undecideds with the unpredictables. A better method would be to create three variables, one for each of the categories. Republican could be coded 0 = no, 1 = yes, for instance. The network will often perform better with each category treated as a separate output and the researcher will be better able to assess the contribution factors for the separate classes and better able to perform sensitivity analysis.

Although coding of input as 0 or +1 is traditional in neural modelling, there is some experimental evidence which shows generalization can be improved by using -1 and +1 (Gallant, 1993: 222).

Naturally, coding should not treat nominal variables as interval. Instead dummy variables should be used for the categories of nominal variables, as is the case in regression analysis. That is, each class of the nominal variable is coded 0 or 1 depending on whether that class is present or absent for a given case. This is sometimes called '1-of-C' coding, meaning one dummy variable is created for each of C categories of a nominal variable. Note that if there is a bias input unit, and if weight decay is not being employed, linear dependency on the bias unit will be created unless one of the C dummy variables is omitted. Omitting a dummy variable when weight decay is used creates a bias toward output for the omitted class.

Sometimes input data are preprocessed by applying principal components analysis. One selects the first few principal axes as the reduction of feature space. This simplifies the problem prior to neural analysis. However, principal components analysis requires the assumption of linear dependencies, whereas a major reason for using neural methods in the first place is the expectation that unknown nonlinear relationships may be present in the data. Also, principal components reduction of the data space only assures inputs with the largest variance will be included in the model, not necessarily the most important inputs.

Coding of Target Data

Since the sigmoidal transfer function used in many networks never reaches 1, sometimes better results are obtained for training cases with binary values if correct outputs are presented as 0.1 and 0.9 rather than 0 and 1, or even as 0.2 and 0.8. On the other hand, from a statistical viewpoint, training to targets in these truncated ranges will give incorrect posterior probability estimates, so this type of coding is not generally recommended. Such coding is not needed when data are relatively noise-free.

For networks with one continuous target variable, coding or normalization of the target variable is not required except to conform to the possible range of output for the selected transfer function. However, when there are two or more continuous target outputs, then it is important that they be normalized (see below). Without normalization, the neural network will assign more importance to the output with the larger range, even to the point of expending all of its learning effort on the variable whose range is larger in magnitude and ignoring the output with smaller range entirely.

Where inputs are continuous in nature, neural models are generally robust with regard to different underlying data distributions of the input variables. Therefore nonlinear data transformations of the input variables are not as critical as in parametric procedures. Nonetheless, in the case of highly skewed or highly kurtotic data, transformation may improve generalization of the model. Highly skewed data may be transformed by applying a power (exponential or root) or logarithm to the data. Highly kurtotic data may be transformed to reduce the distance of extreme data closer to the mean, as through the use of a tanh function:

$$s_i = \tanh\left[c\left(\frac{x_i - \bar{x}}{s_x}\right)\right]$$

where $\bar{x}$ is the mean and s_x is the standard deviation, and c is a constant which determines the severity of the correction.

Normalization and Standardization of Input Data

Better results may also be obtained by using transformations which normalize the data. This need not involve statistical normalization (subtracting the mean, dividing by the standard deviation, to transform the input vector) but might involve such simple procedures as using ratios, percentage change, indexing or other relative measures in place of raw data. For instance, in stock market applications a time series which rises in price and which has a single underlying dynamic may be interpreted by a neural net as a series of patterns rather than as a unified pattern because the network may treat different price levels as different patterns. By using price relative to a baseline, the network may better interpret the time series as a unified pattern.

Statistical normalization is critical in neural networks which use a distance function in the summation of net inputs, as in the case of RBF (radial basis function) networks. The Euclidean distance function in RBF networks reflects the variability of input variables relative to one another. Those with more variability will be construed as more important. Variables with larger raw ranges will generally have more variability simply owing to magnitude. Statistical normalization makes all variables have the same variability, which is to say, allows the researcher to start with the presumption that all input variables are of equal importance. If the researcher knew a priori, however, that a given variable was twice as important as all the others, then it would be appropriate for this variable to be standardized to twice the variance of the rest. Generally, the all-variables-equal assumption is appropriate and normalization is required for RBF networks.

For backpropagation networks and others whose summation function is not directly a function of magnitude and variance, statistical normalization is less critical. Even here, however, normalization may make the training data better behaved and the training process more efficient in seeking to minimize error. Statistical normalization also simplifies the problem of setting small initial weights for each input to hidden layer path in a way that treats all inputs equally at the start.

Statistical normalization is usually called *standardization* in neural network literature, or sometimes 'zero mean unit standard deviation normalization'. This is simply routine statistical standardization (subtract mean, divide by standard deviation, to achieve means of zero and standard deviations of one for all variables) with tail distribution values mapped onto +1 and −1. Standardization is often desirable because when data are normalized in this way, the network usually tends to converge toward weights which are not dissimilar in magnitude. Statistical normalization, of course, involves subtracting the mean and dividing by the standard deviation to make variables comparable because all means are then zero and all standard deviations are one.

Were weights to differ substantially in magnitude, then different learning rates would be appropriate for each weight. Weights with smaller magnitudes require smaller learning rates and vice versa. Without normalization, input fields will have contrasting magnitudes and variances such that inputs which in reality have equal effects on the dependent will not be treated equally by the functions which compute neural weights. Depending on software, you may be able to set minimum and maximum values on input as well, to determine the range.

Statistical normalization aids consistent application of learning rates and facilitates convergence.

Alternative to zero mean unit standard deviation normalization, which to most social scientists is simply ordinary 'standardization' or 'normalization' used interchangeably, neural network researchers may opt for midrange zero, range two normalization, which maps data to a range from −1 to +1, with midrange of 0. Let x_i be the raw value of the ith training case, s_i its standardized equivalent, r the range and m the midrange. The midrange equals half the sum of the minimum x_i and maximum x_i. The s_i becomes

$$s_i = \frac{x_i - m}{r/2}$$

If normalizing to map to 0 to 1, for an activation function with this range of outputs, one may use the corresponding formula

$$s_i = \frac{x_i - x_{min}}{r}$$

where x_{min} is the lower bound of the range of x.

Normalizing in neural network literature can also refer to rescaling by subtracting the minimum and dividing by the range in order to achieve training set input values between 0 and 1. This type of normalization, which is really rescaling, can be performed along with statistical normalization provided it follows it. In general, such rescaling is not recommended. Neural networks are apt to perform better when input values are centred around zero, which statistical normalization (standardization) accomplishes. Rescaling to values between zero and one, if desired with regard to the output variable, is better accomplished through the activation function than through rescaling the input data. For instance, the sigmoidal transfer function (the standard function for backpropagation) yields output values of 0 and 1.

If input values are not scaled to the transfer functions in use, saturation may occur. Transfer functions constrain output to a certain range in response to summed, weighted input values in a corresponding range. When large raw input data values are used, positive or negative, they will result in large sums, even when multiplied by small weights. These large sums may be such that the values for all data cases are beyond the threshold of the function in use. That is, the transfer function may treat all data cases the same. For instance, the derivative of the sigmoid function approaches zero for large summation values and hence such values have no effect as multipliers of weights and therefore no learning occurs for such cases. Data preprocessing avoids this problem by supporting automatic and/or user-directed scaling of data to the sensitivity range of the function in use. Later the same scaling table (called a MinMax table in some neural software packages) is used to rescale neural model outputs back into units of original magnitude.

Normalization is also closely related to weight initialization and bias. To avoid saturation, it is customary to initialize connection weights to small random numbers. To avoid forcing the hyperplanes (error surfaces where net input is zero) defined by each hidden neuron through the origin, it is customary to add a bias input. Statistical normalization of the input data assures that the data will cluster near the origin, which all hyperplanes must pass near if bias terms are all small random numbers, as is customary (since bias determines the distance of the hyperplanes from the origin). That is, statistical normalization assures the input data points will cluster in the appropriate area. Without normalization, or with inappropriate initialization of weights and bias terms, the hidden layer hyperplanes may well fail to pass through the data cloud and the neural net may be unable to reach local minima. This is particularly true when, as in standard backpropagation, the training algorithm is based on the steepest descent method.

A similar consideration is that neurons with greater fan-in (a greater number of incoming connections) will tend to have higher magnitude weights and vice versa. Bottou (1991) therefore calls for computation of local learning rates specific to each neuron, with the rates inversely proportional to the square root of the number of fan-in connections. Some authors have gone further, urging decorrelation of data as well as normalization. This is accomplished by computing the eigenvectors from a principal components analysis of the input vector.

Trouble-Shooting

Inappropriate data adjustment can sometimes be detected by analysis of neural network residuals. Residual error of estimate can be graphed in a histogram, which will be symmetric about the mean of the dependent if the neural model is not biased. Bias will occur, for instance, in time series analysis when the magnitude of the mean rises over time, resulting in model bias toward underestimation. This particular bias is often correctable by substituting difference values for absolute values of relevant inputs.

Training Duration

It is possible to train too much. Neural net software packages recognize this by saving the 'optimum' model and its associated weights. Often this optimum comes at an iteration long before the researcher has decided to end the training process. However, that software has this capacity begs the question of how the optimum is to be determined, whether by the researcher or by the programmer of the software. The previously discussed concept of overtraining posits that this is not a case of 'the more the better'. It is necessary for the researcher to come to some method of determining when it is best to stop the training process.

The length of training is related to the learning rate. When the outputs are very different from actual values from the training set, one wants learning to proceed at a high rate. As outputs approximate desired values, one wants weight changes to become smaller and smaller so overcorrection does not occur. Also, the more homogeneous the training examples, the higher the learning rate can be initially, whereas the more variance in the training set, the lower the learning rate is set to discriminate patterns from noise.

The general dynamic is that early in the training process, neural models uncover much of the underlying input–output structure of the test set data. The longer training proceeds, the more likely it is that refinements to the model's weights will reflect attempts to fit data noise rather than data structure. What is needed is a rule which draws an appropriate line before the iterations of the analysis begin to focus on noise. This is the issue of error function selection, since the error function criterion will be used to stop the training process when error is minimized.

Naturally, the researcher wishes to stop training when some error criterion is minimized. There are three general types of stopping criteria, each with variations: (1) those based on minimizing a measure of cross-validation set error; (2) those based on minimizing training error; (3) those based on minimizing the error gradient.

Early stopping is commonly accomplished by the first of these methods.[25] Indeed, the cross-validation method is the preferable one of the three since it deals directly with generalization and does not depend upon the researcher setting parameters. The drawback, of course, is additional computation and the possible need for additional cases to constitute the cross-validation set. Moreover, early stopping may work better when there are a large number of hidden layer neurons so as to reduce the danger of arriving at poor local minima (Sarle, 1995).

Under early stopping one uses a cross-validation data set in addition to the training and test data sets. One stops training when normalized root mean square error (RMS, the standard for prediction problems; for classification problems, percentage correct is standard) on the cross-validation set is minimized (i.e. at the point before it starts to rise), then one uses that model on the test set for purposes of generalization (Weigend et al., 1990; Chauvin, 1990; Morgan and Bourlard, 1990). Since a one-shot approach to early stopping might well result in a local minimum, because RMS may decline and rise several times over the course of training, it is actually safer not to stop early but instead to train to convergence, then go back and select the 'early stopping' point which had the lowest RMS. *NeuroShell* suggests stopping 20,000 to 40,000 events since an apparent minimum error, more for recurrent models. It can be better yet to repeat training a number of times, each time with a different sampled cross-validation set, to approximate the optimal solution.

A further refinement to early stopping is to use bootstrapping, also known as resampling. In this refinement, one uses multiple cross-validation sets, applying early stopping to each. One then determines the training duration at which the sum of mean square error on the several cross-validation data sets is minimized. This duration is used as the estimate of optimal early stopping when training the master net on the full test set.

In practice, the minimum error is not computed after every training event but is instead calculated at intervals, often in the range of every 50 to 500 training events (e.g. 200). Software allows the researcher to set this error term calculation interval (called the calibration test interval in *NeuroShell 2*).

If cross-validation is not used, then minimum average error for the training set may be used in place of normalized root mean square error on the validation set.

For either cross-validation or training error methods, an alternative to mean square error is one advanced by Hinton (1989), called *cross-entropy*. Cross-entropy is calculated by the formula:

$$E = \sum_{p} \sum_{j} P_{jp} \log_2(Q_{jp}) + (1 - P_{jp}) \log_2(1 - Q_{jp})$$

where P refers to the desired probability of pattern p for output neuron j, and Q refers to the actual probability. In general, the cross-entropy criterion will react more strongly to mismatches between desired and actual results than will squared error criteria.

The gradient method defines a small error gradient such that when the gradient drops below the threshold, training stops.

Determining the Transfer (Activation) Function

As mentioned, the transfer or activation function for a neuron determines when it will fire, given the weighted vector of inputs it receives, and it serves as a multiplier in updating weights.

The *sigmoid function* is continuous, increases monotonically, and assumes constant values as the input approaches positive or negative infinity. It derives its name from the Greek character sigma, in turn chosen to signify an S-shaped curve. The sigmoid transfer function keeps output at 0 until a certain threshold level of input sends it on an increasingly steep upward curve toward an output of 1. As it rises, the curve bends again asymptotically, levelling off at an output of 1. The sigmoid function is also called the semilinear transfer function and takes the following mathematical form:

$$O_j = 1/(1 + e^{-I_{ij} \times \text{gain}})$$

In this formula, O_j is the output of neuron j, I_{ij} is the current sum of weighed inputs, and the gain is a coefficient taken from the learning and recall schedule. Sometimes the gain factor is omitted. Because the sigmoid function squashes high input values to output values in the 0 to 1 range, it is sometimes called a squashing function.

Backpropagation networks generally use sigmoidal activation functions but there are several others from which the researcher may select.

The *linear transfer function* is the simplest possible transfer function. Under linear transfer, the value transferred is simply the sum of weighted inputs:

$$O_j = I_j$$

There are a number of variations on the linear transfer function.

1   The *perceptron transfer function* is the linear transfer function, except that it is set to zero when I_j is less than or equal to zero.
2   The *signum transfer function* is set to minus one when I_j is less than or equal to zero, and otherwise is set to plus one.
3   The *signum0 transfer function* is set to minus one when I_j is less than zero, to zero when I_j is zero, and otherwise is set to plus one.
4   The *step function i* is set to minus zero when I_j is less than or equal to zero, and otherwise is set to plus one.
5   The *brain-state-in-a-box transfer function*, another function used primarily in early neural models, is the linear function modified for gain:

$$O_j = I_j \times \text{gain}$$

Large positive or negative values incurred as a result of the gain factor are later limited by clipping or scaling.

Linear transfer functions are generally restricted to situations where output is continuous rather than categorical, where the number of connections to the output layer is small, and where nonlinear relationships are known to be absent from the data structure. When used, linear functions are often chosen for the connections from the hidden to the output layer, while nonlinear functions are still utilized for input to hidden layer connections. Often the choice of a linear function only serves to reduce the power of a neural model compared with use of more common activation functions such as the sigmoidal or logistic.

The *hyperbolic tangent (tanh) transfer function* is similar to the sigmoid function but constrains output to the range −1 to +1. The sigmoid function, because it varies from 0 to 1, updates weights little or none for low summed weighted input values, and a great deal for high values. That is, learning (updating of weights) is biased toward high input values. Under the tanh function, in contrast, low and high values have an equal impact on learning. Moreover, training time under the tanh function can be half that under the sigmoid function because there is no need to modify weights from neurons whose activation levels are zero. The tanh function is also symmetric whereas the sigmoid is not. For these and other reasons, many experts recommend tanh as the default activation function. The tanh form is the following:

$$O_j = (e^{I_j \times \text{gain}} - e^{-I_j \times \text{gain}})/(e^{I_j \times \text{gain}} + e^{-I_j \times \text{gain}})$$

In this equation, gain may be set to 1 and effectively eliminated. There is a variant, the *tanh15* activation function, which takes the hyperbolic tangent of 1.5 times the input value. This has the effect of exaggerating the function so that an even larger range of upper values are forced toward +1 and an even larger number of low values are squashed toward −1, with a steeper gradient for the midrange. As a symmetric function, tanh has an error gradient which is almost flat when weights are close to zero. This in turn argues for initializing a network using tanh transfer functions to values larger than normal for sigmoid-based models.

Logistic transfer functions increase output according to a logistic growth curve, which is similar to the sigmoid S-curve. Logistic functions have some mathematical advantages, and it is the default in backpropagation models using *NeuroShell 2* software. Logistic functions are generally used in the output layer. In formulaic terms, the logistic growth equation is expressed:

$$\frac{dx}{dt} = I_j x \left(1 - \frac{x}{K}\right)$$

A variant is the *symmetric logistic function*, which maps in −1 to +1, whereas the logistic function maps in the range 0 to +1. Some researchers use the logistic function for continuous output variables and use the symmetric logistic function for categorical outputs.

The *linear threshold function* is somewhat similar to the sigmoid function in that it forms a Z-shaped curve. It keeps output to 0 until a threshold is reached, then it increases output linearly until output is 1, where it stays. The researcher should be aware that a multi-layer neural model which employs linear neurons in the hidden layer is mathematically equivalent to a simple two-layer model with its attendant requirement that input patterns be linearly independent. For this reason, linear functions are not used in most neural models in spite of the superficial similarity of the S- and Z-formed graphs of sigmoidal and linear threshold functions respectively.

The *step threshold function* is one where the linear increase is vertical, which is to say that as soon as the threshold is reached, output immediately goes from 0 to 1.

The *Gaussian transfer function* blurs the input according to a bell curve. Output is increased along a normal curve until a central value of input, after which output is decreased also according to a normal curve. The purpose is to blur input in the hope of increasing the capacity of the model to generalize from the training set. It functions to sensitize the neural model to midrange values. The *NeuroShell 2* manual recommends use of the Gaussian function in the duplicate hidden layer slab of three-layer Ward backpropagation networks, a tanh function in the original hidden layer slab, and a logistic function in the output layer. For classification problems, it also recommends a Gaussian function in the hidden layer and a sigmoid logistic function in the output layer. For prediction problems it recommends a Gaussian function in the hidden layer and a linear activation function in the output layer. A variant is the *Gaussian complement function*, which is an inverse bell-shaped curve which sensitizes the model to high and low input values, and desensitizes it for midrange values.

The *spatio-temporal pattern recognition (SPR) transfer function* was developed by Robert Hecht-Nielsen (1986), based on work by Stephen Grossberg (1969a; 1969b; 1970; 1971). SPR has the characteristic of increasing rapidly whenever the weighted summation is positive, then it decays slowly unless reinforced:

$$O_{j_t} = O_{j_{t-1}} + A(O_{j_{t-1}} \times -\text{gain} + bI_j - \gamma + cX_{t-1})$$

In this equation, b is a mod (importance) factor modifying the input to neuron j. The γ is a global bias term tied to overall network output activity, functioning to let the best match win. Then c is the input clamp value and X_{t-1} is the previous input vector. A is the *attack function*, which adds the parenthetical term to the prior weight when it is more than zero, or adds the parenthetical term times a decay factor, called the firing rate, when the term is less than zero. The SPR function has been used in detecting sound signals, where it has proved robust in classification in the face of variance of signal.

The *sine transfer function* is the trigonometric sine of the input:

$$O_j = \sin(I_j \times \text{gain})$$

The sine function is rarely used. Studies exploring its use usually find the sine function to perform no better than others.

Setting Coefficients in the Learning Rate and Learning Schedule

The learning rate, it will be recalled, determines the extent of weight changes in any given iteration, while the learning schedule varies (almost always decreases) the learning rate as training proceeds. If the learning rate is set too high, large weights will occur which will lock neurons into on or off positions, effectively stopping learning, or the system will become unstable, oscillating and failing to converge. On the other hand, if the learning rate is set too low, training time will lengthen to unacceptable duration.

One wants the learning rate to decrease as training proceeds in order to be sensitive to smaller and smaller refinements in feature detection. A common version of a learning schedule is the *normalized cumulative delta rule*, which decreases the learning rate by the square root of the number of presentations. The *cumulative delta rule* simply decreases the learning rate in a linearly inverse ratio to the number of presentations. Being less severe, it should be replaced by its normalized cousin if it is noticed that significant numbers of large weights appear (most neural software displays a histogram of network weights, allowing one to notice this; a rule of thumb for 'large' is ±5).

Efforts to automate the setting of the learning rate are set forth in the work of Jacobs (1988) and Fahlman (1988).

Improving Generalization

The purpose of neural network analysis is to predict or classify data. Generalization is the capacity of the model to do this. Generalization will be undercut to the extent to which the model is overfitted – that is, the extent to which training for the training data set has been allowed to converge so much that the application has gone beyond learning the true patterns in the data to also learning the idiosyncratic noise particular to that specific training set.

Generalization is not possible for some purposes. For instance, neural networks cannot be trained to generalize to encryption algorithms based on random number generators. More broadly, generalization assumes that the target output results from relatively smooth, non-discontinuous functions. It follows, then, that generalization can sometimes be improved by nonlinear transformations which increase the smoothness of the output function.

Weight decay is the central neural networking approach to preventing overfitting and thereby improving generalization. The weight decay approach adds a penalty term to computation of the error function in neural network analysis such that connection weights tend to atrophy toward zero unless reinforced. That is, under weight decay, weights tend to converge toward smaller absolute values, smoothing the output function, and avoiding large values which are associated with possible discontinuities in the output function. Weight decay makes it less likely the output function will generate out-of-range estimates.

The default under weight decay is to adjust weights by the sum of squared weights to the hidden neuron times a user-supplied decay factor. Neural network software allows researchers to set the weight decay parameter. Note that for weight decay to work properly, the signal transmitted by each input node must be comparable with the outputs of the hidden nodes. This in turn calls for standardizing the input and output data so that they fall, at least mostly, within the 0 to 1 range and have a mean of 0.5 (or in some applications a range of −1 to +1 and a mean of 0).

Neural networking software usually puts selection of decay parameters under the control of the researcher. If the researcher sets too low a decay parameter, overfitting may occur. The resulting model may fit the training data 'too well', yet when out-of-sample validation is implemented, prediction performance may be poor. Weight decay is more effective when the error function is based on cross-validation, discussed in the next section. That is, rather than linking decay to error in the training data set, error is linked to predictions for a cross-validation set which is set aside for purposes of validation of weights derived from the training set. It is also more effective to run the model for several different weight decay constants, then choose the value which minimizes error of generalization.

A variant of weight decay is weight elimination (Weigend et al., 1991). Instead of using the sum of squared weights times a user-supplied decay parameter, weight elimination uses

$$\sum_i \frac{w_i^2}{w_i^2 + c^2}$$

where c is a user-supplied constant. Whereas weight decay shrinks large weight coefficients more than small ones, weight elimination is the opposite. That is, weight elimination is a *pruning* method which tends to simplify a neural model into a subset model.

A recent alternative to weight decay is the Markov chain Monte Carlo (MCMM) method, which is a form of Bayesian learning (Neal, 1993a; 1993b; MacKay, 1992a; 1992b; 1995). Sarle (1995) has shown that Bayesian learning tends to generalize better than early stopping for the case of nonlinear functions (the norm for neural models). Software for implementing a Bayesian approach is now becoming available but is not yet integrated into most off-the-shelf commercial neural packages.[26]

There are a variety of other methods of seeking to improve generalization:

Retraining Retraining is sometimes done by testing a model, determining which cases in the test data set result in wrong model outputs, then adding a representative collection of such cases to the training data set and starting over to see if the retrained model displays greater generalizability to new test sets.

Stacked generalization Wolpert (1992) advocates use of multiple networks, each of whose outputs is used as an input for an overlying neural model whose output represents the combined estimate of the dependent variable of interest to the researcher. Each of the two or more base networks differs from the others in inputs, network architecture, different learning and recall schedules, or other parameters. Stacked generalization improves generalization by allowing base networks to specialize, and also by smoothing estimates in a form of weighted averaging.

Hidden layer reduction Generalization can sometimes be improved by reducing the number of neurons in the hidden layer. Utilizing too many hidden neurons allows the neural model to train to data noise rather than underlying patterns alone. On the other hand, if early stopping is used, such reduction can increase the chance of settling in a misleading local minimum.

Adding noise Adding a noise factor ('jitter') to cases in the training set can sometimes help produce a model which generalizes better. In essence, the researcher, based on an assumption of a smooth output function, creates new training cases by varying the inputs by small random amounts around zero while retaining the same outputs as in the master cases from which the variants are created. The more training patterns already available, the less the need for adding jittered cases. This approach is most frequently used when the number of cases in the training set is very small and the researcher cannot obtain additional cases. For further discussion, particularly of selecting the optimal number of jittered cases, see Holmstrom and Koistinen (1992).

Expanding the size and diversity of the training set   This is the converse of adding noise. Better generalization is frequently associated with a large and especially with more representative training data sets. One conservative rule of thumb is that there should be at least 30 times as many training cases as there are weights in the network.

Henseler (1995: 56) gives five useful tips related to improving network performance, summarized as follows:

1   Training and test set error normally declines gradually, with small disturbances, but if one observes large fluctuations then there may be system instability and the researcher should consider decreasing the learning rate.
2   If the training error approaches zero but test set error remains high, the researcher should consider increasing the size and representativeness of the training set.
3   If the training error declines very slowly even early in the process, there are three possibilities: (a) the learning rate is set too low; (b) the training cases are unrepresentative or confusingly coded; or (c) there are too few hidden neurons.
4   If the training error does not approach zero and does not seem to change, the network may be stuck in a local minimum. The researcher may wish to increase momentum or consider retraining the network initialized to different starting weights.
5   If the training error and test error both decline normally, but then fail to decline, and then training error continues to decrease but test error rises, the network may perform better if additional hidden layer neurons are added.

Cross-Validation

Cross-validation is a form of split-sample model validation. The sample is split into training and validation sets, as a rule of thumb on an 80:20 ratio. The model is developed on the training set and tested on the validation set. This process is repeated a number of times and the average error is computed across split-sample runs. Split-sample validation eliminates tautological findings arising from a high number of hidden nodes overfitting the training data set.

Because neural models can be made to predict arbitrarily closely the training data simply by increasing the number of hidden layers to overfit, it may not be appropriate to compare the effectiveness of a neural network model with that of, say, a regression model of the same training data set. Instead all such comparisons are usually made *out-of-sample* rather than *in-sample*. This is accomplished under cross-validation in a process under which subsets of training data points are dropped from the training set. The model is then trained on the remaining data points and the mean square error for the out-of-sample points is calculated. Usually five to ten such subsets are dropped. Previously dropped subsets are replaced. The average error is calculated for the group of out-of-sample subsets. This is called the *cross-validation error*. Cross-validation was described by Stone (1974) and has been adopted widely by neural network analysts (Moody and Utans, 1994).

Cross-validation error is a statistically unbiased estimator of prediction error, though its variance may be large (Verkooijen, 1996a: 59). On the other hand, it can be argued that the process of model selection optimistically biases cross-validation estimates of the accuracy of prediction (McLachlan, 1992). Nonetheless, the sparseness of data sometimes precludes the possibility of having a training set, cross-validation set *and* final test set. In these circumstances the error from the cross-validation set may have to be used as an estimate of generalization error in a hypothetical test set.

When cross-validation is used as an estimate of generalization error under circumstances of data sparseness, *n-fold cross-validation* is often used. Rather than use error based on a single cross-validation set, the researcher divides the training set into n subsets. The network is trained on $(n - 1)$ subsets and cross-validated on the remaining subset. This is repeated n times, using a different cross-validation subset each time. The mean error of the n trials is used as the estimate of generalization to a test set. Breiman et al. (1984) found an n of 10 provided sound estimates for experimental data, and 10 is often used for n. A special case of n-fold cross-validation is *leave-one-out cross-validation*, which is simply the n-fold method when there are n subsets of one pattern each for the n available cases.

Jean Steppe et al. (1996) have developed an integrated approach to feature and architecture selection for single hidden layer feedforward neural networks trained via backpropagation. They adopt a statistical model building perspective in which neural networks are analysed within a nonlinear regression framework. Their algorithm employs a likelihood-ratio test statistic as a model selection criterion. This criterion is used in a sequential procedure aimed at selecting the best neural network given an initial architecture as determined by heuristic rules. They show that for an object recognition problem, their selection algorithm is effective in identifying reduced neural networks with equivalent prediction accuracy.

Cross-validation is related to the statistical methods known as *bootstrapping* and the *jackknife*. Bootstrapping is an alternative to cross-validation for purposes of estimating generalization error. In simple form, bootstrapping involves repeated analysis of subsamples of the data (not subsets as with cross-validation), using sampling with replacement. Hundreds or even thousands of bootstrap samples may be taken in this repetitive process. Bootstrapping enables the researcher to work with all the training cases, and there is some evidence it frequently outperforms cross-validation based on data subsets. See Efron and Tibshirani (1993) and Hjorth (1994) for further discussion of bootstrapping.

The jackknife is confused with but is not in the same category as cross-validation and bootstrapping, which are methods of estimating generalization error. The jackknife is a method of estimating bias. For any statistic, each input case is omitted in turn and the statistic is computed. The average of all estimates of the statistic is then compared with the statistic computed for the entire sample, with the difference taken as an estimate of bias. One might use the jackknife, for instance, to estimate the bias of statistics used in neural network analysis, such as root mean square error (RMS). See Hjorth (1994) for further discussion.

Causal Interpretation with Neural Networks

As noted at the outset, one reason for neural network analysis not spreading faster in the social sciences is the difficulty in interpreting its results from a causal analysis (as opposed to classificatory or predictive) point of view. In this vein, Caudill noted:

> in a neural network, though we can easily obtain a list of all the weights and connections, it is far from obvious what those values have to do with the problem . . . Unlike the easily understood information resident in an expert system or computer program, a neural network's knowledge is unintelligible to a person. (1989: 36)

Statistical approaches to prediction require the researcher to posit a model relating inputs to outputs, as through multiple equations. Neural models, in contrast, do not require the researcher to articulate a mathematical model. For purposes of prediction and classification, this is an advantage of neural modelling techniques. However, neural networks' ability to recognize ill-defined patterns from noisy data in the absence of explicit input–output rules can be a disadvantage to the researcher whose purpose is causal modelling.

Interpreting Neural Model Results

There are a variety of forms of post-analysis which may lead to further understanding of the phenomenon under study and possibly to later reanalysis.

One form of post-analysis focuses on division of the training cases into quartiles or other divisions according to estimated values of the dependent. The research may then separate the high and low quartiles of the training set to look at their input characteristics. For instance, by comparing the histograms of each input data field between contrasting quartiles, one may be able to discern ways in which the model shifts over the range of the dependent. Some neural packages, such as SPSS's *Neural Connection*, provide three-dimensional fishnet surface plots which trace the relation of two inputs to the estimated values of the dependent. By examining all possible combinations of input variables one can gain insight into the role of each independent in the overall model.

A second form of post-analysis focuses on residual analysis of the difference between neural model estimates and actual values in the test data set. Examination of the set of cases in which residuals are high can suggest variables which are missing from the model, or can suggest the need for multiple models associated with certain classes of the population of cases under study.

Interpreting Neural Weights

The issue of evaluating neural net performance goes far beyond assessing the ability of the net to generalize to a validation data set. No matter how well a net predicts values of the dependent, the social scientist very often will want to know more about the components of the prediction in order to make some assessment of the relative contribution of the independent variables to the result, both for comparative purposes, much as one uses beta weights in multiple regression to establish the contributions of the independents, and for control purposes, much as one uses partial correlation coefficients.

Addressing causal analysis is clearly a weakness of neural network analysis. Precisely because computation is diffused throughout the net, often involving thousands or tens of thousands of weights and connections, it is impossible to approach the problem of causality in the same way as in multivariate general linear hypothesis models such as regression.

What is needed in interpreting backpropagation and certain other neural networks is an approach which focuses on the output rather than input layer connection weights. The connection weights along the paths from the input node to the output node indicate the relative predictive importance of the independents. Caudill (1989) suggested that interpretation could best be done manually, as it were, by presenting a trained network with particular input values, one case at a time, then watching to see if any of the hidden layer nodes reacts strongly.

However, not only is this approach to interpretation extremely tedious but also, as Caudill notes, hidden layer reactions may result from complex relations which are difficult to interpret in this manner.

Interpreting neural networks is often confined to assessment of classificatory or predictive effectiveness. In evaluating neural network performance in terms of ability to generalize, goodness-of-curve-fit measures are appropriate. Pearson's correlation, in contrast, is a poor measure to use when comparing actual and predicted results. This is so because correlation may be high when the order of predicted results corresponds to the order of actual results, even when the magnitudes do not correspond. That is, correlation can overestimate curve fit. However, the social scientist is apt not to be satisfied with mere prediction but rather to want to interpret neural networks from a causal analysis viewpoint.

To a limited extent the magnitude of the weights of the neurons linking input to output layer are a very rough indication of effect. Schrodt (1990) uses the following formula:

$$w_{io} = w_{ih} + w_{ho}$$

The total weight associated with an independent equals the sum of the weight linking it to the hidden layer node with which it is associated and the weight linking that hidden node to the output node associated with the dependent variable of interest.

As Schrodt acknowledges, there are several problems with simply looking at weight magnitudes. The input–output connection is qualified by the squashing function which limits output of a node to the range 0 to 1. In the path from input to hidden to output layers, one connection may be positive and the other negative, making the sum less than meaningful. And where one wishes to compare the importance of independent variables for the output layer rather than a single output node, a partitioning approach is called for. This is the case when, as is common, the output nodes represent values of the dependent.

A simple rule of thumb approach to interpretation of neural weights is to partition the sum of effects on the output layer, using the following equation:

$$\frac{\sum_{j}^{n_H} \left(\dfrac{I_{V_j}}{\sum_{k}^{n_V} I_{V_j}} O_j \right)}{\sum_{i}^{n_V} \left[\sum_{j}^{n_H} \left(\dfrac{I_{V_j}}{\sum_{k}^{n_V} I_{V_j}} O_j \right) \right]}$$

For each j of n_H hidden nodes, sum the product formed by multiplying the input-to-hidden connection weight of the input node I of variable V for hidden node j by the connection weight of output node O for hidden node j; then divide this by the sum of such quantities for all variables. The result is the percentage of all output weights attributable to the given independent variable, excluding bias weights arising from the backpropagation algorithm. While this may seem complicated on first reading, all that has been done is to partition the hidden-to-output connection weights of each hidden node into components associated with each input node.

The reader may wonder why the bias connections are not factored into the partitioning procedure outlined above. Ideally, one would like to partition the bias factors into components associated with the input nodes, adding this complexity to the algorithm just presented. Because of the nature of backpropagation, however, there is no feasible way of accomplishing this purpose. A reasonable estimate of that partition is, in fact, the partition of the connection weights other than the bias weights. If one accepts this assumption, then taking the bias connection weights into account would make no difference in the outcome of the procedure just outlined.

The Contributions module of *NeuroShell 2*, a leading neural package described in Chapter 6, uses a variant of this approach to identifying the most important input variables in a trained neural model. The major drawback is that the partitioning-of-weights method may generate values for nonimportant input variables which are only modestly lower than the values assigned to crucial input variables.

An alternative to the partitioning-of-weights method is to use GRNN or PNN neural architectures. Both utilize a genetic algorithm which constantly smoothes the input variables. Smoothing involves subjecting the input variable to normally distributed Gaussian noise. If a variable is smoothed all the way to a smoothing factor of 0, it is effectively removed from the model. A smoothing factor of 3 indicates minimal smoothing. When more smoothing is applied to an input variable and generalization improves, this is evidence that the variable is less important. If, however, smoothing causes model deterioriation, this is an indicator that the input variable is more important and crucial information is lost by injecting noise. It follows from this logic that the smoothing factor multipliers in GRNN and PNN models are an indicator of the relative importance of input variables. As a corollary, researchers may wish to drop from the model input variables with low smoothing factors (e.g. less than 0.05). Note, however, that smoothing factors are particular to given applications and cannot be compared across network problems.

Both the partitioning-of-weights method and the smoothing factor method become unreliable as the number of input variables becomes large (e.g. more than 20).

In this chapter on interpretation of neural network output, little has been said about issues of statistical significance. The reason is that as of this writing, little work has been done on strategies for dealing with assessment of the probability, using neural network analysis, of accepting the null hypothesis when it is false, owing to sampling error. An exception is the work of Chryssolouris et al. (1996), who have developed a proposed method of setting confidence intervals on neural net predictions, relying on an assumption of associated normally distributed error.

6

Neural Network Software

Most applications emulate neural networks through software, but it may be noted that there have been efforts to design neurocomputers – hardware that emulates neural nets through parallel processors in the computer. Intel Corporation, a leading American chip manufacturer, made available in 1989 the N64 neural network chip, which can perform millions of simultaneous computations. An example of a neural computer is NEC's Neuro-07 computer. Neurocomputer coprocessor boards are also available for existing digital computers. For those constructing neural networks in software, appropriate digital computers are those which can handle large matrices fast, since processing a 400-dimensional array would not be unusual. Appropriate computers have high processing speeds and large memories, and effective compilers are available for them. Even on Sun and VAX minicomputers, neural net problems may run for hours. However, as microcomputers have increased in speed and functional capacity, desktop neural network modelling has become commonplace and is a workable strategy for most social science applications.

The sections below outline how selected neural network software packages approach the problem of implementing a backpropagation model for one's data. The purpose is not to recreate the software manual but rather to demystify the mechanics of neural network analysis for the social science researcher who has not yet approached this topic in a hands-on manner. Although coverage centres on two of the most popular commercial packages, it should be noted that a number of freeware and shareware neural network packages are available.[27] Reid and Zeichick (1992) have provided a description of 50 commercial neural network products. A large list of freeware, shareware and commercial neural networking packages maintained by Warren S. Sarle at the SAS Institute can be found on the World Wide Web at the URL address ftp://ftp.sas.com/pub/neural/FAQ6.html. It is even possible to program one's own neural network software (cf. Dewdney, 1992).

Neural Connection

Neural Connection is the neural network package associated with the *SPSS* statistical package from SPSS Inc., Chicago, Illinois, which in turn licensed it from Recognition Systems, Inc.[28] Though not one of the major neural network development packages, its association with what is perhaps the most used statistical package among social scientists warrants an extended look at *Neural Connection* in this volume. The discussion treats *Neural Connection* version 2.0, the version current in 1997.

Starting *Neural Connection*

After installation of *Neural Connection*, a Neural Network menu choice will be found on the Utilities menu of *SPSS*. Clicking on this choice will launch *Neural Connection*. The researcher then selects File from the menu bar, then selects New, to create a new, temporarily untitled workspace for the neural analysis. This operation is illustrated in Figure 6.1 below. The file will be given a name the first time the researcher selects File, Save As. *Neural Connection* will save the network with the extension .NNT, and this name will appear in the title bar at the top of the screen. As with other *Windows* applications, it is a good idea to save one's work at regular intervals. Later, the researcher may select File, Open, to retrieve a saved model.

The User Interface

The workspace contains a Tools Palette from which the researcher may select graphic icons representing tools and modules. The Tools Palette is illustrated in Figure 6.2. The icons in the Tools Palette can represent data sets; neural modelling tools corresponding to backpropagation, radial basis function, or other types of neural models; operations such as merge; and more. The researcher clicks on a desired tool in the Tools Palette. When the mouse is clicked at a workspace creation, that tool (e.g. the Input Tool) is dropped at that location. The researcher then arranges icons in a flow chart on the workspace to create a neural model for his or her problem. *Neural Connection* refers to the set of connected icons as a 'topology'. All topologies begin with an Input Tool (the only input allowed in a topology) and end with an Output Tool. In *Neural Connection* feedback loops are not allowed in topologies. Valid topologies which conform to the rules and limits of *Neural Connection* are referred to as 'applications'.

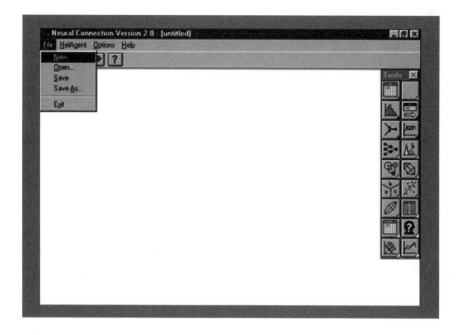

Figure 6.1 *Neural Connection 2.0* user interface

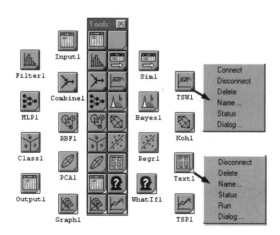

Figure 6.2 *Neural Connection* Tools Palette

The Tools Palette

The Tools Palette contains 17 tools, whose functions are described briefly below.

1   *Input*   The Data Input Tool is the standard means of bringing data into *Neural Connection* from an external file, and displaying them as a spreadsheet. It allows you to specify the format of the data; choose the training, test and validation set sizes; set the uses of individual fields in the data; randomize time series data for use with the Time Series Window; and manually edit entries in the data. In essence, the Data Input Tool is like a separate program (rather than like a dialog window). Data are viewed and edited in spreadsheet fashion.

2   *TSW*   The Time Series Window (TSW) Tool is an alternative data input tool which establishes a database which usually contains one or more input columns, each of which represents a feature which has been recorded at time intervals. Each line in the database represents values recorded at the same time interval. Usually TSW databases do not contain target values since the targets, or forecast variables, are the projected values in the time series.

3   *Sim*   The Simulator Tool produces a continuous set of data for purposes of modelling a problem. It can produce output for any two input fields, and can also produce an output which can vary from fine to coarse. The Simulator Tool is used with the What If? Tool and the Graphics Output Tool.

4   *Filter*   The Filter Tool functions to enable or disable fields of data; to give an analysis of the distribution of a data field; and to scale data fields in various ways. Filtering is critical to the data pre-processing stage of neural analysis.

5   *Combine*   The Combiner Tool functions to combine the output from two or more network objects into a single output. This enables the creation of complex application topologies.

6   *MLP*   The Multi-Layer Perceptron (MLP) Tool is the basic back-propagation neural modelling and forecasting tool. It can be used to classify patterns or to predict values from input data based on training data containing correct targets.

7   *RBF*   The Radial Basis Function (RBF) Tool is an alternative neural modelling and forecasting tool. In contrast to MLP backpropagation, the outputs from the hidden layer are not simple functions of weighted inputs. Instead the inputs to each neuron reflect distance in the network data space. Transfer functions are radial basis functions.

8   *Koh*   The Kohonen Network Tool is used to create unsupervised neural network models. The Kohonen algorithm builds its own representations of the data, and can be used as a clustering tool as

an alternative to PCA (see below). Like PCA, the Kohonen Tool can be used to reduce the dimensionality of data sets and therefore can be used to preprocess data before channelling them into another modelling tool. It can also be used to assign new examples to particular data clusters.

9 *Class*   The Closest Class Means (CCM) algorithm is a simple classifier which, in effect, generates a typical instance for each decision class. CCM is fast and can yield satisfactory results for relatively clustered, homogeneous data. Conversely, the class means are biased when there are a significant number of outliers outside the data space cluster.

10 *PCA*   Principal Components Analysis (PCA) is a form of factor analysis which can be used to reduce data space to simpler dimensions. PCA computes a set of orthogonal vectors (principal components) that account for as much of the data variance as possible. The principal components are derived from the eigenvalues and eigenvectors of the correlation matrix of the data set. The researcher applies PCA in order to be able to work with a smaller number of principal components in lieu of a larger number of possibly overlapping variables.

11 *Bayes*   The Bayesian Network Tool is an alternative to MLP and RBF neural models for classification and prediction. The greatest benefit is that the Bayesian algorithm does not require a validation data set in order to produce a generalized model and, as a result, requires fewer data. The Bayesian Network Tool is applied to MLP as an alternative error criterion, particularly suitable when data are sparse.

12 *Regr*   The Regression Tool provides a well known linear prediction technique useful for benchmarking neural network results, or as a prediction tool in its own right.

13 *Text*   The Text Output Tool prints results in text format, either to the screen or to a file.

14 *Output*   The Data Output Tool exports data to files, displays results as text, and shows the success rate. The Data Viewer spreadsheet is opened to view data output.

15 *Graphs*   The Graphics Output Tool displays results in a graphical form in the Results Window. It requires that the Simulator Tool has been used. The Graphics Output Tool creates a three-dimensional plot of the network output against any two of the inputs.

16 *What If*   The What If? Tool is used for sensitivity analysis, allowing one to see what influence changing one variable will have on another. One can temporarily change one variable, such as income, to see the response of the neural model. A visual output is generated reflecting a mathematical model of a specific area of the response.

17 *TSP*   Used in conjunction with the Time Series Window Tool, the
   Time Series Plot (TSP) Tool displays the results of time series
   prediction against time in the form of a two-dimensional plot.

Input

In *Neural Connection* most data input is handled by the Data Input Tool.
For time series data, the Time Series Window Tool may be used as an
alternative. For exploratory purposes, the Simulator Tool can be used to
generate data for any two input variables.
   The Data Input Tool, also called the Input Tool or the Spreadsheet
Tool, is a data viewer which functions as a separate program with its
own menu bar. It allows up to 750 variables by up to 15,000 cases (while
training) to 32,000 cases (for running a trained model). *Neural Connection*
recommends restricting input data to numbers with fewer than eight
digits. Data may be brought into the input tool by six methods:

1 *Field count data files* (.NNA)   These are a type of ASCII flat file
   format in which fields are separated by spaces, commas or even
   carriage returns. Records may take more than one line since the
   newline ASCII character is ignored.
2 *Delimited ASCII files* (.CSV or .TXT)   These are files in which fields
   are separated by spaces, commas, or other delimiters, and records
   are separated by newline characters. The first line of the file is a
   data row (not a line of variable names), and each succeeding row
   must have the same number of fields.
3 *SPSS files* (.SAV)   These are files saved from SPSS 6.0 or higher.
   Neural Connection has a simpler data structure than *SPSS*, so
   conversions are necessary. For instance, *Neural Connection* does not
   support string data as such. Therefore when *Neural Connection*
   imports *SPSS* data, it converts date, currency and most other *SPSS*
   formats to floating-point numeric, and string data are converted to
   symbolic with a maximum length of 13. *Neural Connection* drops
   variable labels and variable weights contained in *SPSS*.
4 *Systat files* (.SYS)   The .SYS files from the *Systat* statistical package
   can be read directly, for *Systat* version 5.05 and higher.
5 *Excel files* (.XLS)   *Excel 5.0* files can be read directly.
6 *Windows clipboard*   One can also cut and paste from any *Windows*
   application supporting Edit, Copy (or Cut).

To import data from any of the data file types above, one must first
have placed a Data Input Tool instance on the work area. This is done
by clicking on the Data Input Tool, then dropping a Data Input instance
icon at any desired location on the work area by clicking with the

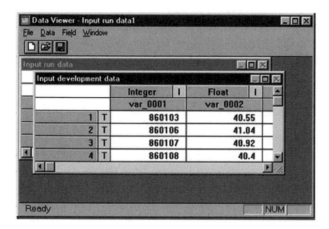

Figure 6.3   *Neural Connection* Data Viewer window

mouse. Next, the researcher clicks on the arrow in the lower right of the Data Input icon, to pull down a menu similar to that shown in Figure 6.2. Unlike the examples in Figure 6.2, however, one of the menu choices will be View. Selecting View will bring up the Data Viewer with a blank spreadsheet. The Data Viewer is shown in Figure 6.3.

In the Data Viewer spreadsheet window, the researcher selects File, then selects Open and clicks on Flat File in the dialog box which then opens. After this, clicking on Configure will give another box which prompts for the file name to import. Alternatively one can type data directly into *Neural Connection*'s Data Viewer spreadsheet. *Neural Connection* will automatically check each column for data consistency (that is, to assure that all data are of the same type – floating-point numeric, integer or symbolic). Rows with inconsistent data will be highlighted with a colour marker. When *Neural Connection* encounters a missing floating-point numeric or an integer value, it replaces it with the column mean of nonmissing values. Missing symbolic values are replaced by the symbol Missing. Missing values are colour-coded in bright blue, replacement values are shown in light blue, and encoded values for previously missing values are shown in dark blue. Out-of-range values are shown in red. Entries inconsistent with the field data type are shown in dark green.

The Data Viewer contains two spreadsheets, as shown in the cascade view in Figure 6.3. The one labelled Development Data is for importation or entry of the training data set. By selecting Data, Data Allocation, from the Data Viewer menu, the researcher can determine the proportions of cases to assign to training, cross-validation and testing. In the second column from the left, these proportions are colour-coded: cyan for training data, yellow for test data, bright green for validation data, and pale blue for run data. Likewise the fields are colour-coded: cyan for input fields, yellow for target fields, and bright green for reference fields (pass-through fields ignored by the neural model but desired in the output data set). The Run Data spreadsheet is for importation or entry of data for testing trained models. As such it need not contain the target field being predicted or classified.

If the allocation percentages (to training, test, validation and run) add to less than 100 per cent, the remaining percentage of records will not be used. It is also possible to specify the usage of individual records manually, one at a time or serially by highlighting a sequence of records to be assigned, say, to training purposes. There is also an option to position test records at the end of the file (this option is required for time series data to assure testing on the most recent records).

The Data Allocation dialog box also allows the researcher to ask the spreadsheet module to randomize the order of the data. This is standard procedure if one is not dealing with time series data. The researcher can enter a random number seed (note that the same seed will always generate the same sequence of random numbers). *Neural Connection* will take the validation and test sets from the end of the randomized list of cases, after having selected out the training set. Later, a separate file which is identical in data format may also be used for further testing.

While in the spreadsheet module, one usually wants to specify the target output variable. By default *Neural Connection* assumes the last column is the output variable and all others are inputs. If the researcher wants to designate a different output variable, this is done by selecting Field, Configuration, from the Data Viewer menu, leading to the dialog box shown in Figure 6.4. The dialog box will pertain to the last-selected field column. In the dialog box the researcher can indicate if the field is to be an input, target or reference (pass-through) variable. Note that target variables must be floating-point numeric or integer for prediction problems, but may also be symbolic for decision problems. The dialog box also allows the researcher to convert data types (from integer to floating point, for instance), to indicate how to handle missing values (ignore, substitute mean, substitute mode, substitute a given value), and to indicate if range checking is appropriate. The Field, Statistics, choice of the Data Viewer gives descriptive statistics for any field, along with information on missing and inconsistent values, which can be useful in making some of the configuration decisions. If only allocation of fields to input, target and reference categories is needed, a dialog box limited to this purpose will pop up if the researcher clicks on the I box in the upper right of each field column header.

While in the Data Viewer module, the researcher can select Field, Equalization, and select the target variable on which to equalize cases. That is, the Data Viewer module can be instructed to adjust the training

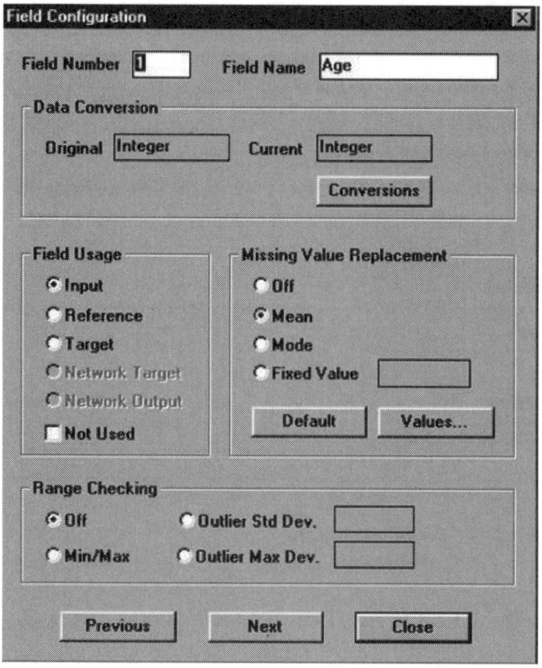

Figure 6.4   Field Configuration dialog box of Data Viewer

data set so that there are roughly equal numbers of cases for each target class. This generally but not always improves the performance of neural models. Various equalization options are offered by the Equalization dialog box. For instance, one can set a maximum number of times any record can be duplicated in the effort to equalize classes.

However the data are imported or entered, after data are in the spreadsheet satisfactorily, one chooses File, Exit and Return, to leave the Data Viewer module.

For time series data, the researcher can divide the series into a specified number of blocks. *Neural Connection* will take the validation set data from the end of each sequential block. Alternatively, the researcher can opt to have *Neural Connection* take the training, cross-validation and test data randomly but in sequence throughout the entire series.

Time Series Input

The Time Series Window Tool is an interpreter for the Data Input Tool. One still drops an instance of the Data Input Tool on the workspace and loads in one's time series data. The Data Input Tool instance is then connected to an instance of the Time Series Window Tool. By opening the dialog box for the Time Series Window Tool (click on the lower

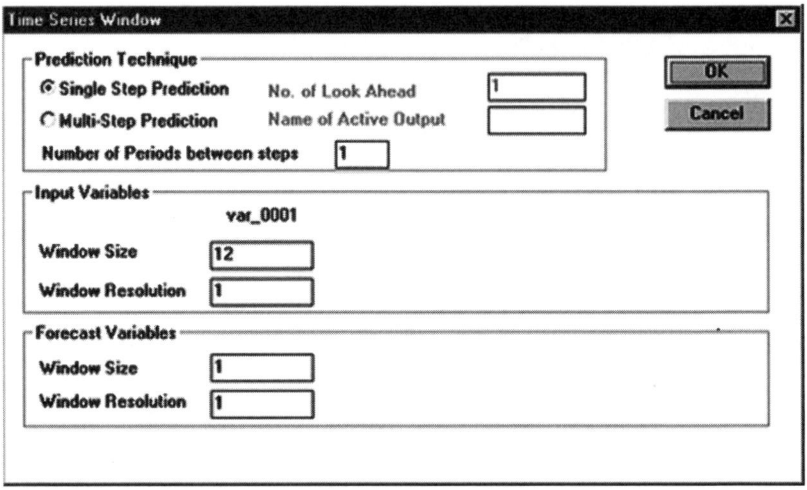

Figure 6.5   Time Series Window dialog box

right arrow in the Time Series Window icon), one can select Dialog. This selection generates the dialog box shown in Figure 6.5.

The Time Series Window dialog box offers a choice between single-step prediction and multi-step prediction. The former generates a series of predictions by using the original window (set) of time series data to predict the datum at time t +1, then advancing the window by one time unit and using the actual (not predicted) datum at time t + 1 to predict the datum at time t + 2, and so on for as many single steps as requested. Multi-step prediction generates the same prediction for time t + 1 but then uses that prediction as input for advancing the window and predicting the datum at time t + 2, and so on.

In Figure 6.5, for either single-step prediction or multi-step prediction, the Time Series Window dialog box lets the researcher specify, for both the input variables and the forecast variables, the window size and the window resolution. Window size is the number of observations in the time series data that are taken to constitute a set, or window, for purposes of forecasting. Window resolution is the number of time steps within the window set to use for purposes of selecting the specific cases used for prediction (a resolution of 1 selects all cases in the window, for instance). Although Figure 6.5 shows prediction based on a single input, if there are multiple inputs then each input can be set to its own window size and window resolution.

With single-step prediction one can predict only one time unit ahead of the actual time series, whereas with multi-step prediction one can generate far into the future. Other dialog box options appearing in Figure 6.5 pertain to multi-step prediction. In the No. of Look Ahead box the researcher can enter the number of time steps to predict. In the Name of Active Output box the researcher can enter the name of the output tool downstream in the model, from which the Time Series Window application will be run (Plot, for example).

Processing

Neural Connection includes a Filter Tool which allows transformation of the data according to various mathematical functions; a Combiner Tool which allows the researcher to join two neural or other tools together in a single application; and a Simulator Tool which formats data for the Graphics Output Tool and What If? Tool.

Filter Tool

Clicking on the Filter Tool icon allows one to transform the input data prior to processing. The objective of transformation is to achieve a relatively uniform distribution of the data since neural models work best under such conditions. If, for example, the data are skewed toward one end of the distribution, learning will concentrate on this end, perhaps at the expense of learning to differentiate cases in the middle, which may be of greater significance for decision-making. Alternative to seeking a uniform distribution, the researcher may seek a transformation which expands the data around the point critical for decision-making (e.g. the midpoint). With the Filter Tool, the researcher can also view descriptive statistics and a distribution histogram for any input variable.

Weighting functions allow the researcher to do things like normalize distributions by applying logarithmic functions to data which are skewed left. Transformations supported by *Neural Connection* include square, cubic, square root, reciprocal, linear ($bx + c$), limiting (sets all values in specified range to 1, rest to 0), exponential, natural logarithmic ($\ln[x+a]$), logarithm of quotient ($\ln[[x-a]/[b-x]]$), base 10 logarithmic ($\log[x+a]$), arcsin square root, Box–Cox transformation ($[[x+a]^b-1]/b$), and trimming (resetting outliers to specified minimum or maximum values).

The Filter Tool dialog box shown in Figure 6.6 is in the form of a spreadsheet. The researcher can click on the Function row cell for any field, then click on the state and weighting change button (the first button in the upper left of Figure 6.6, just to the right of the function box) to select the desired mathematical transformation function for that field. The Use State row is normally set to Yes, but the researcher can disable the field by changing it to No. By disabling a field, the researcher can conduct sensitivity tests for the performance of the neural model with and without that input field. The Parameter *a* and Parameter *b* rows

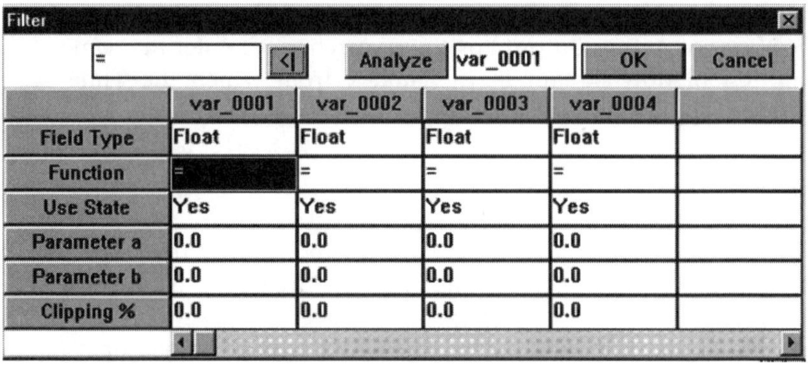

Figure 6.6   Filter Tool dialog box

in Figure 6.6 have meanings related to the specific function selected. For instance, if the researcher chooses a linear transform, whereby observation x becomes $a+(xb)$, Parameter a is the constant and Parameter b is the slope of the transform. The Clipping % row in Figure 6.6 allows a data field to be trimmed up to 50 per cent. For instance, if the Clipping % is set to 25 per cent, then the entire top and bottom 25 per cent of the data range are set equal to the value of the datum at the 25th and 75th percentiles respectively.

The Filter Tool also supports a variety of descriptive statistics for any variable: N, sum, mean, variance, standard deviation, absolute deviation, skewness, kurtosis, range, quartile values, difference of third and first quartiles, and a distribution histogram. These may be used in selecting transformations. For instance, positive skewness indicates right skewing of data from normal, while negative skewness indicates left skewing. Clicking the Analyze button generates statistical information on the selected field (shown in the adjacent box), as shown in Figure 6.7.

Combiner Tool

This is used to join different data tools in a neural model. For instance, in Figure 6.8, the Combiner Tool is used to merge a filtered radial basis function neural model of education and a similar model of wealth into a single output stream. In such a model, all training occurs prior to the Combiner Tool, which simply passes data into the output stream. An implication is that the Combiner Tool cannot be used to create a feedback loop.

Simulator Tool

The Simulator Tool produces a simulated data stream for any one or two input variables, with cases representing the entire range of these

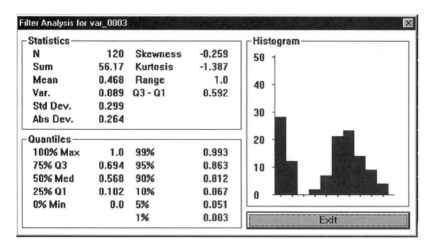

Figure 6.7   Filter Tool analysis box

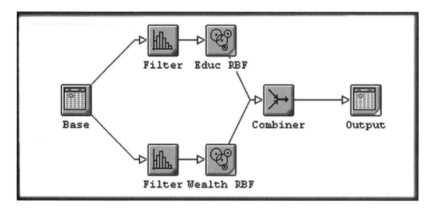

Figure 6.8   A neural model using the Combiner Tool

variables, while holding other variables constant at their mean values (or other values set by the researcher). The tool is placed after the neural modelling tool (e.g. after the Multi-Layer Perceptron Tool) and before the tool which plots results, such as the Graphics Output Tool and/or the What If? Tool. By plotting the output of the neural model against the range of the simulated input variable(s), the resulting plot reflects the function linking the input field to the target output. When the model is working well, this plot will represent a discernible function. When the model is not working well, the plot will not be interpretable. In this way the Simulator Tool provides an optional method of model evaluation.

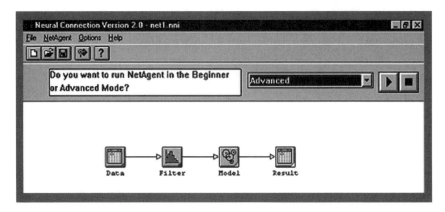

Figure 6.9   NetAgent

Modelling

Neural Connection provides six processing options, three of which are neural models: the multi-layer perceptron (backpropagation), radial basis function models and Kohonen networks. In addition, the data matrix may be analysed using the closest class means classifier, multiple regression and principal components factor analysis – statistical tools not within the scope of this monograph.

NetAgent

The easiest way to create a model in *Neural Connection* is to use the 'NetAgent' guide or wizard that appears automatically upon starting the package. NetAgent builds an application by prompting the researcher for information through a series of questions, as shown in Figure 6.9. In its Beginner mode, NetAgent gives more detailed information than in its Advanced mode. The prompts in NetAgent's Beginner mode are given below. In each case the researcher selects the answer appropriate to his or her problem from a drop-down list of alternatives. The drop-down button is a down-arrow icon. After selecting the alternative wanted, the researcher clicks on the Play button, which is an adjacent right-arrow icon.

NetAgent Beginner mode prompts:

1   *Is this a classification problem or a prediction problem?*   In prediction problems the neural network output for a given case is a numerical value from a continuous open range. In classification problems the output is one of a finite number of values corresponding to different categories of examples. Dichotomous dependent variables are classification problems.

2   *Do you want to use a statistical (linear) or a neural network method for this application?*   By choosing Neural the researcher asks *Neural Connection* to use a neural network model rather than a statistical technique. Kohonen self-organizing neural models cannot be selected for problems relating inputs to predetermined output variables or categories: supervised models are required for such tasks, and *Neural Connection* supports two supervised models – the multi-layer perceptron (backpropagation) and radial basis function models.

3   *Enter the name of your file*   The researcher enters the data filename.

4   *Which data set do you want to use when running your application?*   The researcher selects Training, Validation or Test set data contained in the file cited in the previous step.

5   *Press Play to train the model*   After this step *Neural Connection* will begin training the model. The Play button is a VCR-type button at the top of the NetAgent display. During training a Results screen will appear. The Results screen shows summary data on total number of examples processed, total correct and percentage correct.

6   *Press Play, then select View from the Data Output menu to view your results*   *Neural Connection* completes the analysis. Clicking on the arrow in the lower right of the Result icon will give a popup menu which has the View choice. View in turn will display the Data Viewer spreadsheet, which will include the target values predicted by the neural model.

Menu Mode

More complex models can be created by ignoring the NetAgent wizard and instead simply using the menu mode. The researcher selects File, New, to start a new application as the first step in this approach, which also has the following typical steps.

1   Select Data Input from the Tools Palette, to input the data. (See the foregoing section on input.) The Data Input icon is dragged onto the workspace.

2   To actually load in training data, click on the Data Input Tool and select View. Then, after the Data Viewer spreadsheet appears, from the menu bar select File, Open, and give the filename wanted in the standard *Windows* File Open dialog box. Data are then loaded.

   (a) After loading in the data, one may wish to transform it using the Data Viewer's Field, Configuration, menu option. For instance, dichotomous character data can be transformed auto-matically to numeric by clicking the field header button to give a dialog box of possible type changes, such as from Sym (symbolic) to Num (numeric). While *Neural Connection* and most neural software can process character data, by converting to numeric, the output will take the form of probabilities from 0 to 1.

(b) By default, *Neural Connection* assumes the last field is the dependent variable.

(c) By default, *Neural Connection* automatically divides the input file into training, validation and test data sets.

3   Each of the tool icons has a menu which can be activated by clicking on it to specify parameters. For instance, one menu choice is Connect, which will generate a connection line which can be attached to any other icon by clicking with the mouse.

4   In a similar manner to the Data Input Tool, the researcher moves other tools to the worksheet: the Filter Tool, the Simulator Tool, a neural tool such as the Radial Basis Function Tool, the Text Output Tool and the Graphics Output Tool. The tools are connected by clicking on a tool of origin, selecting Connect from the drop-down menu, and dragging the mouse so that the connection points to the destination tool. A typical application layout would show six icons: Data Input connected to a Filter Tool, in turn connected to a Simulator Tool (to prepare data for the Graphics Tool). The Simulator Tool is connected to a neural network tool such as the Radial Basis Function Tool. The neural network tool is then connected both to a Text Output Tool and to a Graphics Output Tool.

5   The overall task (model) is run from an output icon, such as the Text Output icon, whose popup menu has a Run choice.

Multi-Layer Perceptron Tool

MLP is *Neural Connection*'s backpropagation tool. Its icon is placed on the workspace downstream from the Data Input Tool. Clicking on its Dialog menu choice yields the dialog box shown in Figure 6.10. This dialog box contains a subset of the possible configuration choices for backpropagation:

1   *Normalization of the input layer*   The choices are standard or none. Standard normalization is normally utilized for the input layer so that backpropagation is not biased by field magnitudes and variance. If desired, the dialog box also allows the output layer to be normalized, but this is not necessary from a neural modelling viewpoint.

2   *Hidden layer transfer function*   The choices are tanh, sigmoid or linear. The most often used function is sigmoid, though tanh is also common. Experimentation is needed to determine the optimal function for a particular problem. Transfer functions are rarely linear.

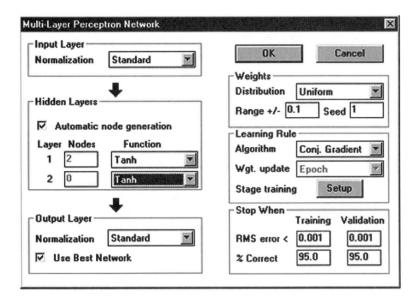

Figure 6.10   Multi-Layer Perceptron dialog box

3   *Distribution of initial network weights*   The choices are uniform or
    Gaussian. Also, the range may be set to be plus or minus a given
    constant for uniform distributions. For Gaussian distributions, the
    variance is set equal to the range setting. The seed determines the
    random number sequence generated. Initial weights can have a
    large effect on model outcomes. Uniform distribution is most often
    chosen within a plus or minus 1 range.
4   *The learning rule algorithm*   The choices are conjugate gradient or
    steepest descent. If steepest descent is chosen, the weight update
    may be set to epoch or pattern. The purpose of the learning rule
    algorithm is to arrive as closely as possible at the lowest point on
    the error surface, avoiding local minima. The steepest descent
    method alters network weights to favour the direction of steepest
    descent. The conjugate gradient method moderates steepest descent
    criteria by also considering the previous direction of change.
    Conjugate gradient is the most common choice. If steepest gradient
    is chosen, it is most common to update not after each pattern, but
    after each epoch of patterns.
       Clicking on the 'Stage training' Setup button will open a
    subordinate dialog box in which the researcher may set the learning
    and momentum coefficients. The learning coefficient has to do with
    the rate at which network weights are changed based on new
    patterns, and momentum has to do with the amount this change is
    moderated in the direction of the average gradient. Normally, as

one moves from the input to the output layers, the learning coefficient decreases and the momentum increases. As a rule of thumb, momentum should be higher when using the steepest descent method rather than the conjugate gradient method.

5   *Stop When criteria*   Root mean square error for the training and/or validation data sets, and percentage correct.
6   *Nodes*   If 'Automatic node generation' is unchecked, then the researcher may manually set the desired number of nodes in each layer. If the model is not performing satisfactorily, increasing the number of hidden layer nodes will generally improve performance on the training set, though it may not improve generalization to the test set. Even if the model is performing satisfactorily, the researcher may want to experiment to see if a more parsimonious model with fewer hidden nodes would also achieve satisfactory results.

Radial Basis Function (RBF) Tool

RBF is an alternative neural model which can also be used for classification and prediction problems. In terms of *Neural Connection* operation, it operates in a similar manner to MLP. RBF models may be more effective than MLP models with noisy data. Only the unique options in the RBF dialog box (Figure 6.11) are discussed here:

1   *Normalization*   Same as MLP.
2   *RBF layer transfer function*   The choices are spline, quadratic, inverse quadratic and Gaussian. These choices of a smoothing parameter can have substantial effects on the results when the data contain an inherent symmetry. Spline and quadratic functions increase with distance from radial basis function centre, while Gaussian and inverse quadratic decrease.
3   *Error distance*   The choices are city block or Euclidean. The latter is the usual, more accurate choice, though it takes longer to calculate.
4   *Number of centres*   The researcher can set manually the number of RBF centres. This determines the number of clusters and must be set in advance.
5   *Extra centres*   In the Optimization group, checking 'Add extra centers' causes the RBF module to repeatedly train, each time adding an incremental number of centres, and it will stop when the Stop When criteria in the lower right of the dialog box are met. When not checked, the RBF module will train once, with a fixed number of centres.
6   *Positioning of centres*   The choices are random, sample and trial. This part of the dialog box determines the initial placement of the RBF centres. Random causes the centres to be distributed randomly in data space. Sample causes the centres to be placed on selected

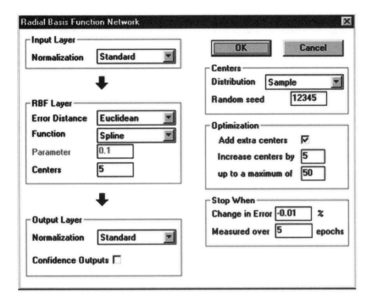

Figure 6.11   Radial Basis Function dialog box

data points evenly distributed in data space. Trial causes the first data point to be selected by sampling, then additional centres are placed on points which are outlying with respect to existing centres. Trial is the most commonly selected method, though experimentation may still be needed.

Kohonen Networks

Kohonen networks, unlike MLP and RBF models, are an unsupervised approach to neural network analysis. That is, they are self-organizing and do not require supplied correct target values in the training data set. As such they can be employed for purposes of clustering analysis The choices in the Kohonen Network dialog box (Figure 6.12) are described as follows:

1   *Normalization*   The choices are none, square or spherical. Square normalization is the regular type of normalization which converts input data to a mean of zero and a variance of one, and is used when Error Response is set to Euclidean. Spherical normalization normalizes input data to unit length and is used when Error Response is set to dot product.

2   *Error Response*   The choices are Euclidean or dot product. This parameter determines how the winning neuron is chosen on each presentation of the input pattern. A Euclidean response function

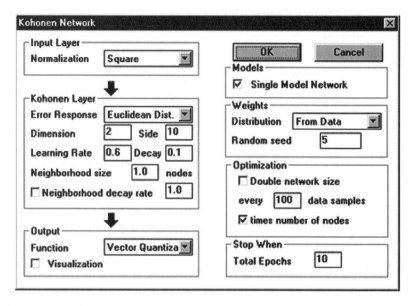

Figure 6.12   Kohonen dialog box

uses the simple Euclidean distance from the input vector to the node
weight vector, and the node with the minimum distance is selected
as the winner. The dot product response function instead uses the
dot product of the input vector and the node weight vector, and the
node with the highest product wins. Experimentation is necessary to
determine which method is superior for a given problem.

3   *Learning rate and decay of the learning rate*   These can be set in the
dialog box as well, determining the rate of change of network
weights in response to presentation of patterns.

4   *Neighbourhood size*   This determines how many nodes adjacent to
the winning node are also modified in weight. Usually a decay rate
is also set so that neighbourhood size decreases with training, as the
network converges on a solution.

5   *Output function*   The choices are vector quantization, VQ codebook
or full response. Vector quantization causes output from Kohonen
layer nodes to be the input vector of the winning node. VQ codebook causes the output to be a reference number associated with the
winning node. Full response causes the output to be the output of
all nodes.

6   *Visualization*   If Visualization is checked, a visual display of the
input space positions of each node is given, along with a graphic
plot of the training run.

7   *Single layer*   If Single Model Network is checked then all features of
the input vector will be mapped to a single Kohonen layer.

8 *Dimensionality*   One- or two-dimensional Kohonen architectures can be selected.

9 *Side length*   The researcher can determine the number of nodes per dimension.

10 *Weights*   The choices are From Data, Random, Small Random, Grid and Small Grid. These settings determine the distribution of initial weights. From Data uses random samples from the input data; Random sets weights to random values from −1 to +1; Small Random uses values from −0.1 to +0.1; Grid distributes weights in a grid pattern; Small Grid distributes weights in a small grid.

11 *Optimization*   If 'Double network size' is checked, then new nodes are added for each block of data samples, as specified by the researcher in the dialog box. If 'times number of nodes' is checked, then new nodes are added according to the product of the number of data samples and the number of nodes passed through the Kohonen layer. The latter is the usual choice.

Output

Neural Connection supports four types of output. Text output is the default. The time series plot is a display of predicted output over time. Graphics output can display a graph showing how the output varies as any two selected input variables change. Finally, the What If? Tool generates a plot which shows how the output varies as any two specified inputs vary, but also gives information on how change in any one input will affect the output.

Text output for a particular application looks like that shown in Figure 6.13. Text output is either an ASCII text file or an *SPSS* .SAV file. Text output is produced by clicking on the Text Output icon in the workspace, then selecting Dialog from the Output Tool dialog box. The dialog box lets one select output to file. The Run option of the Text Output icon runs the model and generates text output such as that in Figure 6.13. The researcher can print the text output report directly from within *Neural Connection*. Text output includes the following:

1 A header, containing the input filename and date.

2 A listing of the input fields and of the target field output.

3 A cross-tabulation matrix in which the columns are the predicted values of the output variable, the rows are the true values of the output variable, and the cell entries are the record counts of each intersection, showing the number of correct and incorrect decisions. For prediction problems, the columns and rows are numeric incremental bins (e.g. 0–0.3, 0.3–0.5, 0.5–0.7 etc.).

```
! Input Data Set : Test
!
! Sun Jun 22 20:20:39 1997
!
!
!
!** Data **
!
! Record No. Input Fields              Target Fields  Output Fields
!            Lifestyle     Wealth      Response       Response
!
  1          50.0          656.0       1.0            0.51845
  2          49.0          842.0       0.0            -0.08773
  3          72.0          1462.0      0.0            -0.09933
...
  248        72.0          295.0       0.0            0.59349
  249        0.0           0.0         0.0            0.00862
  250        51.0          1709.0      1.0            0.30222
!
! ** Confusion Matrix For Output 1 **
!
! True              Predicted
! ----              ---------
!        0.0+ 0.2+ 0.4+ 0.6+ 0.8+
! 0.0+ 42   32   17   18   14
! 0.2+ 0    0    0    0    0
! 0.4+ 0    0    0    0    0
! 0.6+ 0    0    0    0    0
! 0.8+ 7    25   20   43   32
!
! Total number of targets : 250
!
! Total correct : 74
!
! Percentage correct : 29.60%
Output Error Measures
=====================
   Output: RMS Error: Mean Absolute: Mean Absolute %:
   ------- ---------- -------------- ----------------
      1    0.468888   0.381783       75.154174 %
```

Figure 6.13   Text output example

4   Summary data on the total number of examples, the total number of targets, the total correct predictions, the percentage correct; and error data, such as the root mean square error and the mean absolute error.

Text output can be customized from a dialog box which results from selecting Dialog from the Text Output menu, then clicking on the Format button. From the ensuing dialog box one can specify that decision output

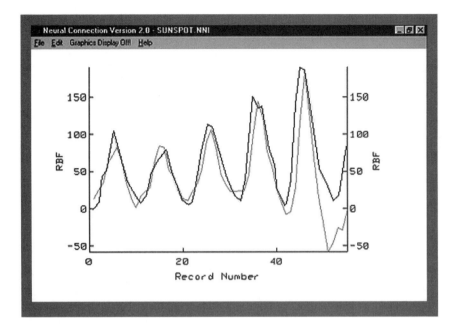

Figure 6.14   Time Series Plot

be 1-of-N Encoded (0 or 1, where 1 is a positive decision); Actual Values (gives output weight for each value of the dependent; since *Neural Connection* treats the lowest weight as the correct prediction, one can see how differentiated that decision is from the weights for other dependent variable choices); Probabilities (same as Actual Values, but with normalized data; note these are *not* statistical probabilities). When text output is saved to a file, the extension .NNO is added.

Time Series Plot Tool

The Time Series Plot gives the plot of predicted results through time, as embedded in the sequence of record numbers fed into the system. Target data for the test data set are shown as a light blue line. Target data for the training set are dark blue. Target data for the validation data set are shown in a green line. Input data are shown in purple. Two such curves can be plotted on a single graph, but the other two can be displayed on a second graph. Figure 6.14 shows an example of a time series plot. The Time Series Plot icon menu also has a Dialog box choice. The dialog box allows the researcher to determine if the plot will use run data or training and validation data. The dialog box also allows the researcher to choose which two items will be plotted from among the actual, target and either of two input variables selected by the researcher, and if the curves are to share a common y-axis.

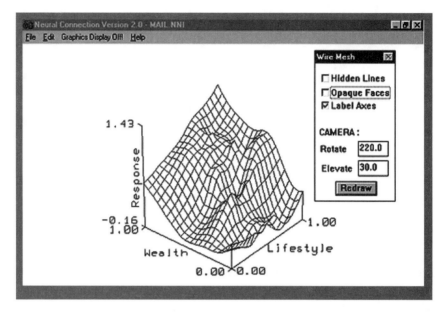

Figure 6.15   Graphics Output Tool

Graphics Output Tool

Graphics Output Tool generates a three-dimensional fishnet plot in which the y-axis (the vertical axis) is the response value for the output variable (Figure 6.15). The other two dimensions are input values for any two selected input variables. At the same time, a Graphics Display window will also open, letting the researcher set whether hidden wire mesh lines are to be displayed, whether axes are labelled, the 'camera' distance, rotation and elevation (angle of view). The particular two input variables which are used for the graphics output are set in the Simulator Tool, which must be an icon which is part of the application. In the Simulator Tool, the Scan Order must be set to 1 and 2 respectively for the two selected variables, and be 0 for all others. Also, the Num Values must be set to some number higher than 2.

The What If? Tool output displays a window with three components (Figure 6.16). As with the Graphics Output Tool, a Simulator Tool must precede this output icon in the application. The particular two input variables of interest are set in the Simulator Tool. The first portion of What If? output is a sensitivity plot. One can move cross-hairs over the space defined by the two input variables. As one does, a text display changes below, which states the numeric level of the two variables at the cross-hair point, and also states how much change in the output variable will occur given a specified change in the input variable on the horizontal axis. A third part of the What If? display is a cross-section

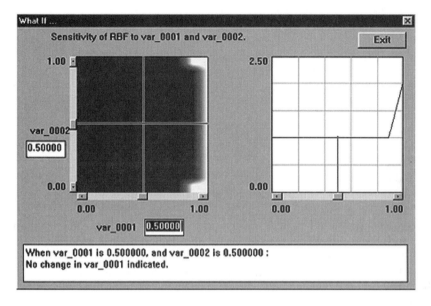

Figure 6.16 What If? Tool output

plot, which shows how output response varies for the entire range of the input variable on the horizontal axis.

Ending the Session

To quit *Neural Connection*, simply choose File from the menu bar, then select Exit.

NeuroShell 2

NeuroShell 2 is a leading neural networking package which is particularly suited for social scientists who are approaching this methodology for the first time.[29] The discussion here treats *NeuroShell* 2, release 3, the version current in 1997. *NeuroShell 2* allows one to select Beginner's Neural Networks to get a quick start, then later to select Advanced Neural Networks for more in-depth utilization of the many possibilities of neural network analysis. There are built-in online tutorials.

The Beginner's System is an enhanced backpropagation network model with default values for parameters like learning rate, momentum and number of hidden nodes. The user supplies data from his or her spreadsheet, specifies the inputs and outputs, trains the network, and then tests the trained network on new data. Beginners are also helped through an online tutorial.

The Advanced System allows the user to choose among 15 neural network architectures, then to set detailed parameters for the selected architecture: learning rate, momentum, activation functions, initial weight ranges (on a layer basis), pattern recognition (rotational or random), criteria for stopping training, method of handling missing data, and option to change weights during training. The distribution disks include sample programs for backpropagation, Kohonen, PNN, GRNN and GMDH networks.

Other features of *NeuroShell 2* include the ability to run several training sessions simultaneously, and a royalty-free Runtime System which allows the researcher to create a Dynamic Link Library (DLL) from the completed neural model, so the model can be executed from within Microsoft *Excel* spreadsheets or other *Windows* programs. The package supports up to 16,000 variables in each layer. There is software implementation of 32-bit high precision calculations for processors lacking maths coprocessor chips (when a coprocessor is present, *NeuroShell 2* uses 32-bit floating-point calculations).

NeuroShell 2 is started like other *Windows* programs. One clicks on its icon (the 'brain' icon) in its program group within *Windows*. When the program appears, the researcher selects File from the menu bar at the top of the screen. From the File submenu, the researcher chooses either New Problem to start a new 'problem' (as *NeuroShell 2* calls a neural architecture applied to a particular database), or Open Problem to open an existing problem. Problems are stored on disk as files with the extension .DSC ('description').

The .DSC files are text files containing a description of the problem in the researcher's words. The actual data are stored in other files:

.PAT   Pattern file, which is the main data file.

.TRN   Training data set, drawn from the .PAT file.

.TST   Test data set, also drawn from the .PAT file, used for cross-validation by *NeuroShell 2*'s Calibration feature. Note that *NeuroShell 2* here uses 'test' to refer to the cross-validation data set, whereas conventional usage applies the term 'test data set' to the final data set to which a fully trained model is applied for purposes of generalization. What would normally be called the test data set, *NeuroShell 2* calls the 'production file' (see below).

.PRO   Production file, a data set to which a trained neural system is applied.

.OUT   Output file, containing the neural system's predictions or classifications after being applied to a .PAT, .TRN, .TST or .PRO data file. All these data files are in .WK1 spreadsheet format, as is the .OUT file.

In addition, still other files are used by *NeuroShell 2* to hold data needed during the training and application of the model. These have the following extensions:

.FIG   Configuration file, specifying the network architecture, including the number of layers, the connection weights, the learning rate, the momentum, etc.

.Nxx   Network file, not readable by the researcher, containing weights associated with the neural model at the present iteration. .N01 files to .N09 files are associated with nine variants of the back-propagation model respectively, .N10 files contain information for Kohonen networks, .N11 for probabilistic neural networks (PNN) and so on.

.Lxx   Last net files, containing weights associated with the last iteration of a neural model.

.MMX   Minimum/maximum files, containing the minimum and maximum values of a network's input and output variables, and related information.

.WTS   Weight file, containing full precision weights for all links in the model.

.Ax   Activations files, which, at the option of the researcher, write out the weights for a particular slab number x in backpropagation models.

.C01   Contributions factors file, containing information on the contribution factor of each input.

.FLA   Formula file, containing source code which may be fed into a calculator to apply a trained network.

.SYI   Symbol input file, containing information on how to translate character values into numeric.

.SYO   Symbol output file, containing information on how to translate numeric outputs back into character equivalents.

.RLI   The if–then–else rules used in the Pre-Network module.

.RLO   The if–then–else rules used in the Post-Network module.

.C   C language source code files, if any.

.VB   Visual Basic source code files, if any.

After a new or existing problem is opened, the main menu window gives the researcher the choice to run *NeuroShell* in one of three modes: Beginner's System, Advanced System or Runtime System. The Runtime System is for completed models, such as those to be run by clients once the researcher has finalized network design. The Beginner's System is simply an abbreviated menu structure which omits optional complexities of the design process, presenting a simplified sequence of tasks for the novice neural model designer. The discussion below treats the

Advanced System, noting which modules or submodules are omitted in the Beginner's System.

Modules are shown in the main menu as columns and submodules are icons within the columns. The Advanced System contains the modules (shown as own-line headings) and submodules (shown as shoulder headings) in the following. The modules and submodules omitted in the Beginner's System are marked by an asterisk.

Problem Input

File Import

This submodule, whose icon is a filing cabinet, is used to import spreadsheet data, or delimited ASCII files, binary files, *NeuroShell 1* files and other formats. The *NeuroShell 2* internal file format conforms to *Lotus 1-2-3*.WK1 formats or to Microsoft *Excel*.XLS formats (up to release 4, not including release 5). A Spreadsheet File Import command allows importation of spreadsheet data in a manner which lets *NeuroShell 2* interpret one row as the column labels and a different row as the first actual data row. There is also support for direct importation of popular stock price retrieval service information, using the Equis International MetaStock file format and Omega Downloader data files created by *Wall St Analyst* and other financial programs. *NeuroShell* exports to delimited ASCII and spreadsheet formats as well as imports.

Data Entry

NeuroShell's built-in spreadsheet, the Datagrid, supports small problems, or one may use one's own spreadsheet. Its icon is a spreadsheet grid and, though not a commercial-level spreadsheet, it does support formulas, formats and other common spreadsheet features. *NeuroShell 2* supports up to 64,000 rows and 16,000 columns for direct data entry, with each row being a data pattern (case). Although text and date data types are supported, all columns used as input and output variables must be converted to numeric type. This will not affect the row of variable labels, which must be of text type. Data types are changed from a selection on the Format Menu. Numeric types may be displayed in the following formats: plain (integer), decimal, thousands separated (comma), money and money separated (comma).

*Pre-Network

*Symbol Translate

This submodule, whose icon is the letters A B C with an arrow to the numbers 1 2 3, is used to convert character data into numeric equivalents which *NeuroShell* can process. The translation process is implemented by filling in rows on a three-column grid whose columns are 'Find this text:', 'Translate to value' and 'Translate in these variables'. For instance, for a survey opinion item, the researcher would enter: Strongly Agree, 2, TaxOpin1; Agree, 1, TaxOpin1; and so on, filling in the three columns similarly. Nominal variables would be recoded as dummy variables, for instance: East, 1, RegionE; West, 1, RegionW; and so on. *NeuroShell 2* applies the translation rules to the .PAT pattern file unless told otherwise by the researcher under the File Menu option to select another file.

*Rules

This submodule, whose icon is a calculator with the words If..Then..Else, is used to create if–then–else rules for data preprocessing. These rules can be used to create new variables as functions of existing ones. The Rules Module allows Boolean recoding of data. One enters rules of the following type:

IF education > 12 AND income > 20000
THEN SES = 1
ELSE SES = 0

This establishes a new dichotomous variable, SES, which by default is zero, but which is recoded to 1 if the case education is more than 12 and its income is more than 20,000.

Rules are established by filling in a four-column grid in which the columns are: Clause, Expression, Rel. and Value/Expression. For instance, if these four columns were filled in respectively with If, C1, >= and 0.5; and if the next row in the grid were filled in respectively with Then, C1, = and 1; then one would have an if–then rule pair which recoded the entry in column 1 (C1) to 1 whenever its current value was more than or equal to 0.5. The researcher begins the rule-making process by selecting in the Template Menu between two rule structures: if-then, or if–then–else. The Edit Menu can be used to insert AND/OR clauses in the rule. Mathematical operators can be selected from the Expression Edit Center.

New variables can be initialized by selecting Append New Variable/ Column from the Variable/Column scroll box. An if–then–else rule which created a new variable might fill in the four columns as follows: If, %sales, >, 6500; Then, bonus (the new variable), =, 500; Else, bonus, =, +0. This example would create a new variable 'bonus' set equal to 500 whenever the variable sales was more than 6500.

*Custom

This submodule, whose icon is a torn sheet with the words Stock Tack, is a specialized *NeuroShell* submodule for preprocessing stock market data and horse racing data.

*Variable Graphs

This submodule, whose icon is a graph, is used to view data in graphical format. There are four graphing choices:

1   Graph Variable(s) Across All Patterns creates a line graph of one or more variables across all patterns (cases) in the file. This is useful when the patterns have an order. For time series data, for instance, the graph would show the value of the variable(s) selected over time.
2   Graph Variable Sets in a Pattern creates a line graph of all the variables for a given pattern (case). This makes sense when all the columns are related measures, such as points on a time series, and each row is a time series. In such a situation the line graph would be a display of the time series for a given row.
3   Correlation Scatter Plot creates a traditional two-variable scatterplot. This allows the researcher, by visual inspection, to determine if two variables are linearly or curvilinearly related. When they are, of course, the points in the scatterplot will approach a straight or curved line.
4   High Low Close Graph is useful for stock market data.

The first two graph types have options for line versus bar graph display, and if the latter, for two- versus three-dimensional rendering. In fact, each type of graph has a variety of associated options for such things as line thickness, colour, fonts, titles, labels, legends, grids, scaling and associated statistics.

Build Neural Network

Define Inputs/Outputs

This module is used to designate which variables in the data file are to be used as inputs, which are outputs, and which are to be ignored. When the researcher double-clicks on the Define Inputs/Outputs icon, *NeuroShell 2* displays the column names. The researcher makes an entry in the Variable Type row beside each name, using a list box to assign one of three values: I (input), A (actual output) or B (blank – not used). There may be more than one output variable. Note that *NeuroShell 2* will revert to its defaults if even one variable is left uncoded. The default is to use all variables in the file, treating the last as the output(s). The number of outputs is determined by the researcher's entry when specifying the size of the output slab.

At the same time the researcher enters the minimum and maximum values for each variable. This information is used by *NeuroShell 2* to scale the data to the 0 to ±1 range needed for calculations. This submodule contains a menu item for calculating the actual minima and maxima for the researcher's reference. It also can calculate a minimum and maximum that are an arbitrary number of standard deviations from the mean. This is one method of eliminating outliers, if so desired. Alternatively the range may be set larger than actual to accommodate application of the trained model to future data sets. Failure to set tight minima/maxima, however, may impair model performance. *NeuroShell 2* stores the information entered in this submodule in a file with the extension .MMX. Note that the .MMX file has to be updated by respecifying minima and maxima whenever the researcher alters the .PAT file by changing the number of input variables or otherwise restructures the data file.

Test Set Extract

This submodule, whose icon is a file card drawer, is used to divide the data file into three sets: a training set (the .TRN file), a cross-validation test set used by *NeuroShell 2*'s Calibration option (the .TST file), and a production (or verification) data set (the .PRO file). The .TST cross-validation test set is used with *NeuroShell 2*'s Calibration feature, which applies to backpropagation, PNN, GRNN and GMDH neural architectures. For other architectures the researcher will not need or want a .TST set. Also, the researcher may not want a .PRO production set if verification is to be done with a set of cases in a separate file from the .PAT original data set file. The sets may be extracted by any of five different methods:

1   Specifying N per cent for the test set and M per cent for the production set. For instance, the researcher may specify that a random 20 per cent of the .PAT file cases be used for the cross-validation .TST test set. If no M per cent entry is made, then the other 80 per cent of the file will default to become the .TRN training set.
2   Specifying every Nth case as the cross-validation 'test' set and every Mth case as the production set (usually called the test set in the literature, but not in *NeuroShell 2* manuals).
3   Specifying the first N cases as the .TRN training set, cases $N+1$ through M as the .TST test set, and the remaining cases in sequence as the .PRO production set.

4   Specifying the last *M* cases in sequence as the .PRO production set,
    then specifying that *N* per cent of the remainder be chosen
    randomly as the .TST cross-validation test set.
5   Specifying a column which contains key codes dividing the cases
    into .TRN training, .TST test and .PRO production sets.

For methods involving random sampling the researcher will have to
specify a random seed number. Note that due to microprocessor
features, the same random number sequence will be generated for the
same seed value each time.

*Design

Set network design parameters, including selection of architecture,
learning paradigm and network training coefficients. The selections
which are made by the researcher are specific to the type of architecture
selected (e.g. backpropagation, Kohonen etc.) as discussed in previous
sections for each architecture. In general, however, the Design submodule allows the researcher to specify the following choices:

1   The architecture: backpropagation (by far the most common),
    Kohonen, PNN, GRNN or GMDH. The architecture selected will
    determine the exact parameters which may/must be entered.
2   Architecture subtypes: for backpropagation, for instance, the
    researcher may specify if there are to be jump connections; if
    recurrent network modelling is to be used and if so, which type; if
    Ward networks are to be used, and if so, which type.
3   Number of hidden layers and number of neurons within layers.
4   Scaling functions.
5   Activation functions.
6   Learning rate.
7   Momentum.
8   Initial weights.
9   Pattern selection: if cases are chosen by sequence (rotation) or at
    random.
10 Cross-validation: if a cross-validation .TST file is to be used, and if
    so, what the test interval will be.
11 Saving training: which network iteration weights are to be saved.
12 Stopping training: criteria for stopping training.

Learning

This submodule is used to train the network. When the researcher
double-clicks on this submodule's icon (an open book), a dialog box
opens in which the researcher may indicate model complexity. Selections here will set the learning rate, the momentum and the number of

hidden neurons. For instance, selecting a complexity of Very Simple will set the learning rate to 0.6 and the momentum to 0.9. There is also a button to Set Number of Hidden Neurons to Default, where default is calculated by this formula:

$$N_h = 0.5 \ (I + O) + \sqrt{n}._{TRN}$$

That is, the default number of hidden neurons is half the combined number of input and output variables, plus the square root of the number of cases in the .TRN training data set (or the .PAT pattern file, if the .TRN file does not exist). The default learning rate, momentum and number of hidden neurons can be overridden by the researcher by hard entry of numeric values in the same dialog box. The dialog box also lets the researcher specify Pattern Selection: if cases are to be presented to the model at random, or rotationally (in sequence). Once all parameters are set, the researcher selects Start Training from the Train menu.

As the network improves in its ability to predict or classify, the error factor diminishes. Four graphs are available to assist the researcher in evaluating the learning process:

1 Average error (*y*-axis) graphed against epochs elapsed (*x*-axis), for the training data set.
2 Average error (*y*-axis) graphed against intervals elapsed (*x*-axis), for the cross-validation 'test' data set.
3 Error factor ranges graphed against training set patterns.
4 Error factor ranges graphed against cross-validation 'test' set patterns.

Associated statistical data are also viewable: the number of elapsed training patterns, the best performance to date, the minimum average error and the number of epochs (passes through the training data set) since this best performance pass. For models other than backpropagation, other graphs and statistical data may be available. For Kohonen networks, for instance, there is a bar chart displaying the number of patterns in each output category of the network, or a similar pie chart format display. Kohonen learning statistics include the current neighbourhood size and the number of unused output categories (that is, the number of available categories not yet used to classify patterns in the training data set). For PNN models, one can view the number of cross-validation test patterns elapsed, the current best smoothing factor, the number of epochs since the minimum number incorrect, and other information. Other graphs and/or data are displayed for other architectures. This information can be used by the researcher to select 'Interrupt Training' from the Train menu.

In the Training window it is possible to turn on Calibration (cross-validation) by setting the calibration interval to a value higher than zero. The calibration interval is the number of training events (patterns or cases presented to the model) allowed to transpire before cross-validating by computing the mean squared error between model predictions and actual values in the cross-validation data set (drawn from the .PAT pattern file). The interval is usually set in the 50 to 200 range. If Save on Best Test Set is selected, *NeuroShell 2* will save the best model.

Apply Neural Network

Contribution Factors

This module, for backpropagation architectures, identifies which variables are most important to the model's predictions. Contribution factors are calculated based on the weights along the path from the input layer to the output layer (see Garson, 1991b). When the number of inputs is large, however, contribution factors may become similar for many variables and therefore will not serve the intended purpose of differentiating among them. In *NeuroShell 2* the View option provides a bar graph of the contribution factors in order of importance.

For GRNN and PNN architectures, if individual input smoothing factors are computed, these can be used for sensitivity analysis. That is, the larger smoothing factors indicate the variables which have more influence on the model in terms of predicting outputs.

Apply to File

This submodule is used to make predictions or classifications on a new data set using an already-trained network. Predicted and actual values are displayed (except for Kohonen models, whose purpose is to cluster input variables rather than predict outputs). Double-clicking on the Apply to File icon (a neural network diagram) brings up a dialog box in which the defaults are 'Compute R squared', 'Include actuals in .OUT file', and 'Include in .OUT file actuals minus network outputs'. The researcher also specifies the file to which to apply the model (e.g. the .PRO production file used for generalization).

The following statistics can be generated for backpropagation models for each output variable:

1   *R squared* This statistic, familiar in multiple regression, is the percentage of the variance in the output variable explained by the network. It is based on the improvement in prediction using

the network compared with simply predicting the mean output for all patterns presented to the network. Where y_p is the predicted value of an output and y_m is the mean output value, the formula is:

$$R^2 = 1 - \frac{\sum(y - y_p)^2}{\sum(y - y_m)^2}$$

2   *Correlation coefficient r*   This is a measure of the strength of linear association between the actual and predicted values of an output variable.

3   *r squared*   This is the squared correlation coefficient measuring the association between a given input and a given output. Called the coefficient of determination, r squared is the percentage of variance in the output variable explained by the input variable.

4   *Mean squared error* (MSE)   This is the average of (actual − predicted)^2 for all cases (patterns).

5   *Mean absolute error*   This is the absolute value of (actual − predicted) for all cases.

6   *Minimum absolute error*   This is the absolute value of (actual − predicted) for the case with the lowest such value.

7   *Maximum absolute error*   This is the absolute value of (actual − predicted) for the case with the highest such value.

NeuroShell 2 also displays graphs of training set and cross-validation 'test' set errors.

For Kohonen networks, the Apply module has a Set Output Neuron Values option. This allows the researcher to view the weights of the winning neuron and runner-ups, to gauge the closeness of competing inputs. Also, the winning neuron can be set to 1 and all others to 0. A bar or pie chart of category distributions can also be displayed.

For PNN networks, the Apply module contains the option which allows the researcher to set the smoothing factor. The Set Output Neuron Values option lets the researcher see how the network classifies a given data pattern (usually 0 or 1). In the Check Boxes option, for each output the researcher can see actual winners (number of times the actual output was set to 1), classified winners (number of times network output was set to 1), actual losers, classified losers, true positives (number of times actual value of 1 was classified 1 by the network), false positives (number of times actual value of 0 was classified as 1), true negatives, true positives, true positive proportion and false positive proportion.

For GRNN and GMDH networks, the Apply module calculates the same statistics as for backpropagation. In PNN and GRNN networks, one also can view a smoothing factor optimization graph.

Attach Output File

This submodule is used to add the new set of outputs (or any data file with the same structure) to an existing data file. After double-clicking on the icon for this submodule (a paper clip), the researcher selects Attach File Side by Side to enter the .OUT prediction data into the original .PAT pattern file. There is also an alternative option to append one file to the bottom of another with the same structure. One can add more cases to an existing .PAT training pattern file and perform other data management tasks.

*Post-Network

*Variable Graphs

This submodule, whose icon is a graph, is used to view output in graphical form. For instance, when the researcher clicks on Graph Variable(s) Across All Patterns, then selects the actual and predictive values of the dependent variable as the variables of interest, *NeuroShell 2* displays a line graph in which the x-axis is the pattern (case) number and the y-axis is values of the output variable. Two lines are displayed representing the actual and predicted values. This graph allows the researcher to see if the model is closely fitting the data, and if the predictions are homoscedastic (fit equally well for the entire range of the data).

Another option, Graph Variable Sets in a Pattern, generates a graph of values by training case. This makes sense when the sequence of cases has a meaning such as would be found, for instance, when dealing with signals from an electrocardiograph machine. The graph would then be the plot of the electrocardiogram.

The Correlation Scatter Plot option produces the standard x–y plot of two variables. The extent to which the graphed points fall on a line reflects the strength of linear or curvilinear correlation between the two variables.

The High Low Close Graph option produces the standard high–low–close stock market plot of variables used in making financial market predictions.

*Custom

A specialized *NeuroShell* module which translates neural model output from the Race Handicapping Pre-Network module back into its original form, with predictions.

*Rules

This submodule, whose icon is a calculator with the words If Then Else, is used to apply if–then–else rules to outputs. For instance, one may want to force all predictions to be zero or one by rounding up or down using the rules: 'If >= 0.5 then 1' and 'If < 0.5 then 0'.

*Symbol Translate

This submodule, whose icon is the numbers 1 2 3 with an arrow to the letters A B C, is used to retranslate numeric outputs back into character strings where appropriate.

Problem Output

File Export

Export data, including predictions, to various types of files: spreadsheet (*Lotus* .WK1 or *Excel* .XLS), ASCII, binary and native *NeuroShell*.

Examine Data

This submodule, whose icon is a spreadsheet grid, is used to view data files, such as the .OUT files containing the model's predictions. Viewing is done on the Datagrid, *NeuroShell* 2's built-in spreadsheet. The Datagrid is not a fully functional spreadsheet, but one can cut, paste and move as well as view data.

*Printouts

This module supports custom printouts of the data columns the researcher wishes to output.

Runtime

Once a network is trained to the researcher's satisfaction, it is possible to program a system in which the network can be called from Visual Basic, C, Pascal, *Excel* and other programming systems. A built-in source code generator can generate Visual Basic or C language source code implementing the trained network. Alternatively, a built-in DLL (Dynamic Link Library) server creates the environment needed to tie the network to such applications as the Microsoft *Access* database or the Microsoft *Excel* spreadsheet. One can, for instance, link an *Excel* spreadsheet cell dynamically to predictions made by a neural network one has constructed.

The *NeuroShell 2* package comes with a Dynamic Link Library module, NSHELL2.DLL, which the researcher is free to distribute. A 32-bit alternative module, NS2-32.DLL is provided for use with *Excel 5* or *Excel 7* for *Windows NT*. These get installed in the \Windows\System directory. The DLL Server option supports the processing of a trained network to create a .DEF file which can be processed by the .DLL modules. The *NeuroShell 2* manual contains detailed prototype code for creating runtime implementations of one's trained network for Visual Basic, C, *Excel* and other environments.

7
Example: Analysing Census Data with *Neural Connection*

Census data are available from numerous sources. One convenient source is the *CensusCD*, which uses new data compression technology to store the entire US Census on a single CD-ROM (as opposed to the 67 CD-ROMs the Bureau of the Census uses to distribute the same information). *CensusCD* is available from GeoLytics, Inc., PO Box 10, East Brunswick, NJ 08816, USA; 800-577-6717; e-mail infor@censuscd.com; http://www.censuscd.com. From this source we selected a target variable, median household income (MEDHSINC), and several independent variables having to do with housing attributes, with the purpose of seeing how well one could predict income levels from real estate data aggregated by ZIP code postal areas.

Data conversion is the first step in the analysis. *Neural Connection* directly imports a variety of data formats, including *SPSS*'s .SAV data format, but it does not import the commonly used *dBASE* .DBF format which the Bureau of the Census, and the *CensusCD* utilized for data distribution. *SPSS*, in contrast, does import .DBF files, so data conversion is a simple matter of loading the *CensusCD* .DBF output into *SPSS*, then immediately resaving it in *SPSS*'s own .SAV format, which *Neural Connection* can read. While in *SPSS* it is a good idea to scale down any fields with large numbers as *Neural Connection* will treat as out-of-range any values over eight digits, and it lacks a convenient method of scaling fields.

The second step is to establish the *Neural Connection* model. This is accomplished by clicking on model components in the toolbar, shown on the left of Figure 7.1. One simply clicks on a tool such as the Data Tool in the toolbar, then one clicks again in the white workspace to set down an instance of that tool. In this case we have set down seven instances of five tools, connected along three paths, each terminating in a Text Output Tool and each originating from a single Data Tool. The middle layer of the model is constituted by three alternative modes of data analysis, represented from top to bottom by the Regression Tool, the Radial Basis Function Tool for neural network modelling, and the

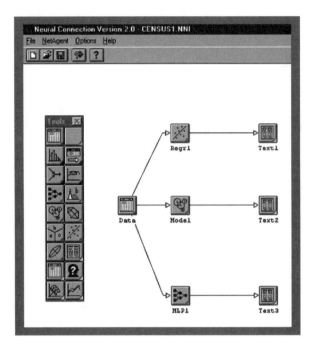

Figure 7.1   Census1 model in *Neural Connection*

Multi-Layer Perceptron Tool for backpropagation neural network modelling. For simplicity, we have not included a Filter Tool intervening between the Data Tool and the three analysis tools, though it is possible that data filtering might improve performance.

The connecting arrows in the model shown in Figure 7.1 are easily drawn. A single right click on any of the tools in the workspace pops up a menu whose first two choices are Connect and Disconnect (except output tools like the Text Output Tool have only the Disconnect choice). By selecting Connect, the cursor can be used to drag an arrow line from the current tool to the tool destination chosen by the researcher. This process was repeated six times in the current example, once for each of the arrows shown in Figure 7.1.

Data

Right-clicking on the Data tool and selecting View brings up the Data Viewer spreadsheet, shown in Figure 7.3. Initially, the spreadsheet will be empty. The researcher selects File, Open, from the Data Viewer spreadsheet, causing the Data Input dialog box to appear. This has two

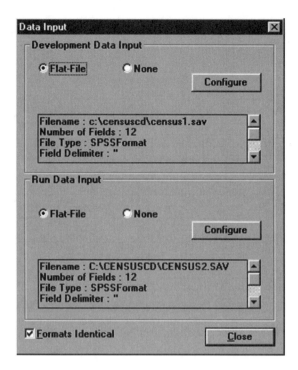

Figure 7.2   Data Input dialog box

sections, one for Development Data Input and one for Run Data Input (Figure 8.2). Only the former is required. The development data are the data set on which the model will be constructed. The set will be partitioned into training, validation and test data subsets. The optional run data can be an alternative data set on which the trained model is run for purposes of further testing. In this example the development data are the ZIP code areas for the state of California, while the run data are the same variables for the ZIP codes in the state of New York. Clicking on the Configure button brings up the customary *Windows* file-selection dialog box (not shown) where the actual directory locations and filenames of these data sets are specified by the researcher. *SPSS* .SAV files are considered Flat Files by *Neural Connection*, so these radio buttons are checked.

Upon clicking on the Close button in the Data Input dialog box, the researcher is returned to the Data Viewer, which will now display the development data as shown in Figure 7.3. The columns will be the fields (variables) and the rows will be the units of analysis (here, ZIP code areas). By default, *Neural Connection* will assume the last column is the target (dependent) variable and will show a boxed T above it in the column heading. An I will show for the independent variables, an

Data Viewer · [Input development data]							
File Data Field Window							
		Float T	Float I	Float I	Float I		
		MEDHSINC	MEDYRBLT	RNTPCHSI	MEDHSVAL		
1	T	36786.0	1981.0	10.0	169500.0		
2	T	30298.0	1975.0	10.0	143100.0		
3	T	33769.0	1971.0	20.0	88300.0		
4	X	38229.0	1979.0	18.200001	108100.0		
5	T	30229.0	1961.0	28.700001	270900.0		
6	X	57077.0	1979.0	28.9	294700.0		
7	T	32093.0	1981.0	26.9	85300.0		
8	X	36950.0	1961.0	30.200001	206800.0		
9	X	23340.0	1969.0	35.099998	70000.0		
10	T	45568.0	1939.0	22.5	143800.0		
11	T	18064.0	1946.0	34.799999	82100.0		
12	X	26437.0	1958.0	22.799999	54800.0		
13	T	51974.0	1974.0	27.200001	267000.0		
14	T	21666.0	1966.0	32.700001	500001.0		
15	T	31222.0	1982.0	30.9	115000.0		
16	T	80101.0	1977.0	31.9	431800.0		
17	T	42953.0	1958.0	28.1	192900.0		
18	T	23351.0	1972.0	30.4	107800.0		

Figure 7.3   Data Viewer with Census1 development data

R for reference variables (ignored by the analysis but displayed as input in the output), and an * for variables not used (ignored in both analysis and output). In this example, the target variable is not the last column, so we must change the last column to an I and change the MEDHSINC target column to a T. Additionally, we change the AREANAME text variable to an * so it will not be treated as an input for analysis.

The rows in the Data Viewer list the identification number followed by a coloured box indicating the case's use, discussed below. The colour indicates the status of the case. In particular, if the case is shown in red, the case has out-of-range data (Neural Connection only handles eight digits). Bright blue cases have missing data. Neural Connection does not have a convenient method of scaling out-of-range data (this is best done at the data conversion stage, as in SPSS), other than manually one case at a time. Missing values, however, can be replaced easily, as by substituting means, medians or fixed values (Neural Connection cannot substitute regression estimates). Clicking on Field, Configuration, in the Data Viewer will bring up a Field Configuration window with easy to follow dialog for replacing missing values (see Figure 7.4). Once missing values have been replaced, they will be shown in a different shade of blue.

Before leaving the Data Viewer, it is necessary to allocate the cases (rows) to training, validation and test data subsets. This is done by

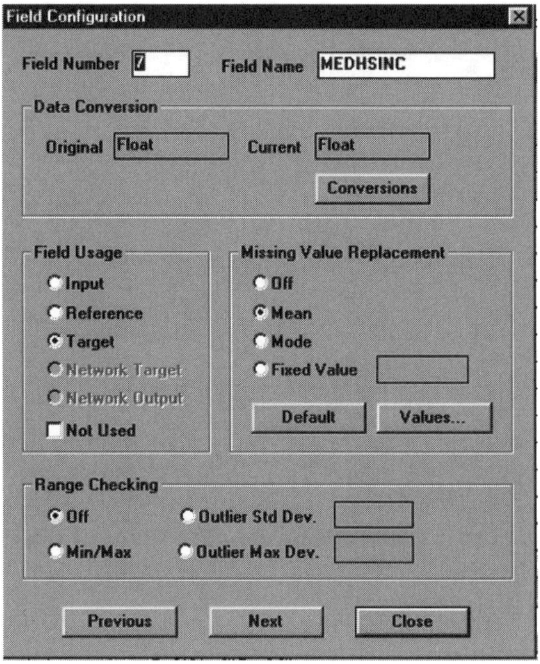

Figure 7.4   Field Configuration dialog box

clicking on Data, Allocation, in the Data Viewer. This brings up the Data Allocation dialog box, as shown in Figure 7.5. The researcher should check Random case selection and likewise check None for data blocking, unless time series data are involved. *Neural Connection* will pick default proportions for the training, validation and test subsets, but the researcher may modify the ratio if desired. After clicking OK and returning to the Data Viewer, training data will be marked T in cyan, test data marked X in yellow, and validation data marked V in bright green.

Neural network analysis is often more effective if the number of training cases is equalized for values of the target variable. The researcher may therefore wish to click on Field, Equalization, in the Data Viewer for this purpose. This brings up the Class Equalization dialog box (Figure 7.6). Cases may be equalized by both duplication and dropping methods. After class equalization, the researcher may return to the model workspace to train the analytic tools which he or she has placed there. In this example, there were three such tools: a regression model, a radial basis function neural model and a backpropagation (MLP) model. To go back to the model workspace, select File, Exit and Return, from the Data Viewer menu bar.

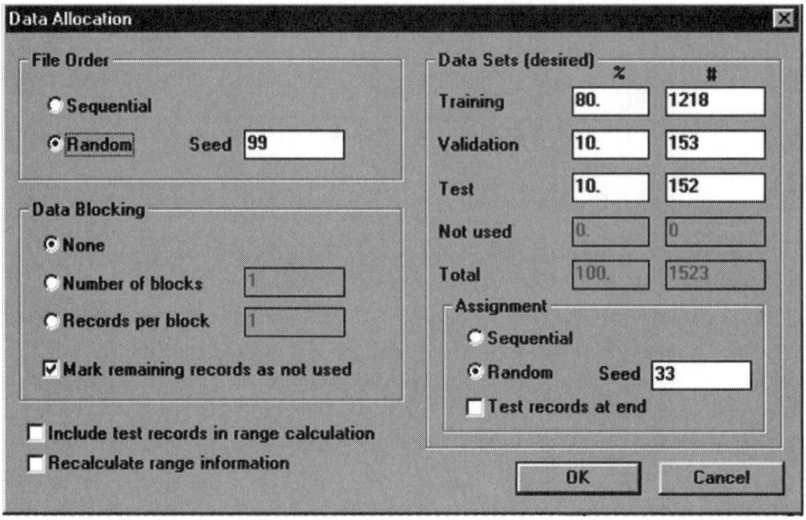

Figure 7.5   Data Allocation dialog box

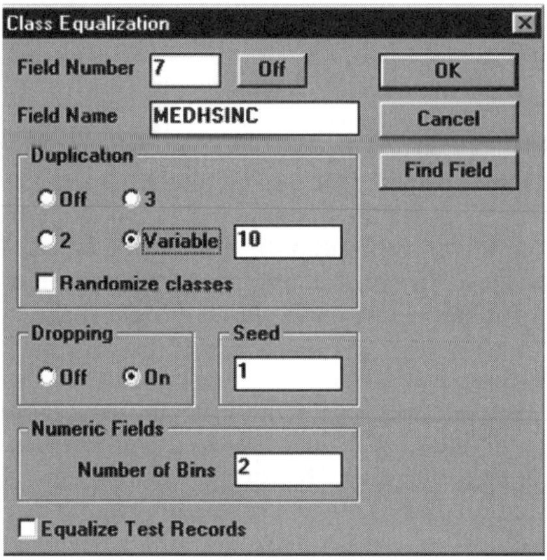

Figure 7.6   Class Equalization dialog box

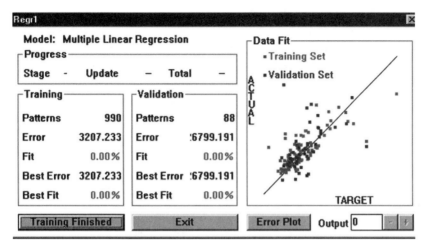

Figure 7.7   Regression progress screen

Regression

To apply regression, the researcher right-clicks on the Regression tool on the modelling workspace. *Neural Connection* will implement multiple regression automatically and will display results as shown in Figure 7.7. (This progress screen will flash off the screen unless the researcher toggles Options, Auto Exit Training, off from the menu bar.) *Neural Connection* does not offer researcher-set computation options for the regression model.

Radial Basis Function Neural Model

The RBF model is implemented in a similar manner, except that researcher-set computation options are available. To access these options, the researcher right-clicks the mouse on the RBF icon in the workspace (recall Figure 7.1) and selects Dialog from the menu which pops up. The RBF dialog screen is illustrated in Figure 7.8. Options are given for data normalization, how the error distance is to be computed (city block or Euclidean), the function to apply (spline, quadratic, inverse quadratic or Gaussian), the number of centres in the RBF layer, whether output is to be normalized or not, whether confidence outputs are to be generated, how centres are to be initially located (random, sample, trial), if additional centres are to be added, and the stopping criteria. *Neural Connection* will suggest defaults for all these choices.

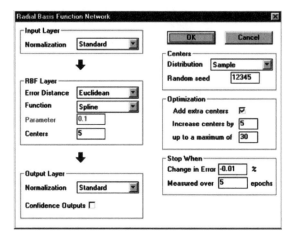

Figure 7.8   Radial Basis Function dialog screen

Only experimentation can reveal if there are better settings than the defaults.

Once parameters have been set, the researcher again right-clicks on the RBF icon and selects Train. In the course of training, a progress screen is displayed as shown in Figure 7.9. This screen is very similar to that for regression (Figure 7.7), but the error values are shown in normalized form. Clicking on the Error Plot button in the progress screen will cause the graphic display of the data fit (on the left of Figure 7.9) to be replaced by a time line chart in real time of error versus time for the training error and the validation error. This error plot is useful when a neural model takes a large number of iterations while seeking convergence, as in the backpropagation model for this example, discussed below.

Multi-Layer Perceptron (Backpropagation) Neural Model

The MLP model is implemented much the same as the RBF model. Of course the dialog screen for setting computation options differs, as shown in Figure 7.10. Here only the data normalization options are the same. Instead there are settings for whether nodes are to be generated automatically or not, if not then how many to generate, what function to use (tanh, sigmoid or linear), the range for initial weights, the learning rule (conjugate gradient or steepest descent) and the stopping criteria. If the researcher clicks the Setup button, another screen pops up (not shown here) which allows changing the maximum number of records

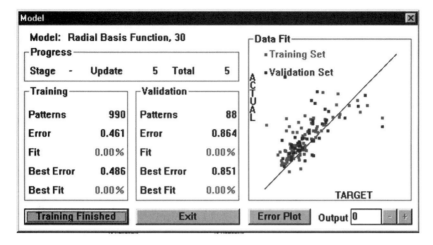

Figure 7.9   Radial Basis Function progress screen

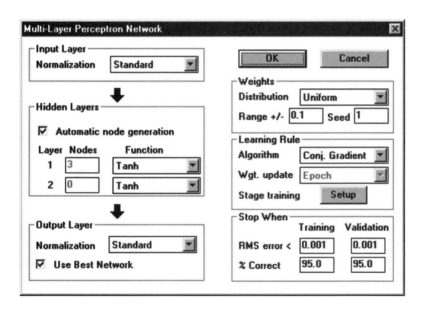

Figure 7.10   Multi-Layer Perceptron (backpropagation) dialog screen

and updates per training stage and, if steepest descent is chosen, what the learning and momentum coefficients will be at each stage.

The MLP model will display a progress screen with a data fit plot as in the previous two forms of analysis. However, Figure 7.11 shows the progress screen with the error plot displayed. As discussed above,

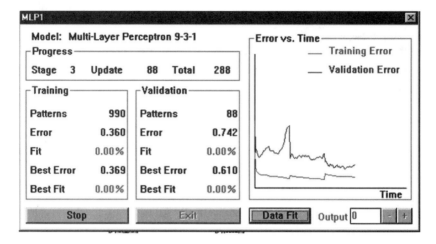

Figure 7.11   Multi-Layer Perceptron (backpropagation) progress screen

the error plot shows in real time how the training and validation error fare. While training error will generally decline, overtraining can occur such that validation error will begin to increase with additional iterations. For this reason, the researcher may wish to monitor the error plot and click on the Stop button when overtraining seems to occur. However, if checked in the MLP dialog box output layer section, the best fit model will be used for output purposes.

Text Output

The Text Output Tool generates a computer printout of the results of each of the three analyses. The output contains a listing of the target field and the output (estimated target) field, as shown in Figure 7.12. In addition to this output, the Text Tool outputs a 'confusion matrix', which is a cross-tabulation in which the rows are the actual value classes of the target value and the columns are the predicted classes. The more the entries are on the diagonal, the better the model is performing in predicting the test set cases. Figure 7.13 below shows the confusion matrix for the MLP (backpropagation) model, which was the best performing of the three models in this example. It shows that 75 per cent of the cases were predicted in the correct class of the target variable. By way of comparison, the regression model's success rate in prediction was 68 per cent, while the RBF model fared least well at only 64 per cent. The confusion matrix also reveals that the MLP (backpropagation) model's errors were about 2:1 on the low side of the actual

```
Target Fields        Output Fields
MEDHSINC             Regr1

38229.0              34701.13672
57077.0              55916.43359
36950.0              27508.19141
23340.0              23353.2832
26437.0              24407.62109
16788.0              27171.1875
22097.0              22178.78125
29653.0              29999.69141
55619.0              44372.53125
48438.0              37301.38672
31161.0              41386.9375
35867.0              38575.00391
24375.0              27976.90234
27952.0              28847.86719
51574.0              47947.67188
69180.0              66190.52344
86254.0              87562.57813
23617.0              20257.68555
25974.0              44803.36328
```

Figure 7.12   Text output: target and output fields, regression model

```
! ** Confusion Matrix For Output 1 **
!
! True              Predicted
! ----              ---------
!            0.0+        25930.8+  51861.6+  77792.4+  103723.2+
! 0.0+       41          16        1         0         0
! 25930.8+   10          62        8         0         0
! 51861.6+   0           2         11        0         0
! 77792.4+   0           0         1         0         0
! 103723.2+  0           0         0         0         0
!
! Total number of targets : 152
!
! Total correct : 114
!
! Percentage correct : 75.00%


Output Error Measures
=====================

  Output:      RMS Error:      Mean Absolute:  Mean Absolute %:
  -------      ----------      --------------  ----------------

    1          10551.155467      6967.731086      22.058926 %
```

Figure 7.13   Text output: confusion matrix and error measures, MLP

values. Also given in the Text Tool output is the RMS (root mean square) error, the mean absolute error and the mean absolute percentage. These measures also reveal that the MLP (backpropagation) model was the most effective in prediction, followed by the regression and radial basis function models in that order.

8

Conclusion

Neural network analysis is used increasingly in social science research. A not untypical 1997 doctoral dissertation (Baker, 1997), for instance, focused on determining the comparative effectiveness of statistical and neural network models for forecasting nationally aggregated educational spending. Two neural architectures, backpropagation and GRNN, were compared with the multiple linear regression model used by the National Center for Education Statistics (NCES) for projecting educational spending. Input variables for all neural network models were the same as those used by William Hussar and Deborah Gerald in the NCES report *Projections of Education Statistics to 2005*. Neural networks were found to outperform such regression models. The author noted that educational expenditures were just one component of a complex economic system and that complex systems required higher levels of behavioural analysis which could not adequately be modelled with linear equations, however common such models have been in government and academia in the past.

A second recent doctoral dissertation (Li, 1997), from the field of economics, focused on oil's critical role in the world economy. Oil tanker markets are among the most volatile yet most important markets in the world. Because of this complexity, traditional econometric and time series modelling methods have had difficulties in modelling these markets owing to their highly dynamic and nonlinear nature and the various noneconomic factors involved. The dissertation developed alternative models using neural networks, fuzzy logic and genetic algorithms. The forecasting performance of the neural networks and time series models was compared. Results showed that the neural network approach was robust in modelling and forecasting complex, nonlinear economic systems and could provide valuable insights into the market behaviour that traditional methods could not.

A third recent dissertation (Vogh, 1997), this from the field of psychology, illustrated the usefulness of neural network analysis as a way of modelling complex human processes such as learning, recognizing and recalling sequences of patterns. This dissertation described a neural network architecture that learns, recognizes and recalls sequences of patterns and also reproduces a wide range of psychological and neurological data. The network replicates the observed human behaviour of learning sequences in an unsupervised manner, recognizing a sequence when part of the sequence is presented, and recalling a sequence when part of the sequence is presented or when a top-down representation of the sequence is presented. The neural network architecture was applied to the problem of three-dimensional object recognition and achieved efficient performance by accumulating temporal evidence and making choices at critical times. The neural network, a variant of adaptive resonance theory (ART) architectures, explained data from various visual memory experiments.

A fourth example, a political science conference paper (Zeng, 1996), compared neural network models with the standard logit and probit models, the most widely used choice/classification models in current social science empirical research. The author explored the application of neural network models to analysis of political choice/classification problems, which in political science often involve nonlinear and unknown functional forms, not to mention noisy data, measuring against baseline data simulated by use of Monte Carlo simulations. The simulation study demonstrated that neural network models performed significantly better than the logit, and were indistinguishable from the 'true' model, at all noise levels. Following the simulation, the author then compared the models on real political data used in several existing studies. Reanalysis of the real data also indicated better performance of the network models compared with the logit/probit models.[30] Finally, the author conducted sensitivity analysis on a network model that significantly outperformed the logit model in predicting the voting behaviour of voters who favoured Perot most in the 1992 election, revealing more convincing substantive relationships than the existing logit model suggested.

These four examples are arbitrarily selected but are representative of why social scientists are increasingly interested in the use of neural network models. They illustrate, respectively, the superior functionality of neural models in forecasting, econometrics, modelling human behaviour, and solving a wide range of classification problems. These examples highlight the applicability of neural methods to the real data social scientists face daily: noisy, nonlinear and with missing measurements. Neural networks are robust under these conditions, whereas many of the more common alternative research tools are not.

Neural network models are useful in prediction, classification, fault detection, time series analysis, diagnosis, optimization, system identification and control, exploratory data analysis and other problems in statistical analysis and data mining. Neural models can serve as a basis for analysing decision-making, reasoning and the filtering of signals, as well as for forecasting, modelling and classification. Neural networks may offer solutions for cases in which a processing algorithm or analytical solutions are hard to find, hidden or nonexistent.

Neural network modelling is evolving rapidly, with the greatest growth in an area which is outside the scope of this work: the combination of neural methods with other modelling tools such as genetic algorithms, fuzzy logic, expert systems, hidden Markov models, belief networks, decision trees, memory-based methods, as well as increasingly sophisticated combinations of these architectures. *Genetic algorithms* employ a form of 'evolutionary selection' which starts with a population of encoded procedures, mutates them stochastically, and then selects mutants meeting some criteria, sometimes combining properties of the successful mutants. *Fuzzy logic* uses linguistic system variables embedded in a rule base and an inference procedure based on a continuous range of truth values rather than strict 0,1 binary values. *Expert systems* derive if–then rules from analysis of data structure, sometimes integrating knowledge engineering studies of the behaviour of human experts, to arrive at selections, and to be able to explain to human experts the reasoning process involved in the selection. In the future, neural models will be increasingly integrated with these and other new orientations to the study of complex data structures.

With the new availability of neural network modelling modules in both of the statistical packages commonly used by social scientists, *SAS* and *SPSS*, the slow but steady diffusion of neural techniques into the methodological toolkits of future generations of social scientists seems all but assured in spite of the obstacles noted early in this volume. Will the proven efficacy of neural procedures force their way into social science graduate methods textbooks treating multivariate analysis? Indeed, will the renaissance in structural equation modelling be extended to a more general understanding of the role of simulation of modelling in social science, with implications for powerful modelling techniques such as neural networks? Time will tell. It has been the purpose of this volume to seek to make a modest contribution to answering such questions in the affirmative.

Notes

1. Later neurophysiological research showed that synaptic knobs did sometimes increase in area as Hebb hypothesized (Tsukahara and Oda, 1981; Anderson et al., 1989), but more frequently forms of reinforcement occur other than physical enlargement of knobs.

2. Minsky himself had contributed to neural network theory earlier. His 1954 Princeton University doctoral thesis was 'Theory of neural-analog reinforcement systems and its application to the brain-model problem'.

3. See also the earlier influential paper by Minsky (1961), titled 'Steps toward artificial intelligence'.

4. The response function was usually the sigmoid function, which is the S-shaped curve of logistic growth equations, forcing values to remain in the range 0 to 1.

5. Parker patented the backpropagation algorithm through Stanford University in 1982, but later allowed the patent to expire.

6. A review of theoretic findings is found in Hornik et al. (1989).

7. At the time of this writing there was a Website by Athanasios Episcopo covering neural network applications to finance and economics at the URL address http://phoenix.som.clarkson.edu/~episcopo/neurofin.html.

8. J.M. Zurada defines neural networks as 'physical cellular systems which can acquire, store, and utilize experiential knowledge' (1992: xv). A. Nigrin defines a neural network as 'a circuit composed of a very large number of simple processing elements that are neurally based. Each element operates only on local information. Furthermore each element operates asynchronously; thus there is no overall system clock' (1993: 11). Finally, Simon Haykin defines a neural network as 'a massively parallel distributed processor that has a natural propensity for storing experiential knowledge and making it available for use. It resembles the brain in two respects: (1) Knowledge is acquired by the network through a learning process; (2) Interneuron connection weights known as synaptic weights are used to store the knowledge' (1994: 2).

9. The term 'hidden unit' or 'hidden layer' was popularized by Rumelhart and McClelland (1986).

10. For more on stochastic approximation as a statistical method, see Robbins and Monro (1951) and Kiefer and Wolfowitz (1952).

11. In *NeuralWorks 2*, this is the Net-Perfect algorithm and option. 'Weight pruning' is an alternative algorithm for the same purpose.

12. The inability of two-layer networks to solve XOR problems can be observed

by using an X–Y graph to plot the data pairs [1,1], [0,1], [1,0] and [0,0]. Simple experimentation will quickly reveal that no straight line can be drawn such that the desired XOR patterns ([0,1], [1,0]) are on one side of the line and those not desired will be on the other. To solve such problems one must employ a nonlinear approach. In neural network architecture, non-linearity requires introduction of an additional, hidden layer.

13   The derivation for the generalized delta rule is detailed in Henseler (1995: 60–4). In numerical analysis literature, the generalized delta rule with momentum is called the 'heavy ball method'. See Bertsekas (1995: 78–9).

14   An example is Vogle et al.'s (1988) variant on backpropagation, which does not update weights after each pattern but only after each epoch (each iteration through all the patterns). That is,

$$\Delta w_{ji}(t+1) = r \sum_{p} e_{pj} a_{pi} + m \Delta w_{ji}(t)$$

The change in weight for the link from neuron i to neuron j in epoch $t + 1$ equals the learning rate r, times the sum for p patterns of the cross-products of the error for neuron j for pattern p, times the activation level for neuron i for pattern p, plus a momentum term m times the previous weight change in epoch t. If the weight change reduces total error, the learning rate is increased by multiplying it by a factor more than 1 for the next iteration. If total error increases, however, then the learning rate is decreased by multiplying by a factor less than 1, the weight changes are cancelled, and the momentum term is temporarily set to 0 until on repetition a step successfully reduces total error.

15   Bengio (1991), in a vowel recognition problem with a large training set, compared deterministic versus stochastic updating in a backpropagation model, finding clear performance gains for the latter. Becker and LeCun (1989) also compared these two approaches, using a small training set, and found little difference.

16   Recall the error surface is a plot of the cost function – the measure of the error signal, commonly mean square error – versus the neural weights.

17   Models incorporating a fixed number of time sequenced frames as inputs are called time-delay neural network (TDNN) architecture when there are time delays between layers as well as time-delayed inputs (Lang and Hinton, 1988; Weibel, 1989). An even simpler architecture is that of fixed moving windows, which utilize time-delayed inputs but not time delays between sequential layers. NETtalk, a text recognition network used to produce pronounced verbalizations of words, is of this type (Sejnowski and Rosenberg, 1986; 1987). Although of simple architecture, by converting English text into highly recognizable speech, NETtalk played a powerful role as a neural network success story. NETtalk demonstrated that neural networks could represent complex relationships which were too difficult to code through conventional programming.

18   See Spieksma (1995), Lenting (1995), Haykin (1994: 55–7).

19   In *NeuralWorks 2* the smoothing factor is calculated automatically if cross-validation (its Calibration feature) is being used.

20   Genetic adaptive PNN models are implemented in *NeuroShell 2*.

21 In *NeuroShell 2* the GMDH equations are given in the Source Code Generator.

22 *NeuroShell 2* offers various options for setting the maximum number of survivors in the first layer and subsequent layers: constant (the maximum is set equal in all subsequent layers to the number of survivors in the first layer), asymptotic (the maximum is decreased asymptotically to a minimum of 2) and linear (the maximum is linearly decreased at a rate set by the researcher).

23 The index is a 'black box'. Ward Systems has chosen not to make this information public, thereby preventing scholarly replication using software other than its *NeuroShell 2*.

24 Probabilistic neural network (PNN) architecture is the same as kernel discriminant analysis.

25 Early stopping is related to ridge regression in that both techniques define a path of steepest descent down an error function. See Sjoberg and Ljung (1992).

26 Such software was available as of 1996 at the home page of David MacKay: ftp://wol.ra.phy.cam.ac.uk/pub/www/mackay/.

27 For instance, *WinNN* is a shareware neural networking package which runs under the *Windows 3.1* environment. Intended for beginners, *WinNN* implements modified fast backpropagation models and comes with extensive online help. Many training parameters are under user control. Output can be to file or to the *Windows* clipboard. It is available at ftp://ftp.cc.monash.edu.au, in the directory /pub/win3/programr/winnn97.zip. It is a 747 kilobyte zipped (archived) file.

28 *SAS*, of course, is the other major statistical package used by social scientists. At this writing, the *SAS Neural Network Application* was not yet at the level of ease of use of the commercial packages outlined in this book. However, much work has been done regarding implementation of neural models using *SAS* code (see Sarle, 1994a; 1994b). At the time of writing, these papers were available by file transfer protocol (ftp) from ftp://ftp.sas.com/pub/neural/neural1.ps and ftp://ftp.sas.com/pub/neural/neural2.ps. The current version of the *SAS NNA* software supported multi-layer perceptrons (by numerical optimization algorithms instead of backpropagation), radial basis functions, statistical versions of counter-propagation and learning vector quantization, and numerous user-controlled parameters controlling such things as multiple hidden layers, direct input–output connections, missing value handling, and multiple preliminary optimizations from random initial values to avoid local minima. For more information contact software@sas.sas.com, or telephone 919-677-8000 (USA).

29 Contact Ward Systems Group, Inc., Executive Park West, 5 Hillcrest Drive, Frederick, MD 21702, USA; tel. 301-662-7950; fax 301-662-5666. At the time of this writing, the undiscounted list price for *NeuroShell 2* was $495. As of time of writing, *NeuroShell 2* required Microsoft *Windows* release 3.1, an 80386 processor, 4 megabytes of RAM and 13 megabytes of hard disk space (18 megabytes under *Windows 95*), or better.

30 For some cases the differences were not statistically significant, owing to low variance in the dependent variables as well as data noise.

References

Ali, J.M. (1995) 'Comparing a neural network model with Brunswik's lens model for analysis of product quality evaluation'. Unpublished doctoral dissertation, Illinois Institute of Technology.

Amari, S. (1972) 'Learning patterns and pattern sequences by self-organizing nets of threshold elements', *IEEE Transactions on Computers*, C-21 (11): 1197–206.

Amari, S. (1974) 'A method of statistical neurodynamics', *Kybernetik*, 14 (4): 201–15.

Anderberg, M.R. (1973) *Cluster Analysis for Applications*. New York: Academic Press.

Anderer, P., Saletu, B., Kloppel, B. and Semlitsch, H.V. (1994) 'Discrimination between demented patients and normals based on topographic EEG slow wave activity: comparison between z statistics, discriminant analysis and artificial neural network classifiers', *Electroencephalography & Clinical Neurophysiology*, 91 (2), 108–17.

Anderson, B.J., Lee, S., Thompson, J., Steinmetz, J., Logan, C., Knowlton, B., Thompson, R.F. and Greenough, W.T. (1989) 'Increased branching of spiny dendrites of rabbit cerebellar Purkinje neurons following associative eyeblink conditioning', *Society for Neuroscience Abstracts*, 15: 640.

Anderson, J.A. and Rosenfeld, E. (eds) (1988) *Neurocomputing: Foundations of Research*. Cambridge, MA: MIT Press.

Anderson, J.A. Silverstein, J.W., Ritz, A. and Jones, R.S. (1977) 'Distinctive features, categorical perception, and probability learning: some applications of a neural model', *Psychological Review*, 84: 413–51.

Angeniol, G. de la Croix Vaubois and Le Texier, J.Y. (1988) 'Self-organizing feature maps and the traveling salesman problem', *Neural Networks*, 1: 289–93.

Anumolu, Vivek (1993) 'A hybrid neural network methodology for studying the development of external memory strategies in problem-solving'. Doctoral dissertation, University of Alabama–Birmingham.

Arrington, Karl Frederick (1993) 'Neural network models for color and brightness perception and binocular rivalry'. Doctoral dissertation, Boston University.

Bailey, David and Thompson, Donna (1990) 'How to develop neural-network applications', *AI Expert*, 5 (6): 38–47.

Bainbridge, William S. (1995) 'Neural network models of religious belief', *Sociological perspectives*, 38 (4): 483–95.

Baker, B.D. (1997) 'A comparison of statistical and neural network models for forecasting educational spending'. Unpublished doctoral dissertation, Columbia University Teachers College.

Bapi, Raju Surampudi (1994) 'Neural network modeling of the role of the frontal lobes in sequence classification'. Doctoral dissertation, University of Texas–Arlington.

Barto, A.G. and Ananden, P. (1985) 'Pattern recognizing stochastic learning automata', *IEEE Transactions on Systems, Man, and Cybernetics*, 15: 360–75.

Barto, A.G., Sutton, R.S. and Anderson, C. (1983) 'Neuronlike adaptive elements that can solve difficult learning control problems', *IEEE Transactions on Systems, Man, and Cybernetics*, 13.

Barto, A.G., Sutton, R.S. and Watkins, C.J.C.H. (1990) 'Learning and sequential decision making', in M. Gabriel and J. Moore (eds), *Learning and Computational Neuroscience: Foundations of Adaptive Networks*. Cambridge, MA: MIT Press. pp. 539–602.

Becker, S. and LeCun, Y. (1989) 'Improving the convergence of back-propagation learning with second order methods', in D. Touretzky, G. Hinton and T. Sejnowski (eds), *Proceedings of the 1988 Connectionist Models Summer School, Pittsburgh*. San Mateo, CA: Morgan Kaufmann. pp. 29–37.

Bejou, D., Wray, B. and Ingram, T.N. (1996) 'Determinants of relationship quality – an artificial neural-network analysis', *Journal of Business Research*, 36 (2): 137–43.

Bengio, Yoshua (1991) 'Artificial neural networks and their application to sequence recognition'. Doctoral dissertation, Computer Science, McGill University, Montreal, Canada.

Bengio, Yoshua (1996) *Neural Networks for Speech and Sequence Recognition*. London: International Thomson Computer Press.

Bengio, Yoshua, Cardin, R. and De Mori, R. (1990) 'Speaker independent speech recognition with neural networks and speech knowledge', in D. Touretzky (ed.), *Advances in Neural Information Processing Systems 2, Denver, CO*. San Mateo, CA: Morgan Kaufmann. pp. 218–25.

Bengio, Yoshua, Gori, M. and De Mori, R. (1996) 'Learning the dynamic nature of speech with back-propagation for sequences', *Pattern Recognition Letters*, 13 (5): 375–86.

Bengio, Yoshua, Simard, P. and Frascioni, P. (1994) 'Learning long-term dependencies with gradient descent is difficult', *IEEE Transactions on Neural Networks*, 5 (2): 157–66.

Bertsekas, D.P. (1995) *Nonlinear Programming*. Belmont, MA: Athena Scientific.

Bishop, C.M. (1995) *Neural Networks for Pattern Recognition*. Oxford: Oxford University Press.

Blackwell, Arshavir W. (1995) 'Artificial languages/virtual brains'. Doctoral dissertation, University of California–San Diego.

Blankenship, R.J. (1994) 'Modeling consumer choice: an experimental comparison of concept learning system, logit, and artificial neural network models'. Unpublished doctoral dissertation, University of Mississippi.

Boardman, I.S. (1995) 'Neural network models of temporal processing in speech perception and motor control'. Unpublished doctoral dissertation, Boston University.

Bobis, Kenneth G. (1991) 'The integration of expert system and neural network techniques in word association examination administration'. Doctoral dissertation, Illinois Institute of Technology.

Bochereau, I., Bourcier, D. and Bourgine, P. (1991) 'Extracting legal knowledge by means of a multilayer neural network application to municipal jurisprudence', in *Proceedings of the Third International Conference on Artificial Intelligence and Law*. Oxford: ACM Press. pp. 288–96.

Boritz, J. and Kennedy, D. (1996) 'Effectiveness of neural-network types for prediction of business failure'. Unpublished doctoral dissertation, University of Waterloo, Ontario, Canada.

Bottou, L. (1991) 'Une approche théorique de l'apprentissage connexioniste: applications à la reconnaissance de la parole'. Doctoral dissertation, Université de Paris.

Breedt, M.F. (1994) 'The application of neural networks to sales forecasting: a marketing perspective'. Unpublished doctoral dissertation, University of Pretoria, South Africa.

Breiman, L., Friedman, J.H., Olshen, R. and Stone, C.J. (1984) *Classification and Regression Trees*. Belmont, CA: Wadsworth.

Broomhead, D.S. and Lowe, D. (1988) 'Multivariable functional interpolation and adaptive networks', *Complex Systems*, 2: 321–55.

Brown, M.A.S.P.E. (1995) 'Simulation of spatial learning in the Morris water maze by a neural network model of the hippocampal formation and nucleus accumbens', *Hippocampus*, 5 (3): 171–88.

Brummett, D.L. (1994) 'Functional estimation with universal approximators: an application of neural networks to production functions'. Unpublished doctoral dissertation, University of Notre Dame.

Bullinaria, J.A. (1995) 'Neural network learning from ambiguous training data', *Connection Science: Journal of Neural Computing, Artificial Intelligence and Cognitive Research*, 7 (2): 99–122.

Burgos, J.E. (1996) 'Computational explorations of the evolution of artificial neural networks in Pavlovian environments'. Unpublished doctoral dissertation, University of Massachusetts.

Carpenter, Gail A. and Grossberg, Stephen (1987a) 'A massively parallel architecture for a self-organizing neural pattern recognition machine', *Computer Vision, Graphics, and Image Processing*, 37: 54–115.

Carpenter, Gail A. and Grossberg, Stephen (1987b) 'ART 2: self-organization of stable category recognition codes for analog input patterns', *Applied Optics*, 26: 4919–30.

Carpenter, Gail A. and Grossberg, Stephen (1988) 'The ART of adaptive pattern recognition by a self-organizing neural network', *IEEE Computer*, March.

Carpenter, Gail A. and Grossberg, Stephen (1990) 'ART 3: hierarchy search using chemical transmitters in self-organizing pattern recognition architectures', *Neural Networks*, 3: 129–52.

Carpenter, Gail A. and Grossberg, Stephen (1992) 'A self-organizing neural network for supervised learning, recognition, and prediction', *IEEE Communications Magazine*, 30 (9): 38–50.

Carpenter, Gail A., Grossberg, Stephen and Reynolds, J.H. (1991a) 'ARTMAP: supervised real-time learning and classification of nonstationary data by a self-organizing neural network', *Neural Networks*, 4: 565–88.

Carpenter, Gail A., Grossberg, Stephen and Rosen, D.B. (1991b) 'ART2-A: an adaptive resonance algorithm for rapid category learning and recognition', *Neural Networks*, 4: 759–71.

Caudill, Maureen (1989) 'Using neural nets: representing knowledge', *AI Expert*, 4 (12): 34–41.

Careur, T.J. and Kelley, P.B. (eds) (1989) *Perspectives in Neural Systems and Behavior*. New York: Alan R. Liss.

Chan, S.-K.J. (1996) 'The theory of mortgage prepayment and the valuation of mortgage-backed securities using neural network with genetic algorithm training technique (investments)'. Unpublished doctoral dissertation, University of Mississippi.

Chang-tseh, Hsieh (1993) 'Some potential applications of artificial neural systems in financial management', *Journal of Systems Management*, 44 (4): 12–16.

Chapell, Mark and Humphreys, Michael S. (1994) 'An auto-associative neural network for sparse representations: analysis and application to models of recognition and cued recall', *Psychological Review*, 101 (1): 103–29.

Chatterjee, Sangit and Laudato, Matthew (1995) 'Statistical applications of neural networks'. Unpublished paper, Northeastern University, Boston, Massachusetts.

Chauvin, Y. (1990) 'Dynamic behavior of constrained back-propagation networks', in D. Touretzky (ed.), *Advances in Neural Information Processing Systems 2*, Denver, CO. San Mateo, CA: Morgan Kaufmann. pp. 642–9.

Cheng, W. (1996) 'Improved forecast performance for neural networks through the use of a combined model (finance)'. Unpublished doctoral dissertation, Cleveland State University.

Chester, D.L. (1990) 'Why two hidden layers are better than one', in *Proceedings of the International Joint Conference on Neural Networks*, Washington, DC, Vol. 1. Hillsdale, NJ: Lawrence Erlbaum. pp. 265–8.

Chiang, W.C., Urban, T.L. and Baldridge, G.W. (1996) 'A neural-network approach to mutual fund net asset value forecasting', *Omega-International Journal of Management Science*, 24 (2): 205–15.

Chiu, Chaochang (1993) 'Reasoning about domain knowledge level for dynamic user modeling in adaptive human–computer interfaces: a fuzzy logic/neural network approach'. Doctoral dissertation, University of Maryland–Baltimore County.

Chryssolouris, George, Lee, Moshin and Ramsey, Alvin (1996) 'Confidence interval prediction for neural network models', *IEEE Transactions on Neural Networks*, 7 (1): 229–32.

Chua, Kim Liang (1992) 'A nonlinear approach to return predictability in the securities markets using feedforward neural networks'. Doctoral dissertation, Washington State University.

Church, K.B. and Curram, S.P. (1996) 'Forecasting consumers' expenditure – a comparison between econometric and neural-network models', *International Journal of Forecasting*, 12 (2): 255–67.

Collins, E. Ghosh and Scofield, C.L. (1988) 'An application of multiple neural network learning system to emulation of mortgage underwriting judgments', in *Proceedings of the Second Annual IEEE International Conference on Neural Networks*, Vol. II, pp. 459–66. Reprinted in 1989 as a technical report from Nestor, Inc., of Providence, RI.

Collins, Judith M. and Clark, Murray R. (1993) 'An application of the theory of neural computation to the prediction of workplace behavior: an illustration and assessment of network analysis', *Personnel Psychology*, 46 (3): 503–24.

Corcella, Karen (1994) 'Buttons the neural net: black box or PhD', *Wall Street and Technology*, 12 (3): 16–19.

Cortez, E.M. et al. (1995) 'The hybrid application of an inductive learning method and a neural network for intelligent information retrieval', *Information Processing & Management*, 3 (4): 177–83.

Cringely, Robert X. (1994) 'Fast money: how computers are used for trading securities', *Forbes*, 153 (8): S74–79.

Crooks, Ted (1992) 'Care and feeding of neural networks: if a neural network won't train, it might be because the data won't let it', *AI Expert*, 7 (7): 35–42.

Cybenko, G. (1989) 'Approximation by superpositions of sigmoidal function', *Mathematics of Control, Signals, and Systems*, 2: 303–14.

Davis, Jefferson Toronto (1993) 'Auditor experience in preliminary control risk assessments: neural network models of auditors' knowledge structures'. Doctoral dissertation, University of Tennessee.

Dayhoff, Judith (1989) *Neural Network Architectures: An Introduction*. New York: Van Nostrand Reinhold.

De Matos, G. (1994) 'Neural networks for forecasting foreign exchange rates'. Unpublished doctoral dissertation, University of Manitoba, Canada.

DeSieno, D. (1988) 'Adding a conscience to competitive learning', in *Proceedings of the Second Annual IEEE International Conference on Neural Networks*, Vol. I. Piscataway, NJ: Institute of Electrical and Electronics Engineers.

Dewdney, A.K. (1992) 'Computer recreations: programming a neural net', *Algorithm: Recreational Computing*, 3 (4): 11–15.

D'Souza, E.J. (1995) 'Neural networks in economic forecasting: a study of stocks in S&P 500 index, from 1983 to 1991'. Unpublished doctoral dissertation, University of Louisville.

Duda, R.O. and Hart, P.E. (1973) *Pattern Classification and Scene Analysis*. New York: Wiley.

Dutta, S. and Shekhar, S. (1988) 'Bond rating: a non-conservative application of neural networks', in *Proceedings of the Second Annual IEEE International Conference on Neural Networks*, Vol. II. Piscataway, NJ: Institute of Electrical and Electronics Engineering. pp. 443–50.

Dwyer, Margaret M.D. (1992) 'A comparison of statistical techniques and artificial neural network models in corporate bankruptcy prediction'. Doctoral dissertation, University of Wisconsin–Madison.

Dybowski, Richard, Weller, Peter, Chang, Rene and Grant, Vanya (1996) 'Prediction of outcome in critically ill patients using artificial neural network synthesized by genetic algorithm', *The Lancet*, 347 (9009): 1146–51.

Eccles, J.C. (1984) 'The cerebral neocortex: a theory of its operation', in E.J. Jones and A. Peters (eds), *Cerebral Cortex*, Vol. 2. New York: Plenum. pp. 1–36.

Efron, B. and Tibshirani, R.J. (1993) *An Introduction to the Bootstrap*. London: Chapman & Hall.

Elman, J.L. (1988) *Finding Structure in Time*. CRL Technical Report 8801. San Diego, CA: Center for Research in Language, University of California.

Elman, J.L. (1990) 'Finding a structure in time', *Cognitive Science*, 14: 179–211.

Elman, J.L. (1996) *Rethinking Innateness: a Connectionist Perspective on Development*. Cambridge, MA: MIT Press.

El-Temtamy, O.S. (1995) 'Bankruptcy prediction: a comparative study on logit and neural networks'. Unpublished doctoral dissertation, Middle Tennessee State University.

Everson, H.T. et al. (1994) 'Using artificial neural networks in educational research: some comparisons with linear statistical models', paper presented at the Annual Meeting of the National Council on Measurement in Education, New Orleans, LA, 5–7 April 1994.

Faggin, F. (1991) 'VLSI implementation of neural networks: tutorial notes', in *Proceedings of the International Joint Conference on Neural Networks*, Seattle, WA.

Fahlman, S.E. (1988) 'Faster-learning variations on back-propagation: an empirical study', in D. Touretsky, G. Hinton and T. Seynowski (eds), *Proceedings of the 1988 Neural Network Model Summer School*. San Mateo, CA: Morgan Kaufmann. pp. 38–51.

Farlow, S.J. (ed.) (1984) 'Self-organizing method in modeling: GMDH type algorithms', *Statistics: Textbooks and Monographs*, Vol. 54.

Feldman, Jerome A. and Ballard, D.H. (1982) 'Connectionist models and their properties', *Cognitive Science*, 6 (3): 205–54.

Feldman, Jerome A., Fanty, Mark A. and Goddard, Nigel H. (1988) 'Computing with structured neural networks', *Computer*, 21 (3): 91–103.

Fleming, M.K. (1997) 'A neural network model of micro- and macroprosody (microprosody, connectionism)'. Unpublished doctoral dissertation, Stanford University.

Forsstrom, Jari J. and Dalton, Kevin J. (1995) 'Artificial neural networks for decision support in clinical medicine', *Annals of Medicine*, 27 (5): 509–17.

Fowler, David (1991) 'A neural network as an instrument of prediction'. Doctoral dissertation, University of Nebraska–Lincoln.

Freeman, J. and Skapura, D. (1991) *Neural Networks*. Reading, MA: Addison-Wesley.

Fritzke, B. (1994) 'Supervised learning and growing cell structures', in J. Cowan, G. Tesauro and J. Alspector (eds), *Advances in Neural Information Processing Systems*, Vol. 6. San Mateo, CA: Morgan Kaufmann.

Fu, LiMin (1994) *Neural Networks in Computer Intelligence*. New York: McGraw-Hill.

Fukushima, Kuniko (1975) 'Cognitron: a self-organizing multilayered neural network', *Biological Cybernetics*, 20: 121–36.

Fukushima, Kuniko (1988) 'Neocognition: a hierarchical neural network capable of visual pattern recognition', *Neural Networks*, 1: 119–30.

Funahashi, K. (1989) 'On the approximate realization of continuous mappings by neural networks', *Neural Networks*, 2: 183–92.

Gallant, Stephen I. (1986) 'Optimal linear discriminants', in *Proceedings of the Eighth International Conference on Pattern Recognition*, Paris, 28–31 October. pp. 849–52.

Gallant, Stephen I. (1993) *Neural Network Learning and Expert Systems*. Cambridge, MA: MIT Press/Bradford.

Garson, G. David (1991a) 'A comparison of neural network and expert systems algorithms for common multivariate procedures for analysis of social science data', *Social Science Computer Review*, 9 (3): 399–434.

Garson, G. David (1991b) 'Interpreting neural network connection weights', *AI Expert*, 6 (4): 46–51.

Geman, S., Bienenstock, E. and Doursat, R. (1992) 'Neural networks and the bias/variance dilemma', *Neural Computation*, 4 (1): 1–58.

Gordon, Jolene Scully (1992) 'A neural network approach to the prediction of violence'. Doctoral dissertation, Oklahoma State University.

Gori, M., Bengio, Y. and De Mori, R. (1989) 'BPS: a learning algorithm for capturing the dynamical nature of speech', in *Proceedings of the International Joint Conference on Neural Networks*, Washington, DC. New York: IEEE. pp. 643–4.

Gotts, Stephen J. and Bremner, Frederick J. (1995) 'Neural network–expert system models of relative-depth perception', *Behavior Research Methods, Instruments & Computers*, 27 (2): 173–7.

Gottschling, A.P. (1997) 'Three essays in neural networks and financial prediction (fuzzy logic system, sigma, sigma pi, S&P 500 index)'. Unpublished doctoral dissertation, University of California, San Diego.

Greene, Rosemary A. (1992) 'Neural nets vs. multivariate analysis of behaviours', paper presented at the Workshop on Neural Networks: Techniques and Applications, University of Liverpool, September.

Greene, Rosemary A. (1995) 'A comparison of the use of artificial neural network and traditional psychometric methodologies in the discriminant validation of a multidimensional self-concept measure (construct validation)'. Unpublished doctoral dissertation, University of Southern California.

Greene, Rosemary A. and Michael, W.B. (1996) 'Using neural network and traditional psychometric methodologies in test validation', paper presented at the Western Psychological Association Annual Convention, San José, CA, 11–14 April.

Griffin, Glenn Ray (1995) 'Predicting naval aviator flight training performance using multiple regression and an artificial neural network'. Doctoral dissertation, Nova Southeastern University.

Grossberg, Stephen (1969a) 'Embedding fields: a theory of learning with physiological implications', *Journal of Mathematical Psychology*, 6: 209–39.

Grossberg, Stephen (1969b) 'Some networks that can learn, remember, and reproduce any number of complicated space–time patterns, I', *Journal of Mathematics and Mechanics*, 19: 53–91.

Grossberg, Stephen (1970) 'Some networks that can learn, remember, and reproduce any number of complicated space–time patterns, II', *Studies in Applied Mathematics*, 49: 135–66.

Grossberg, Stephen (1971) 'Embedding fields: underlying philosophy, physiology, and anatomy', *Journal of Cybernetics*, 1: 28–50.

Grossberg, Stephen (1972) 'Neural expectation: cerebellar and retinal analogs of cells fired by learnable or unlearned pattern classes', *Kybernetik*, 10: 49–57.

Grossberg, Stephen (1976a) 'Adaptive pattern classification and universal recording, I: parallel development and coding of neural detectors', *Biological Cybernetics*, 23: 121–34.

Grossberg, Stephen (1976b) 'Adaptive pattern classification and universal recording, II: feedback, expectation, olfaction, illusions', *Biological Cybernetics*, 23: 187–202.

Grossberg, Stephen (1980) 'How does a brain build a cognitive code?', *Psychological Review*, 87: 1–51.

Grossberg, Stephen (1982) *Studies of Mind and Brain: New Principles of Learning, Perception, Development, Cognition and Motor Control*. Dordrecht, Netherlands: D. Reidel.

Guan, Sang M. (1993) 'Development of optimal network structures for back-propagation-trained neural networks'. Doctoral dissertation, University of Nebraska–Lincoln.

Guenther, Frank H. (1995) 'Speech sound acquisition, coarticulation, and rate effects in a neural network model of speech production', *Psychological Review*, 102 (July): 594–621.

Haefke, Christian and Helmenstein, Christian (1996a) 'Neural networks in the capital markets: an application to index forecasting', *Computational Economics*, 9 (1): 37–50.

Haefke, Christian and Helmenstein, Christian (1996b) 'Forecasting Austrian IPOs – an application of linear and neural-network error-correction models', *Journal of Forecasting*, 15 (3): 237–51.

Hamburg, J.H. (1996) 'The application of neural networks to production process control (nuclear industry)'. Unpublished doctoral dissertation, Kent State University.

Hana, M.A. (1996) 'Qualitative and quantitative near infrared analysis using artificial neural networks (linear neuron, backpropagation, nicotine, tobacco)'. Unpublished doctoral dissertation, North Carolina State University.

Hand, D.J. (1982) *Kernel Discriminant Analysis*. Research Studies Press.

Happel, B.L.M. and Murre, Jacob M.J. (1994) 'Design and evolution of modular neural network architectures', special issue *Models of Neurodynamics and Behavior* of *Neural Networks*, 7 (6–7): 985–1004.

Hartman, E. and Keeler, J.D. (1991) 'Predicting the future: advantages of semilocal units', *Neural Computing*, 3: 566.

Haykin, Simon (1991) *Adaptive Filter Theory*, 2nd edn. Englewood Cliffs, NJ: Prentice-Hall.

Haykin, Simon (1994) *Neural Networks: a Comprehensive Foundation*. New York: Macmillan.

Hebb, Donald O. (1949) *Organization of Behavior*. New York: Science Editions.

Hecht-Nielsen, Robert (1986) *Nearest Matched Filter Classification of Spatio-Temporal Patterns*. Special report, Hecht-Nielsen Neuro-Computer Corporation, San Diego, CA, 23 June.

Hecht-Nielsen, Robert (1987) 'Counter-propagation networks', *Applied Optics*, 26: 4979–84.

Heckert, Teresa Mary (1994) 'Effect of base rate on the applicability of neural network analysis for classification'. Doctoral dissertation, Bowling Green State University.

Hedgepeth, William Oliver (1995) 'Comparing traditional statistical models with neural network models: the case of the relation of human performance factors to the outcomes of military combat'. Doctoral dissertation, Old Dominion University.

Hegazy, T.M. (1994) 'Integrated bid preparation with emphases on risk assessment using neural networks (construction industry)'. Unpublished doctoral dissertation, Concordia University, Canada.

Henseler, J. (1995) 'Back propagation', in P.J. Braspenning, F. Thuijsman and A.J.M.M. Weijters (eds), *Artificial Neural Networks: an Introduction to ANN Theory and Practice*. Berlin: Springer. pp. 37–66.

Hertz, J., Krogh, A. and Palmer, R. (1991) *Introduction to the Theory of Neural Computation*. Redwood City, CA: Addison-Wesley.

Hiemstra, Ypke (1996) 'Linear regression versus backpropagation networks to predict quarterly stock market excess returns', *Computational Economics*, 9 (1): 67–76.

Hill, Tim, Marquez, Leorey, O'Connor, Marcus and Remus, William (1994) 'Artificial neural network models for forecasting and decision making', *International Journal of Forecasting*, 10 (1): 5–15.

Hinton, Geoffrey E. (1989) 'Connectionist learning procedures', *Artificial Intelligence*, 40: 185–234.

Hinton, Geoffrey E. (1992) 'How neural networks learn from experience', *Scientific American*, 267: 144–51.

Hinton, Geoffey E., Sejnowski, T.J. and Ackley, D.H. (1984) *Boltzmann Machines: Constraint Satisfaction Networks that Learn*. Technical Report CMU-CS-84-119. Pittsburgh, PA: Department of Computer Science, Carnegie–Mellon University.

Hjorth, J.S.U. (1994) *Computer Intensive Statistical Methods: Validation, Model Selection, and Bootstrap*. London: Chapman and Hall.

Hobson, J.B. and Slee, D. (1994) 'Indexing the Theft Act 1978 for case based reasoning and artificial neural networks', in *Proceedings of the Fourth National Conference on Law, Computers, and Artificial Intelligence*. Exeter: Exeter University Centre for Legal Interdisciplinary Development.

Hoffman, Ralph E., Rapaport, Jill, Rezvan, Ameli, McGlashan, Thomas H., Harcherik, Diane and Servan-Schreiber, David (1995) 'A neural network simulation of hallucinated "voices" and associated speech perception impairments in schizophrenic patients', *Journal of Cognitive Neuroscience*, Fall: 479–97.

Holland, J.H. (1975) *Adaptation in Natural and Artificial Systems*. Ann Arbor, MI: University of Michigan Press.

Holland, J.H. (1992) *Adaptation in Natural and Artificial Systems*. Cambridge, MA: MIT Press.

Holmstrom L. and Koistinen, P. (1992) 'Using additive noise in back-propagation training', *IEEE Transactions on Neural Networks*, 3: 24–38.

Hopfield, John J. (1982) 'Neural networks and physical systems with emergent collective computational abilities', *Proceedings of the National Academy of Sciences, USA*, 79 (April): 2554–8.

Hornik, K. (1993) 'Some new results on neural network approximation', *Neural Networks*, 6: 1069–72.

Hornik, K., Stinchombe, M. and White, H. (1989) 'Multilayer feedforward networks are universal approximators', *Neural Networks*, 2: 359–66.

Hunter, Andrew (1997) 'Neural networks home page'. At URL http://osiris.sunderland.ac.uk/ahu/nn/nnintro.html. 27 January.

Hunter, D. (1997) 'Commercialising legal neural networks'. At URL http://jilt.law.strath.ac.uk/elj/jilt/ArtifInt/2hunter/1.htm. 27 January.

Husar, W. and Gerald, D. (1989) 'Projections of education statistics', in *Federal*

Forecasts Conference Proceedings. Washington, DC: National Center for Education Statistics.

Huston, Terry Lee (1993) 'Neural network design: a process model development methodology'. Doctoral dissertation, University of Pittsburgh.

Hutton, Larrie V. (1992) 'Using statistics to assess the performance of neural network classifiers', *Johns Hopkins Applied Physics Lab Technical Digest*, 13 (1).

Iyengar, S.S. and Kashyap, R.L. (1991) 'Neural networks: a computational perspective', in Paolo Antognetti and Milutinovic Veljko (eds), *Neural Networks: Concepts, Applications, and Implementations*, Vol. III. Englewood Cliffs, NJ: Prentice-Hall.

Jacobs, R.A. (1988) 'Increased rates of convergence through learning rate adaptation', *Neural Networks*, 1: 295–307.

Jacobs, R.A., Jordan, M.I., Nowlan, S.J. and Hinton, G.E. (1991) 'Adaptive mixtures of local experts', *Neural Computation*, 3: 79–87.

Jagielska, Ilona and Jaworski, Janusz (1996) 'Neural network for predicting the performance of credit card accounts', *Computational Economics*, 9 (1): 77–82.

Jain, Ba and Nag, Bn (1995) 'Artificial neural-network models for pricing initial public offerings', *Decision Sciences*, 26 (3): 283–302.

Jenkins, David (1991) 'Where are neural networks going?', *AI Expert*, November: 50–1.

Johansson, E.M., Dowla, F.U. and Goodman, D.M. (1992) 'Backpropagation learning for multilayer feed-forward neural networks using the conjugate gradient method', *International Journal of Neural Systems*, 2: 291.

Jordan, M.I. (1986) *Serial Order: a Parallel Distributed Processing Approach.* Technical Report 8604. Institute for Cognitive Science, University of California.

Kandel, A. and Langholz, G. (eds) (1992) *Hybrid Architectures for Intelligent Systems.* Boca Raton, FL: CRC Press.

Kashani, Javad H., Nair, Satish S., Rao, Venkatesh G., Nair, Jyotsna and Reid, John C. (1996) 'Relationship of personality, environmental, and DICA variables to adolescent hopelessness: a neural network sensitivity approach', *Journal of the American Academy of Child and Adolescent Psychiatry*, 35 (5): 640–6.

Kasuba, T. (1993) 'Simplified fuzzy ARTMAP', *AI Expert*, 8: 18–25.

Kelly, A.J., Goodman, P.H., Kaburlasos, V.G., Egbert, D.D. and Hardin, M.E. (1992) 'Neural network prediction of child sexual abuse', *Clinical Research*, 40 (1): 99ff.

Kemske, Floyd (1989) 'A new breed of expert', *Information Center*, 5 (6): 28–9.

Kiefer, J. and Wolfowitz, J. (1952) 'Stochastic estimation of the maximum of a regression function', *Annals of Mathematical Statistics*, 23: 462–6.

Kilmer, R.A. (1994) 'Artificial neural network metamodels of stochastic computer simulations'. Unpublished doctoral dissertation, University of Pittsburgh.

Kim, S. (1994) 'Intelligent information retrieval using an inductive learning algorithm and a back-propagation neural network'. Unpublished doctoral dissertation, University of Wisconsin–Madison.

Klimasauskas, C.C. (1992) 'Applying neural networks', in R.R. Trippi and E. Turban (eds), *Neural Networks in Finance and Investing*. Chicago: Probus. pp. 47–72.

Kohonen, T. et al. (1988) 'Statistical pattern recognition with neural networks:

benchmark networks', in *Proceedings of the Second Annual IEEE International Conference on Neural Networks*, Vol. 1.

Kohonen, T. (1989) *Self-Organization and Associative Memory*. New York and Berlin: Springer.

Kohzadi, N. (1994) 'Neural networks versus time series models for forecasting commodity prices'. Unpublished doctoral dissertation, University of Manitoba, Canada.

Kohzadi, N., Boyd, M.S., Kermanshahi, B. and Kaastra, I. (1996) 'A comparison of artificial neural-network and time-series models for forecasting commodity prices', *Neurocomputing*, 10 (2): 169–81.

Kosko, Bart (1987a) 'Constructing an associative memory', *Byte Magazine*, September.

Kosko, Bart (1987b) 'Bidirectional associative memories', *IEEE Transactions on Systems, Man, and Cybernetics*.

Kosko, Bart (1987c) 'Adaptive bidirectional associative memories', *Applied Optics*.

Kosko, Bart (1991) *Neural Networks and Fuzzy Systems: a Dynamical Systems Approach to Machine Intelligence*. Englewood Cliffs, NJ: Prentice-Hall.

Kuan, C. and White, H. (1994) 'Artificial neural networks: an econometric perspective', *Econometric Reviews*, 13 (1): 1–91.

Lang, K.J. and Hinton, G.E. (1988) *The Development of the Time-Delay Neural Network Architecture for Speech Recognition*. Technical Report CMU-CS=88-152. Pittsburgh, PA: Carnegie–Mellon University.

Lapedes, A. and Farber, R. (1987) *Non-Linear Signal Processing Using Neural Networks: Prediction and System Modeling*. Report LA-UR-87-2662, Los Alamos National Laboratory.

Laudeman, I.V. (1994) 'An application of unsupervised neural networks and fuzzy clustering in the identification of structure in personality data'. Unpublished doctoral dissertation, University of California, Berkeley.

LeCun, Y. (1985) 'Une procédure d'apprentissage pour réseau à seuil assymétrique', in *Proceedings of Cognitiva 85: à la frontière de l'intelligence artificielle, des sciences de la connaissance et des neurosciences*, Paris. Paris: CESTA. pp. 599–604.

LeCun, Y. (1986) 'Learning processes in an asymmetric threshold network', in F. Bienenstock and G. Weisbuch (eds), *Disordered Systems and Biological Organization*. Berlin: Springer. pp. 233–40.

LeCun, Y., Denker, J.S. and Solla, S.A. (1990) 'Optimal brain damage', in D.S. Touretzky (ed.), *Advances in Neural Information Processing Systems*, 2, Denver, CO. San Mateo, CA: Morgan Kaufmann. pp. 598–605.

Lee, Tae-Hwy, White, Halbert and Granger, Clive W.J. (1993) 'Testing for neglected nonlinearity in time series models: a comparison of neural network methods and alternative tests', *Journal of Econometrics*, 56 (3): 269–91.

Lehar, Steven M. (1994) 'Directed diffusion and orientational harmonics: neural network models of long-range boundary completion through short-range interactions'. Doctoral dissertation, Boston University.

Lenting, J.H.J. (1995) 'Representation issues in Boltzmann machines', in P.J. Braspenning, F. Thuijsman and A.J.M.M. Weijters (eds), *Artificial Neural Networks: an Introduction to ANN Theory and Practice*. Berlin: Springer. pp. 131–56.

Levine, D.S. (1995) 'Learning and encoding higher order rules in neural networks', *Behavior Research Methods, Instruments and Computers*, 27 (2): 178–82.

Li, J. (1997) 'Oil tanker markets modeling, analysis and forecasting using neural networks, fuzzy logic and genetic algorithms'. Unpublished doctoral dissertation, University of Michigan.

Lin, Daw-Tung (1994) 'The adaptive time-delay neural network: characterization and applications to pattern recognition, prediction and signal processing'. Doctoral dissertation, University of Maryland.

Lin, Frank C. and Lin, Mei (1993) 'Analysis of financial data using neural nets', *AI Expert*, 8 (2): 37–42.

Lippman, R.P. (1987) 'An introduction to computing with neural nets', *IEEE ASSP Magazine* April: 4–22.

Longo, J.M. (1995) 'Selecting superior securities: using discriminant analysis and neural networks to differentiate between "winner" and "loser" stocks'. Unpublished doctoral dissertation, Rutgers State University of New Jersey–Newark.

Lonnblad, L., Peterson, C. and Rognvaldsson, T. (1992) 'Mass reconstruction with a neural network', *Physics Letters*, B278: 181.

Luciano, Joanne Sylvia, Jr (1996) 'Neural network modeling of unipolar depression: patterns of recovery and prediction of outcome'. Doctoral dissertation, Boston University.

Luna, F. (1996) 'Learning in a computable setting: invisible hands, neural networks, and institutions (cooperation)'. Unpublished doctoral dissertation, University of California, Los Angeles.

Luther, Raminder Kaur (1993) 'Predicting the outcome of Chapter 11 bankruptcy: an artificial neural network approach'. Doctoral dissertation, University of Mississippi.

Lynn, P.J. (1994) 'System interaction in human memory and amnesia: theoretical analysis and connectionist modeling (neural networks, inductive memory)'. Unpublished doctoral dissertation, University of Colorado at Boulder.

MacKay, David J.C. (1992a) 'Bayesian interpolation', *Neural Computation*, 4: 415–47.

MacKay, David J.C. (1992b) 'A practical Bayesian framework for back-propagation networks', *Neural Computation*, 4: 448–72.

MacKay, David J.C. (1995) 'Probable networks and plausible predictions – a review of practical Bayesian methods for supervised neural networks'. At URL ftp://wol.ra.phy.cam.ac.uk/pub/www/mackay/network.ps.gz December.

MacQueen, J.B. (1967) 'Some methods for classification and analysis of multivariate observations', in *Proceedings of the Fifth Symposium on Mathematical Statistics and Probability*, Berkeley, CA, Vol. 1. Berkeley, CA: University of California Press. pp. 281–97.

Macy, Michael (1996) 'Natural selection and social learning in Prisoner's Dilemma: coadaptation with genetic algorithms and artificial neural networks', *Sociological Methods and Research*, 25 (1): 103–37.

Martindale, C. (1991) *Cognitive Psychology: A Neural-Network Approach*. Pacific Grove, CA: Brooks/Cole.

Marzban, Caren and Stumpf, Gregory J. (1996) 'A neural network for tornado prediction based on Doppler radar-derived attributes', *Journal of Applied Meteorology*, 35 (5): 617–26.

McClelland, J., Rumelhart, D. and the PDP Research Group (1986) *Parallel Distributed Processing: Explorations in the Microstructure of Cognition. Vol. 1: Foundations*. Cambridge, MA: MIT Press.

McCulloch, W.S. and Pitts, W. (1943) 'A logical calculus of the ideas immanent in nervous activity', *Bulletin of Mathematical Biophysics*, 5: 115–33.

McLachlan, G.J. (1992) *Discriminant Analysis and Statistical Pattern Recognition*. New York: Wiley.

Mcloughlin, N.P. (1995) 'Neural network models of three-dimensional surface perception: da Vinci stereopsis and the McCollough effect'. Unpublished doctoral dissertation, Boston University.

Meley, Kathy Dorien (1995) 'Simulation analysis of a nonlinear system with back-propagation networks'. Doctoral dissertation, Indiana University of Pennsylvania.

Meraviglia, C. (1996) 'Models of representation of social-mobility and inequality systems: a neural-network approach', *Quality and Quantity*, 30 (3): 231–52.

Mesrobian, Edmond (1992) 'A neural network model for textural segmentation'. Doctoral dissertation, University of California–Los Angeles.

Minsky, Marvin (1961) 'Steps toward artificial intelligence', *Proceedings IRE*. Reprinted in E.A. Feigenbaum and J. Feldman (eds), *Computers and Thought*. New York: McGraw-Hill, 1963.

Minsky, Marvin and Papert, Seymour (1969) *Perceptrons: An Introduction to Computational Geometry*. Cambridge, MA: MIT Press.

Moody, J. and Darken, C.J. (1989) 'Fast learning in networks of locally-tuned processing elements', *Neural Computation*, 1 (2): 281–94.

Moody, J. and Utans, J. (1994) 'Architecture selection strategies for neural networks: application to bond rating prediction', in A.N. Refenes (ed.), *Neural Networks in the Capital Markets*. New York: Wiley.

Moore, B. (1988) 'ART1 and pattern clustering', in D. Touretzky, G. Hinton and T. Sejnowski (eds), *Proceedings of the 1988 Connectionist Models Summer School*. Pittsburgh. San Mateo, CA: Morgan Kaufmann. pp. 174–85.

Morgan, N. and Bourlard, H. (1990) 'Generalization and parameter estimation in feedforward nets: some experiments', in D. Touretzky (ed.), *Advances in Neural Information Processing Systems 2*, Denver, CO. San Mateo, CA: Morgan Kaufmann. pp. 413–16.

Mozer, M.C. and Smolensky, P. (1989) 'Skeletonization: a technique for trimming the fat from a network via relevance assessment', in *Advances in Neural Information Processing Systems, 1*. San Mateo, CA: Morgan Kaufmann.

Murre, J.M.J. (1992) *Learning and Categorization in Modular Neural Networks*. Hillsdale, NJ: Lawrence Erlbaum.

Nadaraya, E.A. (1964) 'On estimating regression', *Theory Probability Applications*, 10: 186–90.

Narendra, K.S. and Thathachar, M.A.L. (1974) 'Learning automata – a survey', *IEEE Transactions on Systems, Man, and Cybernetics*, 4: 323–34.

Narendra, K.S. and Thathachar, M.A.L. (1989) *Learning Automata: An Introduction*. Englewood Cliffs, NJ: Prentice-Hall.

NIST (1993) *Comparative Performance of Classification Methods for Fingerprints*.

Report NISTIR-5163, order no. PB93184273. Washington, DC: National Institute of Standards and Technology.

NIST (1994) *Comparison of Hand-Printed Digit Classifications*. Report NISTIR-5209, order no. PB94118213. Washington, DC: National Institute of Standards and Technology.

Neal, R.M. (1993a) 'Bayesian learning via stochastic dynamics', in C.L. Giles, S.J. Hanson and J.D. Cowan (eds), *Advances in Neural Information Processing Systems 5*. San Mateo, CA: Morgan Kaufmann. pp. 475–82.

Neal, R.M. (1993b) 'Probabilistic inference using Markov chain Monte Carlo methods'. At URL ftp://ftp.cs.utoronto.ca/pub/radford/review.ps.Z.

Neuralware, Inc. (1990) *Neural Computing*. Pittsburgh, PA: Neuralware, Inc.

Niebur, Dagmar and Germond, Alain J. (1992) 'Power system static security assessment using the Kohonen neural network classifier', *IEEE Transactions on Power Systems*, 7 (2): 865–73.

Nigrin, A. (1993) *Neural Networks for Pattern Recognition*. Cambridge, MA: MIT Press.

Nour, M.A. (1994) 'Improved clustering and classification algorithms for the Kohonen self-organizing neural network'. Unpublished doctoral dissertation, Kent State University.

Ntungo, C. (1996) 'Forecasting turning points for trading commodity futures using time-series and neural network models'. Unpublished doctoral dissertation, University of Manitoba, Canada.

O'Brien, Larry (1990) 'Developing a neural network with Turbo C++', *AI Expert*, 5 (10): 28–33.

O'Callaghan, S. (1994) 'An artificial intelligence application of backpropagation neural networks to simulate accountants' assessments of internal control systems using Coso guidelines'. Unpublished doctoral dissertation, University of Cincinnati.

Odom, M. and Sharda, R. (1990) 'A neural network model for bankruptcy prediction', in *Proceedings of the International Joint Conference on Neural Networks*, Vol. 2, pp. 63–8.

O'Heney, Sheila (1990) 'Banks finally solve AI mystery', *Computers in Banking*, 7 (8): 30–6.

Ohlsson, M., Peterson, C., Pi, H., Rognvaldsson, T. and Soderberg, B. (1994) 'Predicting utility loads with artificial neural networks – methods and results from the great energy predictor shootout', *1994 ASHRAE Transactions*, 100, Part 2.

Page, M.P.A. (1994) 'Modeling the perception of musical sequences with self-organizing neural networks', *Connection Science: Journal of Neural Computing, Artificial Intelligence and Cognitive Research*, 6 (2–3): 223–46.

Paik, H. and Marzban, C. (1995) 'Predicting television extreme viewers and nonviewers: a neural network analysis', *Human Communication Research*, 22 (2): 284–306.

Parker, D.B. (1982) *Learning Logic*. Invention Report S81-64, File 1. Office of Technology Licensing, Stanford University.

Parker, D.B. (1985) *Learning Logic*. Technical Report TR-47. Cambridge, MA: Center for Computational Research in Economics and Management Science, MIT.

Parks, R.W., Levine, D.S., Long, D.L., Crockett, D.J., Dalton, J.E., Weingartner,

H., Fedio, P., Coburn, K.L., Siler, G., Matthews, J.R. and Becker, R.E. (1992) 'Parallel distributed processing and neuropsychology – a neural network model of Wisconsin card sorting and verbal fluency', *Neuropsychology Review*, 3 (2): 213–33.

Pattie, D.C. and Haas, G. (1996) 'Forecasting wilderness recreation use – neural network versus regression', *AI Applications*, 10 (1): 67–74.

Pessoa, L.A. (1996) 'Studies of human vision: a neural network model of brightness perception and experiments on chromatic textures (texture segregation, Mach bands)'. Unpublished doctoral dissertation, Boston University.

Peterson, Carsten, Rognvaldsson, Thorsteinn and Lonnblad, Leif (1993) 'JETNET 3.0 – a versatile artificial neural network package'. At URL http:// www.thep.lu.se/public_html/jetnet_30_manualk/node12.html. January 1997.

Pitts, W. and McCulloch, W.S. (1947) 'How we know universals', *Bulletin of Mathematical Biophysics*, 9: 127–47.

Platt, J. (1991) 'A resource-allocating network for function interpolation', *Neural Computation*, 2: 25–34.

Poggio, T. and Girosi, F. (1989) *A Theory of Networks for Approximation and Learning*. Technical Report CMU-CS-86-126. Pittsburgh, PA: Department of Computer Science, Carnegie–Mellon University.

Poggio, T. and Girosi, F. (1990) 'Networks for approximation and learning', *Proceedings of the IEEE*, 78 (9): 1481–97.

Postma, E.O. and Hudson, P.T.W. (1995) 'Adaptive resonance theory', in P.J. Braspenning, F. Thuijsman and A.J.M.M. Weijters (eds), *Artificial Neural Networks: an Introduction to ANN Theory and Practice*. Berlin: Springer. pp. 101–17.

Powell, M.J.D. (1985) 'Radial basis functions for multi-variable interpolation: a review', paper presented at the IMA Conference on Algorithms for the Approximation of Functions and Data, RMCS, Shrivenham, UK. Report DAMTP/NA12, Department of Applied Mathematics and Theoretical Physics, University of Cambridge.

Powell, Tim (1995) 'Number crunching is fun: neural computing in market research', *Marketing Computers*, 15 (5): 28–30.

Pugh, G.A. (1991) 'A comparison of neural networks to SPC charts', *Computers and Industrial Engineering*, 21 (1): 253–55.

Pugh, William M. (1996) 'A comparison of multiple regression and a neural network for predicting a medical diagnosis', in *U.S. Naval Health Center Report 91–33*, pp. 1–21.

Qi, M. (1996) 'Financial applications of generalized nonlinear nonparametric econometric methods (artificial neural networks)'. Unpublished doctoral dissertation, Ohio State University.

Quinn, T.S. (1996) 'Determination of the employer–employee relationship: a neural network approach to macro-case analysis'. Unpublished doctoral dissertation, University of Mississippi.

Reid, K. and Zeichick, A. (1992) 'Neural network products resource guide', *AI Expert*, 7 (6): 50–6.

Reynolds, John Huntington (1994) 'Neural network architectures for learning, prediction, and probability estimation'. Doctoral dissertation, Boston University.

Reynolds, Steven Bailey (1993) 'A neural network approach to Box–Jenkins model identification (ARIMA forecasting)'. Doctoral dissertation, University of Alabama.

Ripley, B.D. (1993) 'Statistical aspects of neural networks', in O.E. Barndorff-Nielsen, J.L. Jensen and W.S. Kendall (eds), *Networks and Chaos: Statistical and Probabilistic Aspects*. London: Chapman & Hall. pp. 40–123.

Rivera-Piza, H.A. (1996) 'Towards the forex advisor: a neural network model for forecasting foreign exchange rates'. Unpublished doctoral dissertation, George Washington University.

Robbins, H. and Monro, S. (1951) 'A stochastic approximation method', *Annals of Mathematical Statistics*, 22: 400–7.

Rochester, N., Holland, J.H., Habit, L.H. and Duda, W.L. (1956) 'Tests on a cell assembly theory of the action of the brain, using a large digital computer', *IRE Transactions on Information Theory*, IT-2: 80–93.

Rose, D.E. (1994) *A Symbolic and Connectionist Legal Information Retrieval System*. Hillsdale, NJ: Lawrence Erlbaum.

Rosenblatt, F. (1957) *The Perceptron: a Perceiving and Recognizing Automaton*. Technical Report 85-460-1. Ithaca, NY: Cornell Aeronautical Laboratory.

Rosenblatt, F. (1959) 'Two theorems of statistical separability in the perceptron', in *Proceedings of a Symposium on the Mechanization of Thought Processes*. London: Her Majesty's Stationery Office. pp. 421–56.

Rosenblatt, F. (1961) *Principles of Neurodynamics*. New York: Spartan.

Rumelhart, D.E., Hinton, G.E. and Williams, R.J. (1986a) 'Learning internal representations by error propagation', in D.E. Rumelhart and J. McClelland (eds), *Parallel Distributed Processing: Explorations in the Microstructure of Cognition*, Vol. I. Cambridge, MA: MIT Press. pp. 318–62.

Rumelhart, D.E., Hinton, G.E. and Williams, R.J. (1986b) 'Learning representations by back-propagating errors', *Nature*, 323: 533–6.

Rumelhart, D.E. and McClelland, J. (eds) (1986) *Parallel Distributed Processing: Explorations in the Microstructures of Cognition*. Cambridge, MA: MIT Press.

Russell, G.S. (1996) 'Reentrance and recurrence in early vision: perception, imagery and learning (neural networks, hyperacuity, signal detection)'. Unpublished doctoral dissertation, University of Oregon.

Russell, Ingrid F. (1991) 'Neural networks in the undergraduate curriculum', *Collegiate Microcomputer*, 9 (1): 1–12.

Samad, Tariq (1988) 'Back-propagation is significantly faster if the expected value of the source unit is used for update', in *International Neural Network Society Conference Abstracts*.

Samuel, A.L. (1959) 'Some studies in machine learning using the game of checkers', *IBM Journal of Research and Development*, 3 (3): 210–23.

Sarle, W.S. (1994a) 'Neural networks and statistical models', in *Proceedings of the Nineteenth Annual SAS Users Group International Conference*. Cary, NC: SAS Institute.

Sarle, W.S. (1994b) 'Neural network implementation in SAS software', in *Proceedings of the Nineteenth Annual SAS Users Group International Conference*. Cary, NC: SAS Institute.

Sarle, W.S. (1995) 'Stopped training and other remedies for overfitting', in *Proceedings of the 27th Symposium on the Interface of Computing Science and Statistics*. Fairfax, VA: Interface Foundation of North America. pp. 352–60.

Scarborough, David James (1995) 'An evaluation of backpropagation neural network modeling as an alternative methodology for criterion validation of employee selection testing'. Doctoral dissertation, University of North Texas.

Schiffmann, W., Joost, M. and Werner, R. (1993) 'Comparison of optimized backpropagation algorithms', in *Proceedings of ESANN 93*. Brussels.

Schrodt, Philip A. (1990) 'Prediction of interstate conflict outcomes using a neural network', paper presented at the American Political Science Association Annual Meeting, San Francisco, 30 August to 2 September.

Schrodt, Philip A. (1991) 'Prediction of interstate conflict outcomes using a neural network', *Social Science Computer Review*, 9 (3): 359–80.

Seiler, T.M. (1994) 'An investigation of the use of simulated artificial neural networks to forecast foreign currency exchange (prediction modeling, currency forecasting)'. Unpublished doctoral dissertation, Nova Southeastern University.

Sejnowski, T.J. and Rosenberg, C.R. (1986) *NETtalk: a Parallel Network that Learns to Read Aloud*. Technical Report 86-01. Baltimore, MD: Department of Electrical Engineering and Computer Science, Johns Hopkins University.

Sejnowski, T.J. and Rosenberg, C.R. (1987) 'Parallel networks that learn to pronounce English text', *Complex Systems*, 1: 145–68.

Selfridge, O.G. (1959) 'PANDEMONIUM: a paradigm for learning', in *Proceedings of Symposium on Mechanization of Thought Processes*, National Physics Laboratory, Teddington. Vol. 1, pp. 511–29.

Shanno, D.F. (1990) 'Recent advances in numerical techniques for large scale optimization', in *Neural Networks for Control*. Cambridge, MA: MIT Press.

Shaw, R.S., Huang, H.C. and Chow, L.R. (1995) 'A study of human information acquisition analyzer (IAA) – a neural network approach', *Cybernetica*, 38 (1): 69–84.

Shea, P. and Lin, V. (1989) 'Detection of explosives in checked airline baggage using an artificial neural system', *International Journal of Neural Networks*, 1 (4): 249–53.

Shepherd, G.M. and Koch, C. (1990) 'Introduction to synaptic circuits', in G.M. Shepherd (ed.), *The Synaptic Organization of the Brain*, 3rd edn. New York: Oxford University Press. pp. 3–31.

Silva, F.M. and Almeida, L.B. (1990) 'Accelerations techniques for the backpropagation algorithm', in L.B. Almeida and C.J. Wellekens (eds), *Neural Networks*. Berlin: Springer. pp. 110–19.

Sjoberg, J. and Ljung, L. (1992) *Overtraining, Regularization, and Searching for Minimum in Neural Networks*. Technical Report LiTH-ISY-I-1297. Department of Electrical Engineering, Linkoping University, Sweden.

Sohl, J.-H.E. and Venkatachalam, A.R. (1995) 'A neural network approach to forecasting-model selection', *Information and Management*, 29 (6): 297–303.

Sontag, E.D. (1992) 'Feedback stabilization using two-hidden-layer nets', *IEEE Transactions on Neural Networks*, 3: 981–90.

Soto, R. (1996) 'Three essays on empirical dynamics in macroeconomics'. Unpublished doctoral dissertation, Georgetown University.

Specht, D.F. (1990) 'Probabilistic neural networks', *Neural Networks*, 3: 110–18.

Specht, D.F. (1991) 'A generalized regression neural network', *IEEE Transactions on Neural Networks*, 2: 568–76.

Spieksma, F.C.R. (1995) in P.J. Braspenning, F. Thuijsman and A.J.M.M.

Srivastava, A. (1996), 'Identifying stock winners and losers: a multilayered artificial neural network approach'. Unpublished doctoral dissertation, Carleton University, Canada.

Srivastava, A. (1996) 'Identifying stock winners and losers: a multilayered artificial neural network approach'. Unpublished doctoral dissertation, Carleton University, Canada.

Stanley, Jeannette (1988) *Introduction to Neural Networks*. Sierre Madre, CA: California Scientific Software.

Stent, G.S. (1973) 'A physiological mechanism for Hebb's postulate of learning', *Proceedings of the National Academy of Sciences of the U.S.A.*, 70: 997–1001.

Steppe, J.M., Bauer, K.W. Jr and Rogers, S.K. (1996) 'Integrated feature and architecture selection (single hidden-layer feedforward neural networks)', *IEEE Transactions on Neural Networks*, 7 (4): 1007–8.

Steyaert, J. (1994) 'Soft computing for soft technologies: artificial neural networks and fuzzy set theory for human services', *Computers in Human Services*, 10 (4): 55–67.

Stinchombe, M. and White, H. (1989) 'Universal approximation using feedforward networks with non-sigmoid hidden layer activation function', in *Proceedings of the International Joint Conference on Neural Networks 89*. Washington, DC: IEEE. pp. 613–17.

Stone, M. (1974) 'Cross-validatory choice and assessment of statistical predictions', *Journal of the Royal Statistical Society*, B36: 111–47.

Stone, William Steve (1993) 'Principal selection: an application of neural network forecasting'. Doctoral dissertation, North Carolina State University.

Stork, D.G. (1988) 'Counter-propagation networks: adaptive hierarchical networks for near-optimal mappings', *Synapse Connection*, 1 (2): 9–11, 17.

Stornetta, W.S. and Huberman, B.A. (1987) 'An improved three-layer backpropagation algorithm', in *Proceedings of the First Annual IEEE International Conference on Neural Networks, San Diego*. Washington, DC: IEEE.

Styer, Louis Daniel (1995) 'Control of a biomechanical model of the human postral maintenance system by artificial neural networks'. Doctoral dissertation, University of California–Davis.

Sutton, R.S., Barto, A.G. and Williams, R.J. (1991) 'Reinforcement learning is direct adaptive optimal control', in *Proceedings of the American Control Conference, Boston, MA*. pp. 2143–6.

Tak, B. (1995) 'A new method for forecasting stock prices using artificial neural network and wavelet theory'. Unpublished doctoral dissertation, University of Pennsylvania.

Tambouratzis, Tatiani (1991) 'A neural network implementation of the constraint propagation paradigm in vision'. Doctoral dissertation, Brunel University.

Tapang, C.C. (1989) *An Alternative Matching Mechanism: Getting Rid of Attentional Gain Control and its Consequence 2/3 Rule in ART-1*. Technical Report. Syntonic Systems.

Taschman, Gary Neil (1993) 'A neural network model for spoken word recognition'. Doctoral dissertation, Brown University.

Taylor, W.K. (1956) 'Cortico-thalamic organization and memory', *Proceedings of the Royal Society of London, Series B*, 159: 466–78.

Theng, R. (1996) 'An application of artificial neural networks to target merger prediction and post-merger performance prediction (artificial intelligence)'. Unpublished doctoral dissertation, Mississippi State University.

Toborg, Scott T. and Hwang, Kai (1989) 'Exploring neural network and optical computing technologies', in Kai Hwang and Douglas Degroot (eds), *Parallel Processing for Super-Computers and Artificial Intelligence*. New York: McGraw Hill. pp. 609–56.

Tollenaere, T. (1990) 'SuperSAB, fast adaptive back propagation with good scaling properties', *Neural Networks*, 3 (5): 561–73.

Trafton, J. Gregory (1995) 'A hybrid model using neural networks and ACT-R', *Behavior Research Methods, Instruments, & Computers*, 27 (2): 183–6.

Trippi, R.R. and Turban, E. (1993) *Neural Networks in Finance and Investing*. Chicago: Probus.

Tsukahara, N. and Oda, Y. (1981) 'Appearance of new synaptic potentials at corticorubral synapses after the establishment of classical conditioning', *Proceedings of the Japanese Academy, Series B (Physical and Biological Sciences)*, 57: 398–401.

Usher, Marius and Zakay, Dan (1993) 'A neural network model for attribute-based decision processes', *Cognitive Science*, 17 (3): 349–96.

Uttley, A.M. (1956) 'A theory of the mechanism of learning based on the computation of conditional probabilities', in *Proceedings of the First International Conference on Cybernetics*. Paris: Naumur, Gauthier-Villars.

Van der Velde, F. (1995) 'Symbol manipulation with neural networks: production of a context-free language using a modifiable working memory', *Connection Science: Journal of Neural Computing, Artificial Intelligence & Cognitive Research*, 7 (3–4): 247–80.

Van Eyden, R.J. (1994) 'The application of neural networks in the forecasting of share prices'. Unpublished doctoral dissertation, University of Pretoria, South Africa.

Verkooijen, W.J.H. (1996a) 'A neural network approach to long-run exchange rate prediction', *Computational Economics*, 9 (1): 51–65.

Verkooijen, W.J.H. (1996b) 'Neural networks in economic modelling: an empirical study'. Unpublished doctoral dissertation, Katholieke Universiteit Brabant, The Netherlands.

Vogh, J.W. (1997) 'A sequential memory adaptive resonance theory neural network, with application to three-dimensional object recognition'. Unpublished doctoral dissertation, Boston University.

Vogle, T.P. et al. (1988) 'Accelerating the convergence of the back-propagation method', *Biological Cybernetics*, 59: 257–63.

Von der Malsburg, C. (1973) 'Self-organization of orientation sensitive cells in the striate cortex', *Kybernetik*, 14: 85–100.

Von Neumann, J. (1956) 'Probabilistic logics and the synthesis of reliable organisms from unreliable components', in C.E. Shannon and J. McCarthy (eds), *Automata Studies*. Princeton, NJ: Princeton University Press. pp. 43–98.

Vrieze, O.J. (1995) 'Kohonen network', in P.J. Braspenning, F. Thuijsman and A.J.M.M. Weijters (eds), *Artificial Neural Networks: an Introduction to ANN Theory and Practice*. Berlin: Springer. pp. 83–101.

Wallich, Paul (1991) 'Digital dyslexia: neural network mimics the effects of stroke', *Scientific American*, 265 (4): 36.

Wang, S. (1996) 'Nonparametric econometric modeling – a neural-network approach', *European Journal of Operational Research*, 89 (3): 581–92.

Wasserman, Philip (1989) *Neural Computing: Theory and Practice*. New York: Van Nostrand Reinhold.

Wasserman, Philip and Oetzel, Roberta M. (1989) *Neuralsource: the Bibliographic Guide to Artificial Neural Networks*. New York: Van Nostrand Reinhold.

Watkins, C.J.C.H. (1989) 'Learning from delayed rewards'. Doctoral dissertation, University of Cambridge.

Weibel, A. (1989) 'Modular construction of time-delay neural networks for speech recognition', *Neural Computing*, 1: 39–46.

Weigend, A.S., Huberman, B.A. and Rumelhart, D.E. (1990). 'Predicting the future: a connectionist approach', *International Journal of Neural Systems*, 1 (3): 193–209.

Weigend, A.S., Rumelhart, D.E. and Huberman, B.A. (1991) 'Generalization by weight-elimination with application to foreasting', in R.P. Lippman, J. Moody and D.S. Touretzky (eds), *Advances in Neural Processing Systems 3*. San Mateo, CA: Morgan Kaufmann.

Werbos, P.J. (1974) 'Beyond regression: new tools for prediction and analysis in the behavioral sciences'. PhD thesis, Harvard University, Department of Applied Mathematics.

Werbos, P.J. (1989) 'Backpropagation and neural control: a review and prospectus', in *Proceedings of the International Joint Conference on Neural Networks*, Washington, DC. Vol. 2, pp. 209–16.

Werbos, P.J. (1992) 'Neural networks and the human mind: new mathematics fits humanistic insight', *IEEE International Conference on Systems, Man, and Cybernetics*, Chicago, IL. Vol. I, pp. 78–83.

Werbos, P.J. (1994) *The Roots of Backpropagation*. New York: Wiley.

West, D.A. (1996) 'Neural networks in the decision sciences (manufacturing)'. Unpublished doctoral dissertation, University of Rhode Island.

Westheider, O. (1997) 'Predicting stock index returns by means of genetically engineered neural networks (market efficiency)'. Unpublished doctoral dissertation, University of California, Los Angeles.

Wheeler, M. Andace (1994) 'A comparative case study of neural network analysis and statistical discriminant function analysis for predicting law students passing the bar examination'. Doctoral dissertation, Gonzaga University.

White, A.J. (1996) 'The pricing of interest rate options with futures style margining: a genetic adaptive neural network approach'. Unpublished doctoral dissertation, University of Mississippi.

White, Halbert (1981) 'Consequences and detection of mis-specified nonlinear regression models', *Journal of the American Statistical Association*, 76: 419–33.

White, Halbert (1987) 'Some asymptotic results for back-propagation', in *Proceedings of the IEEE First International Conference on Neural Networks*, San Diego. New York: IEEE Press. pp. 261–6.

White, Halbert (1989) 'Neural-network learning and statistics', *AI Expert*, 4 (12): 48–52.

White, S.C. (1994) 'Forecasting business time series with radial basis function networks (neural networks)'. Unpublished doctoral dissertation, Texas A&M University.

Widrow, Bernard (1962) 'Generalization and information storage in networks of adaline "neurons"', in M.C. Yovitz, G.T. Jacobi and G.D. Goldstein (eds), *Self-Organizing Systems*. Washington, DC: Sparta. pp. 475–61.

Widrow, Bernard and Hoff, M.E. (1960) 'Adaptive switching circuits', in *Institute of Radio Engineers WECON Convention Record*. Part 4, pp. 96–104.

Widrow, Bernard and Stearns, S.D. (1985) *Adaptive Signal Processing*. Englewood Cliffs, NJ: Prentice-Hall.

Widrow, Bernard, Rumelhart, David E. and Lehr, Michael A. (1994) 'Neural networks: applications in business, industry, and science', *Communications of the ACM*, 37 (3): 93–105.

Wolpert, David H. (1992) 'Stacked generalization', *Neural Networks*, 5: 241–59.

Wyse, L. (1994) 'Neural networks for segregation of multiple objects: visual figure–ground separation and auditory pitch perception'. Unpublished doctoral dissertation, Boston University.

Xenakis, John J. (1990) 'Brain thrust', *InformationWEEK*, no. 255: 41–2.

Xia, X. (1996) 'Neural network models in predicting insurance insolvency and detecting insurance claim fraud'. Unpublished doctoral dissertation, University of Texas at Austin.

Xiong, Momiao (1993) 'Mathematical theory of neural learning and its applications to statistics and molecular biology'. Doctoral dissertation, University of Georgia.

Ye, Julia Xiaozhu (1994) 'An application of the feedforward neural network model in currency exchange rate forecasting'. Doctoral dissertation, Washington State University.

Zeng, Langche (1996) 'Prediction and classification with neural network models', paper presented at the Annual Meeting, American Political Science Association, Los Angeles.

Zhuo, Jiayin (1995) 'Stock market valuation the neural network way'. Doctoral dissertation, University of Nevada–Reno.

Ziegler, Uta Maria (1991) 'A neural network which rapidly learns to perform a multistep task (navigation)'. Doctoral dissertation, Florida State University.

Zurada, J.M. (1992) *Introduction to Artificial Neural Systems*. Boston, MA: PWS.

Index